A CENTURY OF SILENCE

The author expresses his heartfelt gratitude to the following Patrons whose generous support made the publication of this work possible:

Bill & Tess Evans, Aix en Provence, (FR)
Richard Staveley & Patrice Murphy, Dublin (IR)
Denis & Ilse Mongan, Dublin (IR)
Padraig & Pamela O'Curry, Paris, (FR)
Peter & Carmel Lennon, Bruxelles, (BEL)
Brian & Mary O'Carroll, Roscommon, (IR)
Mark Mongan & Imelda McKay, Melbourne (AUS)
The late Peter, and Lorna Murray, Dublin, (IR)
Carol Mongan, Dublin, (IR)
The late Michael, and Vera O'Duffy, London, (UK)
Alan & Nina Skelly, Dublin (IR)
John C. & Peter Wooloughan, London, (UK)
Brian & Lisanne Berry, Dublin, (IR)
Ciaran & Patricia O'Carroll, Marbella, (SP)

Norman Mongan was born in Dublin and studied at the NCAD. An ardent Francophile and European, he moved to Paris in 1962, where – apart from spells in New York and Milan – he has resided since.

By vocation a writer, photographer, film maker and musician, he was a free-lance creative consultant with major advertising agencies throughout Europe, and contributor to publications in France, Ireland, the UK and the USA.

He published *The History of the Guitar in Jazz* in New York (1984) and Paris (1986) and *The Menapia Quest* in Dublin (1995). His Arts documentary *Oranje & Green* was featured at the Irish Film Institute, Dublin in 2006.

He is now based between Dublin and Paris.

ALSO BY NORMAN MONGAN
The History of the Guitar in Jazz
The Menapia Quest

REVIEWS OF *THE HISTORY OF THE GUITAR IN JAZZ*

'This is the book we've been waiting for, painstakingly researched, clearly written, virtually encyclopaedic, a formidable achievement'
Pete Welding, *JAZZ TIMES* (USA)
'Rarely does one come across a guitar-orientated work so comprehensive and detailed that it approaches perfection. *The History of the Guitar in Jazz* is one of those works'
Jim Ferguson, *GUITAR PLAYER* (USA)
'A highly informative chronicle. Turn to Norman Mongan's book for guidance'
Peter Clayton, *SUNDAY TELEGRAPH* (UK)
'All jazz-guitar lovers must have this book'
Thierry Fribourg, *GUITARE MAGASINE* (FRANCE)
'A veritable Bible for guitar lovers'
Maurizio Franco, *MUSICA JAZZ* (ITALY)
'Mongan's enthusiasm comes through loud and clear'
Ken Stewart, *RTÉ GUIDE* (IRELAND)
'He has presented the people, their guitars and the music in such a way that even if you never met them... they live. More than this an author cannot do'
Barney Kessel, Guitarist

REVIEWS OF *THE MENAPIA QUEST*

'An astonishing achievement ... of sound scholarship, speculative and antiquarian'
Alfred Smyth, Chair of Medieval History, University of Kent, Canterbury
'[In] this well researched work... of considerable interest... by taking one Celtic tribe, the author has found an angle from which the history of Celtic Europe, and in particular Celtic Ireland can very usefully be viewed... I salute the diligent research'
Prof Liam de Paor, Boston College, Boston, MA
'With its painstaking detective work, Mongan's book coincides with a renewed interest in Celtic culture across Europe: London's British museum recently opened a permanent display of Iron Age artefacts; while new exhibitions in Belgium explore the country's Celtic heritage'
Ian Ramsay, *PASSPORT SABENA*, Sept, 1997
'I sincerely recommend this book to anybody interested in our past and people... for the deep amount of research it contains'
Dr Hugh Weir, *CLARE CHAMPION*, Feb. 1996
'The author has taken sources, provided them with credibility, building up a work which well could be an example for further studies of the histories of Celtic tribes of Europe. Most commendably of all, for such a difficult subject, is the reliability of this book'
FAMILY HISTORY MAGAZINE, Canterbury, UK

Norman Mongan

A CENTURY

ECHOES FROM A MASSACHUSETTS LANDSCAPE

OF SILENCE

My quest to find my ill-fated granduncle in America

THE HERODOTUS PRESS

Library of Congress Cataloging-in-Publication Data

Mongan, Norman

A CENTURY OF SILENCE –
Echoes from a Massachusetts landscape –
My quest to find my ill-fated granduncle in America

I. Title

ISBN: 978-0-9525414-1-7

Includes Bibliographic references and Index
1. Mullingar – Aldershot, UK – Massachusetts – Boston, MA -
Irish in America – Irish Americans – South Boston, MA – Cambridge, MA –South Shore –
Brocton, MA – Weymouth, MA – Abington, MA – Holbrook, MA – Worcester, MA –
Irish Emigration Studies – biographical memoir – Ireland/America

Typeset in Bembo 11 on 13pt
Text design by Bill Bolger

Manufactured in the United States of America
by Create Space Inc., N.Charleston, SC. 29418

Contents

List of Illustrations

All photos are by author unless otherwise indicated

Introduction

I believe that one of the most fundamental human needs is to belong: to a tribe, a clan, a family, a townland, a team, a parish, a county, a nation, a society. Revealingly, the three most consulted subjects on the internet today are money, sex and family history – the basic human instinct to find out where we have come from and where we belong. It's at the very backbone of our sense of self-identity.

Blood is thicker than water and leads adopted children to seek out unknown parents or sperm-donor children to search for their anonymous biological parent and siblings. Emotional reunions with long-lost relatives have been a feature of newspaper and TV reports around the world for years but the advent of the world wide web has greatly facilitated the research for long-lost relatives and ancestors.

This book represents an attempt to examine transatlantic history. Emigration has been a major factor in the history of this Atlantic isle for over two centuries, even as recently the 1980s it was still a feature of Irish life. As Frank McCourt, author of the bestselling *Angela's Ashes* has remarked, 'The study of the Irish in America is still virgin territory. The Irish have only begun to reflect on their past.' Anne Enright, in her *Sunday Times* review (Jan 1, 2006) of Nuala O'Faolain's book *The Story of Chicago May*, eloquently highlighted this trend: 'We are bringing them all back home: it is not just recent emigrants who are returning to Ireland, but the dead, the lost, the long-ago disappeared – their ghosts are being repatriated one by one. This is a necessary task. So deep was the shame of emigration that, for many generations, we never dared to ask what really happened to them, once they were gone.' This book will hopefully contribute to a better understanding of the dynamics of this major aspect of Irish history.

Much has been written about the success stories of the Irish-American diaspora. This book tells the darker side of that diaspora following the destiny of one family – my own. The Mongans were endemic of the millions of post-Famine Irish families who faced hardship, struggle and tragedy in the New World. Uprooted from familiar ancestral rural homelands, most emigrants had to face the challenges and uncertainties of a fiercely competitive, urban-industrial landscape. They had to fend for themselves, while suffering discrimination, which bordered on racism, and religious intolerance. And yet many preferred to confront these stresses and struggles of life in America rather than resign themselves to a life of misery and despair in Ireland. All emigrants in America experienced some degree of estrangement, where they encountered both poverty and prejudice. They suffered homesickness, yet encouraged their relatives and siblings to follow them.

From the early 17th century until the establishment of the Irish Free State in 1921–22, as many as 7 million people emigrated from Ireland to North America, an exodus that was to shape the history of both countries. Fleeing from this small island, Irish men and women played an important role in the commercial, cultural and industrial revolution that transformed North America.

Bald statistics starkly reveal the rush to escape Ireland in the mid-19th century. In the fifty years from 1851 to 1901, 3,846,393 people emigrated and, during the years 1851, 1852, 1853, 1854, 1863, 1864 and 1883, over 100,000 left the country annually – with 90 per cent settling in the United States. Today some 44 million Americans claim Irish ancestry.

Research is like gold mining; you have to sift through thousands of tonnes of ore to extract a few grams of the precious metal. The story of my family took shape as my Boston researcher, Ed Hines, gradually brought to light the factual evidence of my family's long-hidden destiny in America which revealed the disintegration of a family unit on both sides of the Atlantic as tragedy struck. I never imagined the quest for my ancestors would come to dominate my existence to such a large extent and that its innate poignancy would make it such a challenging and emotional experience. However, in spite of its sad nature, this journey has enabled me to reinstate my father's ancestors to their rightful place in the overall clan/family story. I trust it will also be an iconic story of countless Irish families in America and across the worldwide Irish diaspora.

I have traced the history of my family based on the available, sometimes fragmentary, documentary evidence extracted from the archives both in Ireland and America. The resulting story looks at the process of emigration: why emigrants decided to leave, the ocean voyage itself and how they financed the voyage, and how these emigrants faced their involuntary exile. How they had to develop an ability to adapt to their new surroundings, to adjust and prosper abroad, and the consequent tensions and stresses of that adjustment. How they became able to leave the past behind them and embrace their future in the New World while ensuring that they never lost sight of their Irish identity.

I had some fortuitous encounters on my journey. My late mother Agnes (Staveley) Mongan visited America in 1978. At the time, I suggested that she contact her (unrelated) namesake, the eminent Fogg Art Museum curator at Harvard University, when she was in Boston. Although they never met, they did speak by phone. My mother's namesake mentioned a friend and fellow Harvard graduate, retired US Air Force Colonel Edgar 'Pat' Mongan, an also unrelated, Sacramento-based attorney who had developed a passionate interest in what he called 'Mongan-hunting'.

I developed an engrossing correspondence with Col Pat over the following years and later flew out to California where we spent several stimulating days exchanging ideas and took a road trip to explore San Francisco. Col Pat Mongan sadly passed away in 1994, leaving me to continue this quest on my own, regretting that I no longer had him as a sounding board.

When I made my initial trip to Boston in 1980, I had the pleasure of being invited to lunch by my mother's namesake, Agnes Mongan (1905–96), and her distinguished physicist brother, Charles, at her rooms in Harvard. She was the daughter of Dr Charles Mongan, a Sommerville physician whose ancestors came from Roundstone, County Galway. At seventy-five years old, Agnes was a very gracious host to myself and my researcher Ed Hines. The wide-ranging conversation naturally turned to Irish roots, and my burgeoning quest for the long-lost American branch of the family. Erudite, witty and charming, with expressive round eyes and doll-like features, Agnes encouraged me to continue my research, and locate the missing family members in the archives. It was a memorable and, for me, historic meeting, and a memory to be cherished.[1]

During his official visit to Ireland in 1963 with First Lady Jackie, President Kennedy had stressed how much the Irish had contributed to America. He pointed out that his own grandfather had left New Ross, County Wexford, after the Famine, and that his grandson had been elected President of the United States. Kennedy was received by the Irish President Eamon de Valera at Áras an Uachtaráin in the Phoenix Park. In his speech to the Dáil on 28 June 1963, President Kennedy underlined how 'our two nations, divided by distance, have been united by history'.

> No people ever believed more deeply in the cause of freedom than the people of the United States. And no country contributed more to the building of my own country than your sons and daughters. They came to our shores in a mixture of hope and agony, and I would not underrate the difficulties of their course of action once they arrived in the United States. They left behind hearts, fields and nation yearning to be free. It is no wonder that James Joyce described the Atlantic as a bitter bowl of tears. And the poet W.B. Yeats wrote: 'They are going, going, going, and we cannot bid them to stay.'

Fitting the pieces of my quest together has been both a challenge and a fulfilment. It has been a titanic, emotional roller-coaster, a demanding struggle with history, and with myself, as I strove to assemble the disparate pieces of the vast mosaic together. I have found the writing down of my family tragedy to be a form of catharsis, a healing act, that helped to redeem what was a catastrophe and turn it into a positive epiphany. It has removed the family's 'skeleton' from the cupboard and laid it to rest. It has lifted a baleful historic pall from our past.

I trust that this story may be an inspirational example of what can be unearthed by persistent research, and encourage others to seek out their missing ancestral links. I found it ironic, almost perverse, that, as an Irishman, I was led to search for my long-lost family in America. It is usually the exact opposite, with Americans coming to Ireland to seek out their ancestral heritage.

It also highlighted the risks of indepth genealogical research – you may not always like what the factual evidence reveals, as shown by the popular TV series *Who Do You Think You Are?* This quest obliged me to put many other projects on hold, so its with a sense of relief that I feel I can now let go of the past and move on. For any errors or ommissions that may have slipped into the text, I beg the reader's indulgence.

Norman Mongan
Dublin, 2009

Acknowledgments

Firstly, I'm forever deeply indebted to my Boston researcher, Mr Edward Hines, an inspired historical and genealogical detective, whose minute forensic trawling of the archives brought to light the essential evidence for the lives of my grandaunts and granduncle in America. Without his profound knowledge of the sources, and deep interest in Irish-American history, this work would never have been possible. He led me to St Paul's Cemetery, Arlington, last resting place of the elusive Michael J. Mongan. I much appreciated the generous hospitality of his wife Betsy and himself at Marshfield Hills during my trip to Boston. The fact that his own maternal grandfather had been an emigrant Irish streetcar motorman may have stimulated his great enthusiasm and support for this project.

I also wish to acknowledge the inspiration and encouragement of the late Col. Edgar J. 'Pat' Mongan, Sacramento, USAF (Rt) and Harvard Law School graduate, who was most generous with his advice and knowledge of his own 'Mongan-hunting', and his hospitality during my trip to California. The late Ms Agnes Mongan, Cambridge, Mass, (my mother's American namesake) renowned pioneer female Keeper of the Fogg Fine Art Museum, Harvard University, Cambridge, MA, and finally its Director from 1969 –71. She had been instrumental in putting me in contact with Col. E.J. 'Pat' Mongan. I enjoyed her kind hospitality and sparkling erudition at Harvard during my first trip to Boston in 1980. The Agnes Mongan Center for Drawings and Prints at Harvard's Fogg Museum is an enduring monument to her pioneer work.

My most heartfelt thanks to Dr Thomas O'Connor, Professor Emeritus of History, Boston College, Chestnut Hill, MA, whose inspirational writings, kind hospitality and exceptional knowledge of Boston history provided essential information to my understanding of his native South Boston; to Dr William Reid, President, South Boston Historical Society, who helped me explore his area, while sharing his vast knowledge generously; to Mr Jake Manning, a true 'Southie' who generously took the time to guide me around his home neighbourhood, and share his knowledge; to Mr Tim Hayes, 23 M Street, South Boston, who evoked the life in his area and invited me into his home; Charles Bahne, Boston Street Railway Association, Boston, MA, who kindly elucidated the development of the West End Street Railways; Mr George Brown, Archivist, Groton School, Groton,

MA, who graciously provided information oh the history of that distinguished institution, and my grandaunt Delia's time as a member of staff there.

My sincere thanks to Prof Joseph P. Morrissey, Ph.D, Professor of Social Medecine, Health Policy and Psychiatry, and Deputy Director of Research, Cecil G. Sheps Center for Health Services Research, University of North Carolina, Chapel Hill. N.C. who provided invaluable insights into the history and functioning of Worcester State Hospital, where he was a member of staff in the mid '60s and 1970s. My thanks to Prof Gerald G. Grob, Sigerist Professor of the History of Medecine, Institute of Health Policy, Rutgers University, NJ, who most generously contributed invaluable advice on the history and care of the mentally ill in the late nineteenth century.

My sincere thanks to former Massachusetts State Commissioner for Education, Dr Owen Kiernan, Centerville, MA, on Cape Cod, his daughter Joan, who cooked up a New England feast, to celebrate our historic reconnection after a hundred years of separation; to his son John, wife Susan and family, his nephew Stephen and his wife, for their generous hospitality in Milton, his nephew Vincent and his wife Debbie, East Falmouth, MA, who kindly presented me with important material on James H. Keough, all whose warm welcome made all the many years spent seeking out their family so worthwhile.

My thanks to Dr John Aherne, his mother Mary, (Ms Charles Aherne), his sister Mary and her husband Clyde Boucher, who were most gracious hosts during my field trip to Abington, and led me to my grandaunts graves at St Patrick's Cemetery, Rockland, MA. My gratitude to Councillor Kevin R. Donovan , Abington, who finally connected me with the Ahernes. To Mr David Evans, Abington, who kindly shared his knowledge of the history of the former Aherne property on 33 Charles St, and Ms Mary Minihane (Dr John Aherne's assistant) for her kind assistance; to Ms Patricia McKenna, Town Clerk, Abington, MA, for her valued help with my research.

To Mr Phillp Smith, and Debbie Sullivan, Weymouth Historical Society, who shared their deep knowledge of their home town, and led me to the former Keough property at 21 Oakdale Ave there; to Mike Burns, family historian, Weymouth, MA who shared his knowledge generously; to Ms Shirley Austin, Town Clerk, Holbrook, Mass, and her staff, who showed amazing forbearance while being bombarded with requests for local lore, and who kindly pointed me in the right direction; Mr Rick McGaughey, who shared his memories of the late, revered sports Coach and local hero, Bob Burns; to historian Wesley Coty and his wife, whose hospitality and kind guidance were much appreciated; to Ms Edna Bowers, Holbrook Historical Society, who kindly provided me with an 1980 taped interview with the late Bob Burns.

To the late Ms Ellen McLaughlin, who forwarded precious images from her cousin Robert Burns' collection; to former Officer Jack Reddy, Holbrook, Mass.

Police Dept, who provided clues that led to the discovery of the Holbrook connection; to Mr Norman Burns, Braintree, MA, who provided me with important information on Helene Burns' New York U.N. career. My thanks to the late Ms Mary (Smith) McAvoy, formerly of Holbrook, and her daughter Eileen, whose recollections of her Keough neighbours were invaluable.

To the Librarians and staff of the following institutions; Ms Nancy B. Reid, Librarian, and staff, Abington Public Library, Abington, MA; Ms Marian Delaney, Dyer Memorial Library, Abington, MA; Ruth A. Hathaway and Cathy Fox, Holbrook Public Library, Holbrook, MA; the Librarian and staff at the Boston Public Library, Copley Square, Boston, MA; My thanks to Dennis Ahern, Ahern Clan Association, an Arlington, MA,- native, who guided me around his home patch, and located former family homes there.

To Ms Marguerite (Sennott) Lechiaro, former Head Reference Librarian, Cambridge Public Library, Cambridge, MA, who contributed unique recollections of her erstwhile colleague, Charles J. Mongan. It was a moving experience to talk to someone who had actually personally known 'Charlie of the Library' and brought his existence into sharper focus; Ms Susan Ciccone and Roxane Combes, Reference Librarians, Cambridge Public Library; Councillor Michael Sullivan, Cambridge City Hall; Mss Sarah J. Zimmerman, former Director, (now with the Masschusetts Historical Commission) and Kathleen L. Rawlins, Assistant Director, Cambridge Historical Commission; who extracted vital information from the Cambridge City Directories; to Lieut. John Walsh, and Capt Bongiorno, Cambridge Police Dept; Ms Donna Wells, Boston Police Archives, Jennifer De Remer, Robbins Library, Arlington, MA,

My sincere thanks to the Hasia Diner, NYU, New York, whose writings on the destinies of Irish women domestics in America were inspirational; George Young and George Sermuksnis, National Archives and Records Administration, Waltham, MA; to Dr Michael Crawford, Naval Historical Center, Washington, D.C. who kindly pointed me to the story of the USS Louisiana; Mr Dana Essigmann, Archivist, Massachusetts National Guard Military Museum, Worcester, who brought to light valuable information on James H. Keough; Ms Dawn W. Stitzel, Photo Archives, United States Naval Institute, Annapolis, who provided a photo of the USS Louisiana; Mr R. M. Shrader, Navy Reference section, Military Personnel Records Center, St Louis, MS; the Photo Service, Naval Historical Foundation, Washington, D.C.; Mr Timothy O'Leary, Historian, Post 44, American Legion, Boston, MA; Mr T. O'Brien, Veterans Service Center, Dept of Veterans Affairs, Boston, MA, who kindly provided me with invaluable material of Charles J. Mongan's career in the US Navy; Mary M. Gallant, Librarian, Medford Public Library, Medford, MA; Teresa M. Scahill, Town Clerk, Barnstead, NH.

My thanks to Mss Mary Lou Dennehy and Mary Lowe, Archivists, Catholic Archdiocese of Boston, Brighton, Mass; who carried out essential research in extracting the baptismal records of the Mongans in South Boston; to the Librarian, The John F. Kennedy Library, Boston for valuable information on the 43rd President and his forebears; to the late Ms Arlene Fitzpatrick, and Mary Feragamo, Medford, MA., whose clear memories brought fascinating insights into the personality of their friend and psychic medium Mary Mongan vividly to life; researcher Dorethy Dingfelder, Chico, CA; Charles B. Edgerly, Center Barnstead, NH, Bonnie Brannigan, Librarian, Oscar Foss Memorial Library, Center Barnstead, NH; J. Edward Foster, Attorney, Boston, MA; Ms Carole A. Persia, Director, Medical Records,, Raymond Robinson, Hospital Administrator, Dr Christopher Kennedy, MD, Director of Clinical and Professional Services, Worcester State Hospital, Worcester, MA; Ms Charlene Sokal, Worcester Public Library; Ms Maria Padan, Holyoke Public Library, Holyoke, MA; and also to Ms Peggy Schibi, Chapel Hill, NC, and Ms Sue Fry, San Francisco, CA; for their enduring encouragement and friendship.

My thanks to Ms Kieran (Murray) Hondrich, whose generous hospitality and unfailing high spirits were stimulating during my stay on her front-room sofa at Dana St, Cambridge, Mass, where the ambiance inspired the title for this opus; to Ms Jean O'Hara, and Mr Dick Johnson, Gloucester, MA, whose delightful B/B was my base during my initial foray into the family story in Cambridge;

My everlasting gratitude to Ms Maryse Wyser-Pratte, Leesburg, VA, a long-time supporter of my creative endeavours, for her much appreciated hospitality during my research trip in America; Ms Melita Clarke, London, an inspiring muse who accompanied me along part of the path on my search; Ms Michelle Leca de Monbrison, who encouraged artistic pursuits even when the spirits were flagging; Ms Charlotte Lejeune, Paris, who always had tremendously positive attitude to overcoming obstacles; historian and writer and former American diplomat, Mr Francis de Tarr and his wife Geraldine, Paris and Four Mile House, Roscommon, who actively encouraged me to seek out the lost generations in America; Mr René Dedienne and Marie-Helene Coulaut, Paris, my French 'family', to the late Murray Stuart Smith, and Ms Sibyle Debidour; to Ms Michelle Smith Gril and their late daughter Sabrina, whose great friendship and support have been of tremendous importance to my endeavours; to Mr Michel Rivlin, Paris, who by his example in difficult periods, showed what can be achieved by persistence; to Ms Valerie and Christophe Gainfoleau, Paris, who always listened sympathetically to my projects; to Mr Philippe and Evelyne Lesca, Biarritz, who enthusiastic support has never flagged over the years; Gregoire and Angelika Lacroix, Paris, for their friendship; to Krystof Dubienko, Paris, for his unflagging support; to the late Francisco Coll, San Juan, Puerto Rico, and Ms Susan Scott, Montreal, Quebec, whose wise council showed me that fitting these pieces together was both my challenge and fulfilment.

In Spain, my sincere thanks to HSH Doña Ana, Condesa de Ofalia, and Don Ignacio, Duque de Segorbe, Casa de Pilatos, Seville, and Madrid, for their kind assistance and hospitality during my field trips to Spain; to Doña Theresa Maldonado, Madrid, for her kind permission to photograph her ancestor Doña Alexja O'Connor Phaly's portrait; to Mr Eric Berman, author and researcher, Madrid, for extracting the army file of Don Vincente Mongan Losada in the Archivo Militar in Segovia; to the staff of the Archivo Nacional, Madrid, my gratitude.

In the UK, my sincere thanks to Dr Alfred P. Smyth, Canterbury University, Kent, and his wife Marguerite, for his inspirational writings and ever generous and much appreciated encouragement in my research; to Mr Robert O'Hara, consultant archivist, who extracted invaluable information on my granduncle's military career with the British Army, at the PRO, Kew, Richmond; to Joseph T. Warden, Royal Logistic Corps Museum, Deepcut, Camberly, Surrey; Aldershot Military Museum, Aldershot, Hampshire; Patricia Field, consultant graphologist, Shipdam, Thetford, Norfolk, who teased out valuable insights from the fragmentary examples of Michael J. Mongan's handwriting; John C. Wooloughan, Windsor, Berks, who patiently listened to, and encouraged this endeavour; to Ms Veronica O'Duffy and the late Michael O'Duffy, London, and their talented offspring, Alan, Cormac, Rowan and Paul, for their constant encouragement over the years.

In Ireland, I am indebted to many people who encouraged and supported me in this venture; Mr K. C. Nichols, Cork University, whose writings on Gaelic Ireland were inspirational, and who generously shared his vast knowledge of the O Connor Faly lordship; to Michael Byrne, Offaly Historical Society, Tullamore; to Ms Marian Keaney, former Mullingar Librarian, author and broadcaster, who generously shared her vast knowledge of Belvedere House and its owners, and accepted to read an early draft of this work; to Mr Leo Daly, Mullingar, historian, novelist, and broadcaster, who graciously shared his wide knowledge of his native place; to Ms Mary Farrell and Mr Tony Cox, Westmeath County Library, Mullingar, for their sterling support and patience during my research; Ms Mary O'Donoghue, Mullingar, who revealed the destiny of Mary Duignam Jr, former Housekeeper at Belvedere, and erected her grave stone at Meedin Cemetery, Tyrrellspass; Capt. Kieran Milner, Archivist, Columb Barracks, Mullingar; the late Capt Peter Young, and Commt V. Laing, Irish Army Archives, Portobello Barracks, Dublin; Mr James Geogeghan, Walshestown, Mullingar; neighbour of the Mongan's former homestead; Ms Catherine Magan, former Director, and Bartle D'Arcy, present Director, Belvedere House, Mullingar; Mr Dick Hogan, editor of the Topic newspaper, Mullingar; Mr Dudley and Vonnie Stewart, the chatelains of Charleville Castle, Tullamore, who kindly invited me into their home to soak up the athmosphere, where Ms Mary Duignam had often seen service; Jude Flynn, Longford Museum and Heritage Center, Longford; Mary Morrissey, Librarian, Longford County Library,

My thanks to former Chief Herald Donal Begley, and Fergus Mac Giolla Easpaig, Keeper, and the staff of the Genealogical Office, Dublin; to Aongus O' hAonghusa, and his ever-patient, courteous and helpful staff at the National Library of Ireland, Dublin, to Dr David Craig and the most helpful staff at the National Archives, Dublin; to Mr James V. Rogers and the staff at the Valuations Office, Dublin, to Mr Peter Harbison, and the staff of the Royal Irish Academy, Dublin; to W.E. Shephard, and Brendan Pender, Irish Railway Records Society, Hueston Station, Dublin.

My thanks to the late Peter Paul Murray, and Lorna Madigan, who kindly read the typescript, for their continuing support and encouragement; to Mr Ciaran O'Carroll and Patricia Cahill, Marbella, Paris, and Dublin, whose enduring friendship, support and encouragement, have kept me going on this long quest, to Brian and Mary O'Carroll, Roscommon, enthusiastic believers and stimulating architectural historians; Richard Staveley, Dublin, and Dr Patrice Murphy, St Loman's Hospital, Mullingar, to Kenneth and the late Joan Staveley, Dublin, all whose support and hospitality over the years has been a constant encouragement; to Denis and Ilse Mongan; Carol Mongan, Dublin, for their support and patience as I wrestled with this undertaking; to Nina Mongan and Alan Skelly, to Brian and Lisanne Berry, whose unquestioning support was most appreciated. Mr Bernard Share, (and the late Elizabeth Coleman), whose sterling friendship, encouragement and editorial expertise metamorphosed this vast meandering text into a legible shape; to Claire Rourke, my brilliant copy editor who transformed a disjointed monster into a flowing narrative, to Jonathan Williams, my intrepid literary agent who left no stone unturned in his attempts to find a home for this work, and Bill Bolger, whose design artistry and elegant typography has enhanced every page of this book ; to all those many helpful individuals I met during my years spent in researching opus, may I offer my sincere and heartfelt gratitude.

1

The young boy and his grandfather

I can remember exactly where it all started as if it were yesterday. It was one of those dreary, damp Dublin days in the dismal post-war early 1950s. A leaden, grey sky hung over the city like a pall and the rain came up the Liffey to hang its wet blanket over the capital. The old man sat hunched over on an upturned wooden box puffing contentedly on a white clay pipe – *a dúidín* – his lips uttering soft, wet popping sounds – like a freshly landed carp – as he sucked on his pipe. A navy-blue waistcoat sported a gold fob pocket watch, regularly consulted to ensure that time was passing; probably an instinctive gesture for a former railwayman.

His pale-blue eyes stared out through the open garage door as raindrops exploded on the garden path. Periodically, he would remove the pipe and spit on the garage floor; his long narrow face crowned by snowy strands seemed deep in contemplation of things past. Lacy tendrils of smoke curled slowly upwards to become clouds floating under the ceiling. He hummed a barely audible tune under his breath, his right boot marking time. I stood next to him silently waiting and wondering.

My mother interrupted the reverie when she popped her head around the kitchen door. Out of the blue she asked, as if reading my thoughts, 'Where's all your family now?' My grandfather turned, removed his pipe, tapped it against the side of the wooden box, cleared his throat and said slowly, 'Well, I have a brother and sisters in America but we never write. Couldn't be bothered.'

I listened intently to the words. It seemed strange that my grandfather never wrote to his family in America where 'the streets were paved with gold'. Very curious indeed. I wanted to ask him why, but hesitated. He had come to live with us in our south Dublin home after his sister-in-law died and had been given a small room for himself at the back of the house.

Born in Mullingar, he had become a maintenance foreman with the Midland Great Western Railway in Longford and, in 1919, transferred to the main Broadstone terminal in north Dublin where he worked until his retirement in 1925. He received a small pension each month which was quickly splurged on a few pints in the local village pub before he rambled back tipsy to his room to sleep it off. At the dinner table, he would lower his mouth to his plate and loudly slurp his soup through trembling lips. He also had periodic bowel upsets that soiled the upstairs toilet and made our noses rankle.

A tall, taciturn, reserved man, he was a shadowy presence in the house. Occasionally, I could hear his muffled curses across the upstairs landing, as he vented pent-up frustrations over old grievances. Although we saw him every day until his death in 1954, we never came to know him that well and any family stories he had went with him to the grave.

I remember my father weeping at my grandfather's funeral in Glasnevin Cemetery. Grandfather was laid to rest next to his wife, sister-in-law and only daughter, who had died tragically young during an operation. For me, life moved on as present priorities left no time to dwell on the past. Yet, unknowingly, my grandfather had sown a seed in my young mind that would later blossom and seek out the truth.

2

The quest. Seeking the truth

Life is full of the unexpected. I never in a thousand years thought I would feel compelled to spend a large chunk of my existence chasing something when I did not even know exactly what it was I was seeking. If that makes any sense. It reminded me of U2's emblematic song with Bono's probing lyrics *I Still Haven't Found What I'm Looking For.*

Growing up, I vaguely recall that my father had spoken with some pride that, around 1900 as a four-year-old child, he had travelled to America with his parents and had visited Springfield, Massachusetts. Why he remembered Springfield more than anywhere else I never knew. There must have been a reason why his parents had visited the western Massachusetts city – to visit a sister, relative or friend there? I never did find out.

I also have a vague recollection of a menu from an old transatlantic liner printed in silver which had been kept as a souvenir. I have the impression that the liner's name began with 'L'. The menu eventually disappeared from the writing desk drawer where it had been kept, largely ignored, for years. It's all a hazy memory now.

Maybe part of my curiosity about my father's family stemmed from the fact that, although I had lived under the same roof as my father, I never really got a chance to know him as an adult, on a man-to-man basis. He had married my mother late and died relatively young. In my late teen years, I went through the normal teenage rebellious patch and, as the eldest son, relations with the *pater familias* were tense at the best of times. I was straining at the leash for independence, and use of the family car, while my father was doing his best to inculcate his Victorian values of family, faith and fatherland. Impatient, I wasn't listening when he wanted to talk – I just wanted to get out of the house.

I never got around to asking him about his family history or where his family had settled in America. I just wasn't interested at the time. I was teenager discovering the exciting world of art, music, literature and cinema. I was much more interested in borrowing the car to head for the tennis clubs, and in girls, girls, girls. I had just started playing guitar with a local rock 'n' roll group, and the world was a non-stop party. Nothing was further from my young mind than rooting around in the past.

I knew very little about my father's family background. On the other hand, my mother was one of nine brothers and sisters, there were numerous maternal aunts and uncles, along with an army of cousins. On my father's side, I felt more like an orphan, my sense of identity undermined by my grandfather's sealed lips.

Little did I know that the search for answers would become a predominant obsession in my life. It's strange how long-ignored matters can creep up on you, bubbling up from the subconscious, to take over your existence.

On 17 March 1962, I left home for the first time. I was heading for Paris to meet up with a student friend to explore the magic *Ville Lumière* and possibly find work in the Gallic capital. As I left the house, my father, just recently retired, said strangely prophetically, 'You'll probably never see me alive again.' Already stressed, his words unnerved me. I felt torn by my emotions – I felt guilty about leaving home and yet knew I had to go. I mumbled something about being back in no time and headed for the airport as my mother shed tears. Three months later, on 16 June, my brother called to say that my father had died during the night and I flew back to Dublin for the funeral.

I returned to Paris and after a decade in the multicultural city, I began to feel the need to find out more about my own family background. I suppose it was a need felt by many Irish emigrants. On a trip back to Dublin in 1973, I spent three weeks at the National Library digging for immediate family roots in Mullingar, County Westmeath. After hours of systematically pouring over microfilms of Mullingar parish birth registers, I finally located the birth dates for some of my grandfather's family and I learned that he had had several sisters and an elder brother. It was a start.

Over the next few years, Paris provided far too many distractions for a young man to become much involved in researching his family roots. Then it all changed. In December 1979, on the annual trip back to Dublin for the Christmas festivities, serendipity led me to direct evidence on the possible whereabouts of relatives in America.

Something drew me to looking through the family writing desk. I found an old family photo album and was leafing through its pages looking at photos of people I did not recognise. I then noticed the edge of a photo hidden behind another. Curious, I pulled it out to discover a sepia image – a professional studio portrait – of an infant in swaddling clothes. The baby was dressed in a long, white lace dress with large bows down the front; the sort of baby clothes favoured by proud mothers around the 1890s. Wondering to myself who on earth this child might be, I turned it over. There my startled gaze leapt to a carefully pencilled inscription: 'Mary Mongan, Boston, USA.'

I suddenly realised that I was looking at the missing link in my attempts to discover what had become of my grandfather's relatives in America. My grandfather had spoken of his sisters and brother in America but had never given any

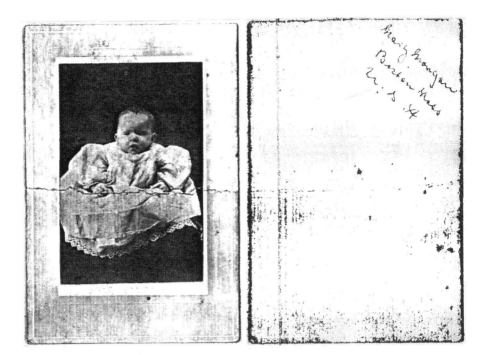

The photo that started this quest. It lay hidden in a family album for eighty years until rediscovered in 1979. Mary Elizabeth, Michael J. Mongan's, daughter was born on 29 May ,1896, when her proud parents send this image from 21 M Street, South Boston, to their brother James back in Ireland.

The vital missing link with the family in America was made clear by the pencilled inscription on the back, probably written by her mother Maria (Hurd) Mongan, 'Mary Mongan. Boston, USA' Mary Elizabeth was just a few months old when this only surviving image of her was sent.

clues as to where they lived. The sepia photo definitely looked as though it had been taken at the turn of the 20th century. Immediately, my mind raced. Was this the daughter of my grand-uncle Michael, my grandfather's long-lost elder brother? If it was, it suddenly pinpointed his location in America.

Now my search could really begin in earnest. I had learned from the Mullingar Cathedral registers that Michael J. Mongan had been born in 1863, son of Patrick Mongan and Anne Murray. That made him five years older that my grandfather, James. A simple deduction suggested that he must have emigrated to America in the 1880s. He probably married around the late 1880s or early 1890s in Boston.

As I scrutinised the image of the baby girl, a thought flashed across my brain. If this baby had be born around 1890–95 then she might still be living – aged about eighty – in Boston! I knew I had to find her and meet her. She would be my starting point into discovering the destiny of my long-lost family.

In early 1980, with this minimal, yet exciting, information, I wrote to Ed Hines, a genealogical researcher who had been recommended by a fellow researcher. I immediately sent him what little information I had. Two weeks later, he replied with the news that he had found a trace of Michael J. Mongan, son of Patrick Mongan and Anne Murray, in the local archives! I was elated and stimulated by this speedy detective work.

He found evidence that Michael had married an American girl, Maria Hurd, daughter of Elisha Hurd and Hannah McCarthy, on 5 April 1894 in Cambridge, Massachusetts. He was also able to reveal that the couple had had three children: Anne, born in 1894, who died in infancy; Charles Joseph, born 1895; and, more importantly, Mary, born in 1896. This wonderful news confirmed the identity of the infant in the sepia photo. On my return to Paris, I recontacted Ed Hines straight away.

Ten days later, he replied. He had been lucky and explained that he had located three Mary Mongans, one of whom was a daughter of Michael J. Mongan. He even had found an address for her – at Church Park Apartments, 221 Mass Ave, just opposite the Christian Scientist Church on Copley Square in downtown Boston. Eureka! I had located a living American cousin.

I plunged back in to a busy demanding schedule in the rough and tumble Parisian advertising world where deadlines came racing up. However, now I was determined to get to Boston as soon as I possibly could. After many delays, I finally flew to New York on 6 July 1980, primarily to discuss an upcoming book contract with a publisher. I had made arrangement with Ed Hines to fly up to Boston for a few days to call on my new-found cousin.

I flew in to Boston's Logan Airport and jumped in a yellow taxi, giving the driver Mary's address. My heart pounded excitedly in expectation of the meeting and the joyous reunion in view. We had so many stories to exchange and destinies to discover. Already I was thinking about all the questions I wanted to ask this cousin about her family. Why had they not remained in contact? How many of them had married? How many descendants were still living? What had happened to her Irish-born aunts? All these questions would be answered if I could talk to her. Maybe she had married and had had children, and maybe grandchildren, of her own?

The taxi dropped me off in front of Church Park Apartments. I entered the building, took a lift to the third floor and knocked on Mary's apartment door. I could hardly believe that I was actually there. I thought of her surprise to receive a visit from a long-lost Irish cousin.

No reply. I knocked again. Still no reply. Was she out?

Then the door to the left opened and a grey-haired, elderly lady asked who I was looking for.

'Mary Mongan,' I said.

The lady replied, 'Oh, she just died in February this year.'

My heart plummeted. No! No! Not possible.

This lady said her name was Mary O'Toole and she told me that Mary had passed away quietly in her sleep. I felt totally robbed and frustrated. She suggested I contact the attorney who had handled Mary's affairs and burial arrangements and gave me his phone number. She mentioned that Mary had had friends in Methuen, a suburb north of Boston, who used to call to take her out for the day. However, as Mary did not want to bother them, she always refused the invitations. Feeling totally disappointed and dejected, I thanked her and left.

I later contacted the manager of Church Park Appartments, who, sadly, knew very little about Mary or her life. I also contacted Mary's attorney but he had little information on any surviving relatives, apart from a mention of two nieces. However, he said he had some of Mary's correspondence dealing with her apparent psychic powers, which he promised to forward to me. I wondered if Mary, as a psychic, had seen that I was coming to find her.

It was both sad and ironic that Mary, whose photo I had discovered at Christmas 1979, had still been alive at that point. She had only died – alone – two months later. Desperately disappointed, I consoled myself with the idea that I still might have some American cousins out there somewhere. The following day, I checked the Boston phonebook and called the few Mongans listed. No connections. Before I left, I met my Boston researcher Ed Hines and gave him the sad news.

He promised to continue the search for Michael's obiturary and burial place. With time and deadlines closing in, I flew back to Paris with this enigma racing through my mind.

I knew I would be back.

3

Belvedere House. Upstairs, downstairs

Throughout the 18th century, Mullingar was dominated by the harsh Penal Laws. Life was extremely difficult for the Catholic majority, with worship severely restricted. Mass and other religious ceremonies had to be undertaken in private houses or Dowdall's tannery – or, more often, at a Mass Rock in some hidden location around the town. In a century of total British domination in Ireland, most Catholics were excluded from owning property or land. However, for the Protestant Ascendancy, this was a period of growth and expansion that saw the creation of elegant landlord estates around the Lough Ennell and Lough Owel, such as Tudenham, Belvedere, Middleton, Ballingall, Mount Murray, Bryanstown and Ladestown. With increased travel by coach to these estates, the road system across the county began to improve and there was considerable work carried out on the roads to the east, between Mullingar and Kinnegad, and to the west, between Mullingar and Kilbeggan.

Situated on the northeastern corner of Lough Ennell, Belvedere House was built in 1740 as a fishing and hunting lodge by Robert Rochfort, first Lord Belfield, who later acquired the title Lord Belvedere.[1]

The house certainly merited its name; from the Italian *bel, bello*, meaning 'beautiful' and *vedere* meaning 'to see'. The awe-inspiring, breathtaking views over Lough Ennell must have uplifted the hearts of all those who gazed rapturously across the panorama of its calm waters to the horizon.

It consisted of two storeys over a basement, with an exceptionally long frontage (almost 33 metres) and curved end bows. However, the house was relatively small, being barely more than one room deep. Maurice Craig, the distinguished architectural historian, believed it to be the first bow-ended house in Ireland.

The gardens at Belvedere were believed to be designed in 1740 by a professional landscape designer, though Robert Rochfort would have contributed to the informal layout, which has survived largely intact. Beech trees thrived in the limestone soil on the estate, while limes and oaks were mixed in to give more colour, shape and form.

The outstanding beauty of the building and gardens were in stark contrast with the history of its owners. The story of the tyranny and cruelty perpetrated on

Mary Molesworth, the second wife of the first Lord Belvedere, marred its history. Robert Rochfort, the first earl, born in 1708, was an infamous character noted for his selfish traits, and was known as the Wicked Earl. He married the talented 16-year-old Mary Molesworth, who, under constant pressure from her family, gave her unenthusiastic consent to the union in 1736.[2]

After the marriage, the couple settled at Gaulstown House, near Rochforts-bridge, not far from nearby Belfield, home of his younger brother Arthur. Regular socialising between the houses went on for several years until tragic events overtook the family in 1743, when Arthur was accused of having an affair with Lady Belfield. After he fled abroad, Lady Belfield was imprisoned by her husband at Gaulstown House, while he moved to an indulgent bachelor life at his new home at Belvedere. She was to remain there for thirty years, isolated, confined against her will and deprived of visits from her children, until Lord Belvedere's death in 1774. Arthur Rochfort's inability to pay the huge sum of £20,000 damages incurred by the legal battle, resulted in his incarceration in a debtor's prison for life.[3]

An enigmatic photo was to be the family link with Belvedere House.

During research in Dublin, I had come across a family photo album containing an old sepia image of a group of people, all wearing smart tweed uniforms with black velvet collars. Looking like members of staff, the group was posed in front of an ivy-covered doorway. Intrigued I turned over the photo to discover a strong, penned inscription: 'Belvedere, 1913.'[4] I was totally intrigued by the image, wondering who these people were, or why they were in our family archive. I had heard of Belvedere House in Mullingar, but didn't know of any family connection to it.

It was only after examining the Mullingar parish birth registers again, that I found the link. Amongst the many Mungan/Mongan names listed, I noted the name of Mary Mongan, great-great-granddaughter of William of Walshestown South, whose father, Michael, was one of the first to move into Mullingar town from Walshestown. Born in 1837, the marriage register showed that she had married a John Duignam of Ballinae around 1862. Finally, I found the birth certificate of their youngest child which indicated that John Duignam had been the coachman at Belvedere. What a surprise indeed!

It later transpired that Mary had joined the staff at Belvedere around 1853-56, when it was the new residence of Charles Brinsley Marlay. This was the missing connection. John and Mary were to have four children, two daughters and two sons: Mary Josephine, born in 1869; John in 1870; Francis in 1872 and Elizabeth in 1874. They had brought up their family in the coachman's cottage

Belvedere House was designed by architect Richard Cassels for Robert Rochfort, 1st Earl of Belvedere as a shooting lodge in 1740, and inherited by Richard Brindsley Marlay (1831-1912) in 1847. Mary Mongan joined the Belvedere staff in 1855 and in 1861 married John Duignam, the coachman, with whom she had two boys and two girls, and resided in the coachman's cottage near the main entrance avenue. Mary was appointed housekeeper around 1865, a position she held until her death in Novembe 23, 1918, after sixty-seven years at Belvedere. The house was inherited by Everest explorer, politician and photographer Col Charles Howard-Bury in 1912. Mary Duignam's daughter, Mary Jr, took over the position of husekeeper until she retired in 1937. (*Courtesy Berlvedere House archives*)

located on the main entrance avenue until Mary was widowed around 1892–97 and William Yeoman became the new coachman. In 2004, I finally found the cottage'sdesolate ruins barely visible in thick shrubbery to the left of the avenue.

At the time, Belvedere House, although an intimate, elegant villa, consisted of a drawing room, dining room, ante-room, hall and stairs, with four bedrooms, passage landing, dressing room, slumber room, Blue room and the Ebony room, which contained Brinsley Marlay's most antique and exquisite furnishings and collections. The housekeeper's room was located on the ground floor (near the present back entrance). There was a linen collection, china and glass store, butler's pantry, kitchen, footman's room, servant's hall and basement hall. The housekeeper's room and footman's room were furnished to an exceptionally high standard which, as Marian Keaney noted, 'only people of substance and opulence – who were very scarce indeed in the late nineteenth/early twentieth century Ireland – would have enjoyed'.[5]

Mary's connection to Belvedere was, however, more than just through marriage. In 1869, after a decade on the domestic staff, she was appointed its housekeeper, with responsibility for managing the female staff, ordering food supplies, ensuring that household chores were completed efficiently and on time, keeping fires burning, and running what was, essentially, a boutique luxury hotel. A constant stream of distinguished visitors made great demands on everyone. Among the visitors was Lady Charleville of Charleville Castle in Tullamore, who was related to Charles Brinsley Marlay. A photograph of Lady Charleville was another to emerge from the family archive.[6] This sepia image, no doubt taken by Col Howard-Bury, showed a well-dressed, aristocratic lady and her daughter, Marjorie, having tea in the garden.

The importance of the role of domestic staff, and especially senior members like butlers and housekeepers, was highlighted by Terence Dooley in his comprehensive 1990s study, *The Fall of the Big Houses in Ireland, 1860-1960*. Dooley stresses the lifelong commitments of staff who spent their entire careers in the service of Anglo-Irish landowners. He noted that 'house servants formed a hierarchical structure from butler and housekeeper down to hall boys and scullery-maids'.[7]

In many houses, servants received no regular wages, and rates varied widely from one household to another, or one servant to another. In 1884, the housekeeper at the Duke of Leinster's seat at Carton, County Kildare, received £60 per annum. Advertisments in *The Irish Times* for April 1911 suggested wages of £40 being quoted for smaller mansions like Belvedere.[8]

Servant life was not an easy choice, especially in smaller mansions where there were fewer, less-specialised servants who had to deal with most types housework. Although it may have been a life of drudgery, employment in a stately home offered job security, good food and reasonable living conditions, with a possible pension on retirement. It was also perceived as a glamorous lifestyle, far removed from growing up in a simple cottage. Job perks could include travel to London and the continent or outings to race meeting or the theatre.

However, these comforts came with a price tag. Live-in servants had little time for socialising and were at the owner's disposal at all times of the day. There were no fixed hours and they would work as many hours as their employer required, for six and a half days per week.[9]

As Brinsley Marlay (and later Colonel Howard-Bury) remained single, Mary Duignam, as housekeeper, had no wife to deal with, and as a result was probably able to develop a more authoritative position as the leading female in the house-hold, which comprised ten to fifteen employees.

There were other built-in perks for senior staff too. They had their own reasonably comfortable, furnished rooms and ate at least as well as their employers. On marriage, some staff partially furnished their homes with their employer's former chattels.

As an important post with serious responsibilities, candidates for the position of housekeeper were closely scrutinised by prospective employers. Employees from outside the locality were often chosen over local people for positions at the top of the staff hierarchy. In a sample of seventy-eight housekeepers, research found that fifty-five were born in Britain, thirteen outside the county of employment and only ten were born locally.[10] At Belvedere, Mary Duignam, and later her daughter Mary Josephine, were part of a very small number of locally born housekeepers to have merited the trust and consideration of a Protestant owner. Mary's long service as housekeeper was even more remarkable as she had a Catholic background. From a religious perspective, research also revealed that out of a sample of 717 servants, 71 per cent were Protestant, so Mary's employment as housekeeper was quite exceptional for the period. However, the extended Marlay–Charleville–Henry Grattan family had been prominently associated with the Catholic cause for several decades before Daniel O'Connell's 1829 Catholic Emancipation Act and this may help to explain her employment.

When Mary Mongan joined the Belvedere staff around 1853–56, Charles Brinsley Marlay was considered one of the best landlords in Westmeath. He was also had a reputation as an 'amiable rogue' with an eye for the ladies. Partial to entertaining wealthy widows, his favourite place for 'courting' these ladies of independent means was along the 'Widow's Walk', a path between the house and the lake. His portrait depicts a handsome, aristocratic, moustachoed, yet sensitive, face of an refined aesthete, avid art collector and admirer of women. After an ill-fated attempt to enter politics, he gave many lectures on his favourite theme The Nobility of Women, privately publishing a monograph on the topic in London.

In 1866, Brinsley Marlay purchased the Bloomfield Estate along with the adjoining estate of Lynnwood (part of St Colmán's former monastic lands). He intended to amalgamate the lands into one substantial park-type property, to be known collectively by the name of Belvedere. In 1870, the Marlay estates in Meath and Westmeath comprised 12,617 acres.[11]

The 1901 census showed that Mary Duignam, by then a sixty-four-year-old widow, was still employed as housekeeper at Belvedere, with her two daughters, Mary Josephine and Elizabeth, employed as part of the household staff. A decade later, she was still at her post when she completed the 1911 census form in her distinctive, strong, authoritive broad-nibbed hand.

In 1912, Charles Brindsley Marlay died at his London residence. He left

This 1913 staff photo on the steps of Belvedere House, taken by Col Howard-Bury, shows (from left to right): farm worker Michael Casey; Ms Mary (Mongan) Duignam, a smiling sprightly 76-year-old, and still official housekeeper, in her black widow's weeds. She is surrounded by staff members; daughter Elizabeth (standing), son John and daughter Mary Josephine (seated on steps), an unknown lady, (standing) coachman William Yeoman and wife (standing). (*Courtesy Reginald Mongan archives*).

Belvedere House to his cousin, Colonel Charles Kenneth Howard-Bury (1881–1963) and left one year's salary to each of his domestic staff. An inventory of the house was drawn up at that time and mentioned 'Ms Duignam's Room' and the 'Housekeeper's Room'. As a trusted retainer, Mary Duignam drew up an inventory of the fifty pieces of household silver for Belvedere's new owner.[12]

Colonel Charles Howard-Bury was a seasoned traveller, linguist, botanist and photographer – and future Everest explorer. No doubt he took the staff photo in front of Belvedere House in 1913, just before he set out on a six-month exploration of the Tian Shan mountains of Central Asia; an account of these travels was recalled in his book *The Mountains of Heaven*, edited by Marian Keaney in 1990.[13] Colonel Howard-Bury served with the British army, spending the First World War leading the King's Royal Rifles in the trenches before being imprisoned at Furstenburg prison camp after the fall of Ypres.

During his five-year wartime absence from Belvedere, Mary Duignam and her daughter, Mary Josephine, were responsible for the upkeep and day-to-day running of the Belvedere property. Mary never saw the colonel again, as she died on 23 November 1918, when he was still being held at Furstenburg (he was released in 1919).

The 1913 staff photo on the steps of Belvedere House, taken by the colonel, showed Ms Mary (Mongan) Duignam, then a smiling, sprightly seventy-six-year-old, and still official housekeeper. Seated on the left, dressed in her black widow's weeds, she was surrounded by members of her staff, including her own two daughters, Mary Josephine and Elizabeth, wearing smart tweed uniforms with black velvet collars. Other staff members then were her son John, English-born coachman, William Yeoman, and his wife; and farm worker Michael Casey.

Mary had provided a sixty-year presence in her gilded cage at Belvedere House. After her death, her youngest daughter, Mary Josephine, then aged fifty-seven, took over the housekeeper's position.

At the end of the First World War, Colonel Howard-Bury made Bloomfield House available to the International Red Cross to be used as an Auxillery Hospital for invalided soldiers. The house continued as a hospital for several years, and was frequented by a local committee who provided entertainment for the wounded men, arranging transport for them into Mullingar town.

Mary Josephine attended on many distinguished visitors to Belvedere during her time as housekeeper. Among them was Sir John Betjeman, later British poet laurate, who penned a major poem sequence entitled *Sir John Piers*, which he first published under the pseudonym 'Episilon' in the *Westmeath Examiner* in 1938. Betjeman was so impressed with the grandeur and setting at Belvedere, that he used poetic licence to transfer the action of the poem to its idyllic location and immortalised Belvedere for ever:

Oh, gay lapped the waves on the shores of Lough Ennell,
And sweet smelt the breeze 'mid the garlic and fennel,
But sweeter and gayer than either of these,
Were the songs of the birds in Lord Belvedere's trees.[14]

Mary Josephine remained on at Belvedere until her retirement in 1937, aged sixty-eight, when she went to live at 40 Mount Street, Mullingar, where she took in boarders, until her death in 1957. Family tradition recalled that my father had visited her (a first-cousin once removed) in Mullingar with his new bride in 1937. She must have proudly given him the precious 1913 Belvedere staff photo bearing her mother's strong, broad-nibbed inscription.

When Colonel Howard-Bury died in 1963, Belvedere passed to its last owner, his close friend and companion Rex Beaumont, whom he had met in 1942 when the colonel was Assistant Commissioner of the British Red Cross. In 1947 Colonel Howard-Bury bought a citrus farm in Tunisia, building a magnificent villa at Dar-el-Oud, where he and Rex entertained a wide range of writers, statesmen and explorers; including the first Tunisian President, Colonel Bourgouiba and French politician André Malraux. Beaumont also had a passion for racing, and owned a number of promising racehorses, including one called El Khekni, the winner of some twenty races. A keen gardener, for many years he helped to maintain the celebrated gardens at Belvedere. He was also a generous patron of local charities, hospitals and churches, as well as the Rose of Tralee Festival in Kerry.

In failing health, Rex finally sold the estate to Westmeath County Council in 1981 and died in October 1988. A grant from the 'Great Gardens of Ireland Restoration Programme' in 1998 enabled work to start on restoring the dilapidated estate. The restoration was a huge undertaking, and represented an investment of

Colonel Charles Kenneth Howard-Bury, Assistant-Commissioner of the British Red Cross, made Bloomfield House available to the International Red Cross as an Auxiliary Hospital for invalided soldiers in 1918. Mary Duignam Jr was a volunteer nurse, shown here with fellow volunteers [seated front row right] at Bloomfield, wearing her ornate silver buckle. (*Courtesy Mary O'Donohue archives*)

almost £6 million by the Westmeath County Council and the Irish Tourist Board.

In 2000, I had no information on who the people in the 1913 photograph were, so I visited Belvedere House, just reopened after restoration, and met the then manager, Ms Catherine Magan hoping that she might be able to give me some clues – but she couldn't help. I was still intrigued, so I wrote to the local *Topic* newspaper,[15] who published the images along with a brief article asking for information.

Shortly after publication, one reader wrote back to say that she had known Mary Josephine Duignam.[16] Mary Josephine had been a distinguished lady around the town, who was obviously used to dealing with the gentry and who was known for her idiosyncratic fashion of wearing only one earring in her left ear.

As a child, Mary O'Donohue, remembered that Mary Josephine had regularly visited Molloy's, her father's grocery store, to purchase household items. She even produced a photo from her archives taken in 1918 showing Mary Josephine posing with a group of seven fellow volunteer nurses at Bloomfield. She stood out because of the large ornate silver buckle she wore around her waist, which emphasised her impressive physical presence and looked capable, efficient and determined. Mary Josephine was the last surviving member of the Mongan–Duignams in Mullingar. She had been the missing family link with Belvedere House. On her death in 1957, having outlived all her siblings, she was buried at Meedin cemetery near Tyrrellspass, where a memorial gravestone was erected by Mary O'Donohue in 2002.

At Belvedere, I felt certain that the spirits of Mary Duignam and her eccentric daughter roam serenely through the silent rooms of the house at night, pausing to cast a glance through the window over the moonlit waters of Lough Ennell. All was peaceful now.

4

Patrick Mongan. Mullingar railway pioneer

On Monday, 2 October 1848, a train, belching smoke, eased into Mullingar station for the first time.[1] In spite of the historic nature of the event, the assembled onlookers were not inclined to celebrate. The country was in the implacable grip of the Famine and, in 1849, Mullingar was to register its worst famine fatalities ever – a high of 4,504 deaths were recorded, in contrast to a pre-Famine average of 1,200. Despite the depressing context, the arrival of the trains would change the town for ever.

Like most European countries, from the 1750s onwards the Irish population rose rapidly: by 1801 it was heading for 5½ million and continued this trend to a peak of over 8 million at the start of the Great Famine.

Ever since the Williamite army had partially fortified the town with ramparts in 1690, when 8,000 soldiers had been billeted there, Mullingar had been a long-established garrison town. In 1807, land west of the town was purchased by the War Department for the site of Wellington Barracks. On the completion of the construction in 1819, the first regiment to move in to the barracks were the 78th Highlanders. There was also other building work being undertaken at the time as the town developed at a rapid rate – the Royal Canal, begun in the 1780s, a hospital, convents, a workhouse and a mental asylum. In spite of all this construction activity, the town was not a pleasant place for its inhabitants; *Wally Cox's Magazine* for 18 August 1815, had reviled the town for displaying: 'all the character which landlords wish should invariably distinguish our country towns, a restricted population, an appearance of decay and a settled poverty… this most wretched town is in ruins… in a few years it must disappear altogether'.[2]

During the Famine years, some inhabitants of Mullingar were fortunate enough to find steady, well-paid work right on their doorstep with the railways. The railways were Victorian high-tech and, at the time, to be employed in the industry was to be involved in the technological cutting edge, with the promise of economic development and hope for the future. Railway employment was a much sought-after prize. On 13 March 1847, *Railway Times* ran an advertisement seeking employees for positions in the new company. Among the salaries proposed were: assistant superintendent at £1.5s.0d.; ticket clerk at £1.5s.0d. per week; parcels clerk at £1; and ticket issuer at £1.5s.0d. per week. Senior staff were offered remuneration such as two first class station masters at £5 per month plus house, four second class at £4 plus house; along with twenty-five policemen at £0.13s.0d. plus clothes and twenty-five porters at £0.12s.0d. plus clothes.[3]

A year later, in March 1848, tenders were invited for the construction of a temporary station house at Mullingar. At that time, 1,761 men and ninety-eight horses were employed on the line construction along with eleven engines.

When the line finally opened on Monday, 2 October 1848, *The Packet*, a Dublin newspaper, reported that a very comfortable but temporary station house had been erected at the Mullingar terminus: 'which is finally intended for an engine or other storehouse; and the approach to the town is very commodious and ample for any increase of traffic that may arise. There was scarcely any curiosity exhibited amongst the local peasantry to witness the arrival of the first train,

Built in 1848, Mullingar station remains unchanged to the present day. Patrick Mongan worked with the MGWR from 1850 until 1886 and his sons Michael and James followed his footsteps into the burgeoning railway transport industry.

and not a cheer was given to welcome the directors, who so far most successfully, through good and evil report, had accomplished this great project – one calculated to extend civilisation, promote trade and agriculture, and increase the wealth and comfort of the people'.[4]

Among the early pioneers at Mullingar railway station was Patrick Mongan, born in 1832, son of Michael Mongan and Margaret Donellan, and great-great-grandson of William Mongan. He had a brother, Michael, who lived in Ballina-carrigy, and a sister, Mary, born in 1837, who was to find steady long-term employment at Belvedere House. As the Mongans had begun to leave the ancestral farmstead in Walshestown South, they moved into Mullingar seeking urban employment. Patrick, after a primary school education, had been apprenticed as a carpenter around 1847, and was hired by the railways probably around 1852 and was posted to the permanent way staff, responsible for the daily supervision, laying and maintenance of the railway line.

There were harrowing scenes at the station too. On 16 June 1853, 100 female paupers from the Mullingar workhouse were accompanied to the station by a large crowd of friends, relatives and town inhabitants as they were forced to emigrate. Patrick Mongan was probably among the witnesses to the poignant event. Three third-class carriages were waiting for the women and, when the Galway train arrived, the carriages were attached and they left at 9.00 a.m. for Dublin where they embarked aboard the ship *Odessa* for Quebec.

John Mongan, another great-great grandson of William of Walshestown, lived in Mary Street, near the cathedral. An older cousin of Patrick, he was employed as town sergeant in 1857. By then, this was largely ceremonial role even if it did give the holder the right to carry a gilt or silver mace before the mayor (a tradition stretching back to an Edward II charter of 1354). In Mullingar, the role of town sergeant had become that of caretaker of the property of Mullingar Town Commissioners. In 1857, John Mongan's report showed that there were 164 cabins in the town 'without rere or Sanitary accommodation of any kind'.[5]

Patrick Mongan prospered in this new permanent way position and, in time, his mind turned to romance. On 31 July 1854, aged twenty-one, he married a local girl, Anne Murray, at the Cathedral of St Mary. She was the daughter of Phillip Murray, a strong farmer from Slanestown, near Walshestown, who rented 138 acres there from Sir John Nugent of Ballinlough Castle.

Completed in 1836 to replace the old Chapel House in the Catholic quarter of town the cathedral had been dedicated on 15 August of that year, with a Pontifical Mass celebrated by Dr Denver, Bishop of Down and Connor, and Dr John McHale, Archbishop of Tuam. The Mongan-Murray marriage ceremony was witnessed by his friend Peter Walsh and the bride's sister, Rose.

For the lucky few like Patrick and his new wife, the arrival of the Midland Great Western Railway heralded an era of regular employment and the hope of

The Chief Freight Clerk's parcels office lies just inside the main entrance of Mullingar Railway Station, where Michael J. Mongan was employed from 1878 until he left to join the British army in 1884.

better times and Mullingar station and the MGWR became one of the major employers in the area. One enduring feature was 'the fact that whole families were involved in railway service, often over a number of generations'.[6] The railway was not just employment, but a way of life.

The numerous and dedicated people who worked in and around Mullingar station were proud of their work and jealously guarded access to their ranks. Prospective candidates had to be vetted before even being considered for an MGWR position. Personal references and recommendations were of the utmost importance.

Over 300 men and women found employment in the Mullingar station area and positions there conferred a definite status on those working for the railway amongst the townspeople, who considered MGWR workers to be as highly esteemed as midwives, priests and doctors.[7] The workers were considered respected, reliable and well-known members of the community, with stable, pensionable employment entitling those in senior positions to company housing.

At Mullingar station at one time there were nineteen drivers, nineteen firemen and dozens of cleaners, steamraisers, firedroppers, callboys and messengers, attached to the locomotive shed. The crafts were well represented by fitters, boilermakers, blacksmiths, vicemen and carpenters with their mates and helpers.[8] At the Broadstone shops, the standard working week was fifty-four hours, only reduced to forty in 1879 when there was a drop in business.

By 1888, the MGWR employed 168 drivers and firemen, with forty-one passenger and twenty-five goods guards, 124 signalmen and twenty-eight shunters. Manager Joseph Tatlow felt that all MGWR staff were treated liberally and most were satisfied with their employment conditions. As a perk, men could benefit from a week's paid leave and an added bonus was the 465 houses owned by the company, excluding the station masters' homes; those in Dublin were rented at 1 shilling per week to drivers, guards and porters while gate keepers had their houses gratis.[9]

By the end of 1869, Patrick Mongan, was living near the station with Anne, his wife of thirteen years, and their six children: Elizabeth, aged thirteen, born in April 1856; Mary Anne, just eleven, born in 1858; Bridget, nine years old, born in June 1860; Michael aged six, born in August 1863; Catherine, aged four, born on July 1865; and James, born on 23 September 1869. The following year, Patrick was provided with a company house located on Clown Road (now Railway Terrace), near the station.[10]

A permanent way inspector like Patrick, who was responsible for the proper laying and maintenance of the line over a number of miles, and with fifteen men under him earned £1 (€1) per week, with a house and garden. Labourers were paid 10 shillings (€0.50) per week, and gangers earned 13s.6d. (€0.67.5). At the time, this was considered a fair remuneration. Strikes of trade dispute were rare, as the penalty of two months imprisonment for 'leaving the service of his master' acted as a deterrent.[11] It was company policy to reduce the pay of all persons working in the neighbourhood where outrages occurred, like a local murder case, where the station master, Thomas Anketell had been killed in his home in 1869. In August 1869, all permanent way men had their pay reduced from 10 shillings (€0.50) to 9 shillings (€0.45) per week for twelve months after the murder.[12] This edict inevitably affected Patrick Mongan's wages, already under strain by the demands of raising six young children.

Because of my research, I went on a pilgrimage to Mullingar station in 2000 and discovered that little had changed since my great-grandfather Patrick had worked there as a pioneer permanent way maintenance supervisor from 1852 until 1886.

The principal station building, designed by company architect George Wilkinson in 1855, was still in use. I walked though the front entrance, admiring the fine granite walls and carved window surrounds, into the main concourse. The No. 1 platform, witness to so many sad departures into exile in America, had remained untouched since Patrick's day. Just inside the front entrance to the right was the former chief freight clerk's office, dominated by a large fireplace. Now used as a store room, Patrick's son, Michael, had been employed there for six years from 1878. If only walls could talk.

From around 1870 until 1886, Patrick Mongan and his family lived at Railway Terrace (formerly Clown Road) where all his children grew up.

I walked down to Railway Terrace and saw the station master's house, next to the engine shed which had fallen into disrepair with rampant ivy climbing all over it. The four, two-storey employees houses had survived, the windows boarded up, with only one still lived in as a home. Patrick Mongan had lived here when it was known as Clown Road, with his family for seventeen years. His children had grown up in these surroundings until events took them away. I stood in the sunlight and photographed the peaceful scene. It was an eerie feeling to stand next to so much family history that had lain undisturbed for 150 years. As I looked at the ramshackled houses, I thought how Patrick and Anne had probably never suspected that they would lose seven of their children to emigration.

5

Michael. Taking the Queen's shilling

Ownership of the town of Mullingar had changed hands in 1858 for the first time since the Forbes family, earls of Granard, had been granted the manor in 1661. With funds running low, they decided to dispose of their Westmeath properties, and the town was put up for sale. The new owner, Colonel Fulke Southwell Greville Nugent (later Baron Greville) purchased the town for £120,000.[1] The rents Greville imposed were deemed reasonable, even enabling some main-street residents to make a profit by subletting parts of their tenements. By the time of the Greville purchase, the town's main problems were housing and water supply. In 1863, one inhabitant complained that there was 'literally nothing doing in the way of improvements'.[2] Lodging houses were also a 'monster grievance' with some small hovels home to eight or nine people and a pig. Many dwellings lacked a backyard, while middle-class householders had provided their own private wells or pumps to ensure supply.

By 1870, the Mongan family were fortunate to be living in a comfortable, stone-built, two-storey, four-bedroom MGWR company house at Railway Terrace. Every day, Patrick headed off with his team of permanent way gangers to inspect and repair the railway tracks.

Patrick Mongan's eight children had grown up in these townscapes. The Presentation Sisters had founded their first convent in Bishopgate Street in 1826. They provided excellent educational facilities for young girls through primary school and for boys up to First Class. However, schooling really began to improve when Daniel O'Connell pushed the Catholic Emancipation Act through Westminster in 1829. In 1833, Mullingar businessman James Hevey had left his extensive property legacy in trust for the 'support, maintenance and education… of the poor children resident in the parish of Mullingar'.[3] This funded the building of St Mary's College, which opened on 20 October 1856 under the management of the Christian Brothers and which educated generations of Mullingar children up to first and second level. Patrick Mongan's eldest girls, Elizabeth and Mary Anne, made the daily walk with their mother from their Railway Terrace home to their school throughout their formative years.

In 1872, the family's oldest daughter, Elizabeth, decided her future lay in America and she emigrated to Boston. She was soon followed by her sister Mary Anne who emigrated, aged just sixteen, in 1874.

Patrick and Anne Mongan were no doubt traumatised at the idea of never seeing their beloved daughters again, as they saw each off at platform No. 1 in Mullingar station, surrounded by their sorrowful siblings. The two sisters established a bridgehead in America from where they could send funds to their siblings to enable them to follow in their footsteps. The third girl, Bridget, left soon after in 1878, only to disappear into the vast American continent, although some evidence suggested she might have settled in Springfield, in the western part of Massachusetts.

Michael, Patrick and Anne's eldest son, left school in 1877 aged fourteen, having been at the top of his class in Mr Curtin's school.[4] Through his father's intervention and influence at Mullingar station, he was soon taken on as an apprentice shipping clerk in the MGWR Freight Department Parcel Office, next the main entrance. He had fallen on his feet with a good job and was earning his keep. He could look forward to a long career with the railways, and even a pension when he retired. Within six years, he had risen to become head freight clerk in charge of the freight department at the station.

The MGWR had developed the freight side of the business with the introduction of cheap stamped parcels in March 1870. Within six months, it became clear this had been a good initiative, and the service continued to grow for several years until 1882. Its success was judged by the increase in parcels traffic from 30,000 to 120,000 items during its first five years of operation.[5] Patrick was no doubt proud of his eldest son's efficient work in the flourishing section.

Michael had been living on his own in the town since 1881 and, with his increased financial independence, had begun to explore Mullingar's seedier side. His medical records later revealed that, in 1882 aged eighteen, he contracted a bout of syphilis after consorting with a local garrison prostitute and the infection was treated with mercury. Whether his parents found out about this youthful transgression is unclear.

Mullingar had its *filles du regiment*, frequented by the soldiers from Wellington Barracks. In a garrison towns like Mullingar, prostitution was a well-known fact of life. *The Westmeath Examiner* on 6 September 1884, reported a case where Sergeant Callan apprehended Bridget Shanley, a prostitute, for loitering on Barrack Road for immoral purposes. Sergeant Callan deposed that at 11:30 on Friday night, he had found the defendant in the company of some soldiers. 'Her language was filthy.' She was fined 20 shillings or fourteen days in jail. Another reported case dealt with Anne Moran, a prostitute, who received the same punishment for the same offence. In court, the defendant said, 'Long life to Your Honor, I'd do that on the top of my head.'[6]

Leo Daly, in his *James Joyce and the Mullingar Connection*[7] notes that, when Joyce visited Mullingar around 1900-01, 'courting the soldiers' was an unforgivable crime and many young girls, and some not so young, were ostracised for years by the townspeople for fraternising with the garrison.

In contrast, the judicial attitude to public intoxication was relatively tolerant when Michael was a young man. A report in the *Westmeath Examiner* (6 September 1884) noted at the Mullingar Petty Sessions that Sergeant Donohue had arrested Peter Allen for being drunk of 3 September. 'Defendant was fined 5 shillings and costs.'[8] In Ireland, public inebriation was still viewed with some tolerance, meriting nothing more than an night in jail and a nominal fine.

In 1884, Michael was still living alone in town, while his four younger siblings, Catherine, James, Delia and Maria Theresa, lived at home at Railway Terrace. Tragedy struck the family when their beloved mother Anne became ill. After a short period of fibricula, a contagious fever, she died suddenly aged only fifty-two, with, as her death certificate noted, her eldest son Michael 'at her bedside'.

A few days later, the grieving family followed the horse-drawn hearse to Walshestown cemetery where so many previous generations of the family had been interred. At twenty-one, Michael was most affected by his mother's passing and fought to hold back the tears. His younger brother James, fifteen, and his sisters, Catherine, nineteen, Delia, twelve, and little Maria Theresa, just five, supported each other as the trap bumped along the rough country road. Their devastated father, Patrick, sat silent and grim-faced next to the coachman. At Walshestown, their mother's coffin was lowered into her last resting place and a simple wooden cross erected over her grave, with a few flowers to grace the dark earth. Times were difficult and money too scarce to afford a permanent carved stone memorial. Mary Duignam, and her family, along with neighbours and friends from the railways murmured condolences and tried to comfort the family.

With the loss of their mother, Michael, James and their sisters began discussing their plans for the future with their father Patrick. Catherine had decided she wanted to emigrate to Boston where her sisters Elizabeth, Mary Anne and Bridget, were gainfully employed. They had promised to send money for her transatlantic ticket and she was determined to join them there.

Michael was fortunate to have a good, steady, if humdrum, job as chief freight clerk at Mullingar station. However, at twenty-one, he was beginning to feel restless, bored with the small-town life, and harboured ideas of seeing the world. After all, he was now working in the technologically advanced railway transport industry. Friends had suggested that the best way to see the world was to join the British army and be posted to exotic places across the vast Empire – to India, Africa or other far-flung colonies. His mother's passing had finally broken the bonds he had with his hometown. Devastated by the loss, and feeling the urge to get away from the scene of such loss and sadness, Michael decided to abandon his employment. He felt too young to settle down, so he chose adventure.

The information I have gathered came in fragmentary dribs and drabs over time, like parts of a gigantic jigsaw puzzle. I was totally surprised to learn that Michael had served in the British army and only discovered this when I obtained his Boston medical records in 1999. This was something that had never been mentioned in the family and was an amazing revelation for me. During interviews with his doctors, Michael stated that he had served with the British army in Suakin.

As the name 'Suakin' was totally unfamiliar to me, I called the Military Attaché at the British Embassy in Dublin but he was also totally stumped. I then checked the internet, which revealed that it had been a major British campaign against the Madhi uprising in Sudan in the 1880s. With this evidence, I decided to contact the Public Record Office at Kew, Richmond, and found a independent researcher, Robert O'Hara, who finally brought Michael's military career files to light. It was to make fascinating reading.

The large ledger format photocopies showed the amount of detailed information on each soldiers in the army, pay lists, company postings, numbers of day serve at basic pay, etc. The short service questionnaire detailed his military career. It traced his postings from unit to unit within the Commissariat and Transport Corps.[9]

On 29 October 1884, three weeks after his beloved mother Anne's death, Michael left his home and headed for Wellington Barracks. Accompanied by his friend Corporal James Taffe, he walked the half mile to the barracks on the western edge of town.[10] From the early 19th century, a soldiering tradition had developed between Mullingar and the army with many townsmen joining the Leinster regiment as well as other units.[11]

Michael reported to the recruiting officer, a Sergeant Major Finlay of the 9th Battallion Rifle Brigade. Michael was just one of the many Irishmen who at the time formed one third of the soldiers in the British army. Not only were they found in famous Irish regiments like the Connaught Rangers, Munster Fusiliers, Irish Guards or Royal Irish Lancers, but were spread throughout all other regiments. From 1884–85, the 2nd Battallion Welsh Regiment was stationed in Mullingar, later followed by the Royal Dublin Fusiliers from 1886–90.

Michael stood five feet nine inches tall and, on sitting in the recruits weighing chair, the scales registered 136 pounds. He had a fair complexion, grey eyes and brown hair. He gave his religion as Roman Catholic and his occupation as Head Freight Clerk at Mullingar station.

As next of kin, he gave the name and address of his father, Patrick Mongan, Mullingar. He stated he was single and confirmed he had been living alone in Mullingar for the previous three years and was a British subject. As character witness he gave a Mr H. Rogers, 30 Greville Street, Mullingar. Asked what unit he was willing to enlist in, he named the Commissariat and Transport Corps, which would benefit from his training and experience. He signed the recruitment form with his characteristic, slanted, fluent copperplate, with a stylish flourish on his capital Ms.

After undergoing a medical examination, he was passed fit for service by the Surgeon Medical Officer, G.W.F. Dooley. Surgeon Dooley failed to notice any sign of Michael's syphilitic infection, even though it was a proscribed condition for army recruits. A list of other proscribed medical conditions was also given: from scrofula, phitisis, impaired constitution, defective intelligence, defects of vision, voice or hearing, hernia, haemorroids; varicose veins (beyond a limited extent); marked variocele with unusual pendant testicle; to inveterate cutaneous disease, chronic ulcers, or traces of corporal punishment, or evidence of having being marked with the letters D or BC.[12] The examination required the recruit to see at the required distance with either eye, that his heart and lungs were healthy, that he had free use of his joints and limbs and that he declared that he was not subject to fits of any discription. Michael's habits were noted as 'Very Good, Sober and Steady'. After answering all the questions, and confirming that he was willing to serve in the army, new recruit Michael J. Mongan took the oath of allegiance to Queen Victoria, which stated that he would obey all orders of the general and officers set over him. The certificate was signed by the attesting officer and he was given the army regimental number 5831. With his signature, Michael

Michael J. Mongan enlisted with the British army at Wellington Barracks, Mullingar, on 29 October 1884. He travelled to Buller Barracks, Aldershot where he was posted to No 1 Company, Commissariat & Transport Corps, dealing with the horse-drawn wagons handling supplies and logistics. (*Courtesy John Sutton*, Wait for the Wagon, *Pen & Sword Books*)

had signed up for a minimum seven years service, initially being posted to the 100th Rifle Regiment. On 29 October 1884, aged twenty-one, Michael joined Her Majesty's forces at Mullingar.[13]

Queen Victoria's reign saw the high point of British imperial expansion in Africa. In 1867, British forces under General Napier had briefly invaded Ethophia and defeated the armies of Theodore, who killed himself. The Suez Canal, opened in 1869, needed protection while the 1880s saw the rise of Anglo-French imperialist rivalry, with the British generally prevailing in Egypt. In Sudan, Mohammed Ahmad was proclaimed Madhi and embarked on a bloody campaign of recovery of indigenous power. In 1885, British forces under Sir Gerald Graham had failed to relieve General Gordon in the Sudanese capital, Khartoum. In the Sudan, British forces found themselves confronted by a Dervish army, led by a slave trader named Osman Digna. His forces were composed of first-class fighting-men essentially from the predominant Hadendowa and Amarar tribes.

These fiercely fanatical warriors were known as 'Fuzzy Wuzzys', because of their distinctive large frizzed hairstyle, saturated with grease and sandalwood dust (Ruyard Kipling is credited with coining the name in his ode to the British army) and the battles around Suakin on the Red Sea were among the bloodiest ever fought by the British army. They were unique in British military history for the automatic killing of the wounded.[14]

Now enlisted in the British army, Michael prepared to leave Mullingar for the first time. But, before he left, he travelled out to Belvedere to say goodbye to his favourite aunt Mary Duignam, and his cousins, Mary Josephine, Frances and Patrick. Well-ensconced in her position as housekeeper with Charles Brindsley Marley, Mary led him into her private parlour, where she gave him a cup of strong sweet tea and potato farls before sending him on his way.

After an emotional farewell to his father Patrick, brother James and sisters Catherine, Maria Theresa and Delia, Michael took the Dublin train from platform No. 1 at Mullingar, and travelled by steamer across the Irish Sea. Another train trip brought him to Aldershot, where he reported to the Office-in-Charge, Capt W.H. Cole on 5 November 1884. Famed as 'Home of the British Army', Aldershot Barracks had sprung from barren heath land in the 1850s to become the largest garrison anywhere in the British Empire. With his head freight clerk experience, Michael was posted to No. 1 Company, Commissariat & Transport Corps the day he arrived.[15]

The history of the corps stretches back to 1794 when, as the Royal Waggoners, the first British army logistics company was formed. In 1881, the Commissariat & Transport Corps got its name, and adopted a navy-blue uniform with silver braid epaulets and cuffs, with Prussian-style spiked blue helmets. Off duty, the men sported pillbox hats and trews with twin stripes on the side seam. The Royal Garrison Church of All Saints (Church of England Episcopalian), in Aldershot town, was where the garrison prayed and where fallen comrades were remembered with commemorative plaques and flags and the corps motto 'We sustain.'

In Aldershot, Michael, now in his smart new navy-blue uniform, underwent several months basic military training and also attended the army school to further his education. On 19 March 1885, he was transferred to the 18th Company.[16]

The Commissariat & Transport Corps had a vital task of transporting food supplies, ensuring that the soldiers were properly watered and fed, that the horses had fodder, and they also handled the postal services. At Suakin, immense supplies of water were necessary for men, horses and camels in the furnace of the Sudanese desert.

In his interviews with doctors in his American medical records, Michael had claimed that he had actually served with his corps during the Suakin campaign in Sudan between 1885–88. It is possible that he was shipped out briefly to aid with the huge logistical task of disembarking supplies at Suakin but there is no listing for him being posted there in his army record.

Some of Michael's comrades in the 2nd, 3rd, 6th and 14th companies had been on board HMS *Crocodile* from 10–12 September 1885, and 'Suakin' had been marked next their names in the pay lists.[17] Men of the 3rd and 7th C&T companies, as part of the Indian Brigade, were later awarded a Suakin medal, or bar, for their services there between 1 March and 14 May 1885.[18]

The army records showed the company muster rolls for the 2nd, 5th, 7th, 9th and 11th companies that served in Egypt in 1884–85,[19] but not for Michael, nor for companies 3 or 17.[20]

However, the muster for 18th Company stationed at Aldershot showed that Michael had transferred to the 6th Company on 21 April 1885.[21] The 6th Company muster [22] showed them stationed in Dublin in 1885–86. From there, Michael moved to 12th Company on 8 August 1885, which was stationed at Porto-bello Barracks, Rathmines, Dublin.[23] Michael was again moved from this unit to 16th Company in September 1885.

Michael appears to only have joined 12th Company, shortly after their return from Suakin, when they were posted to Dublin. Unless these records contain errors, the evidence gives no indication that Michael had served with 12th Company at Suakin. Further confirmation from Michael's official military history sheet showed he had served in the 'Home' country only during his army years. Had his alleged service in Suakin been a simply self-aggrandising fiction? Or had he slipped through military records unrecorded? The truth may never be known through one possible clue remained.

There is one small clue to support Michael's claim in his medical records in America. During an interview with doctors, he mentioned in passing that, as a street railwayman in Boston, he had worn 'blue glasses' or sunshades to protect his eyes. Similar 'blue goggles' had been British army standard-issue sunglasses, as a form of protection against glaring sun and the invasive sand and dust during the Suakin campaign. Had Michael carried a pair of these shades with him to America as a souvenir of his army service days? Or had he been given a pair from one of the returned soldiers?

A reorganisation of the entire Commissariat & Transport Corps took place on 1 April 1887, when the existing seventeen transport companies were divided into thirty-four in order to provide sufficient cadres for the mobilisation of the two army corps: lines of communication and base.

The 12th Company was split in half, as new 12th and 32nd companies. From 1887–88, 12th and 7th companies were stationed at Portobello Barracks as the Horse Transport Company, under the command of Deputy-Commissary Prendergast. Michael had been posted to 12th Company of 8 August 1885, and then in September, a further transfer posted him 16th Company at Portobello.[24] From 8 TO 14 August 1885, Michael was hospitalised with a mild bout of gonorrhoea. The following year, he contracted another dose of venereal disease and remained in his hospital bed from 9 July until discharged on 16 August 1886. He was spending much of his off-duty time in the notorious Monto red-light district, off Dublin's Sackville (now O'Connell) Street. During the period from 1860–1900, the area had at least 1,600 prostitutes.

No medical supervision was provided and venereal disease was rampant. One notorious Madam, Bella Cohen, owned an infamous house at 82 Mecklenburgh (later Tyrone, now Waterford) Street Lower, between 1888 and 1905. This was later immortalised as the setting for the famous brothel scene in James Joyce's *Ulysses*.[25]

The British garrison in Dublin had seen a considerable increase in numbers for over fifty years since after the alarm caused by the abortive Robert Emmet Rising in 1803, and the subsequent threat of Napleonic invasion. From high-ranking officers to privates, British army units stationed at barracks in Dublin were well aware of the red-light zone, and made constant use of its services. Medical students also frequented Monto nightly after hospital duty, along with every social class from noblemen, wealthy businessmen, sea captains, to shop assistants, mechanics and sailors.

In 1886, Michael is likely to have travelled to Longford to spend his Christmas leave with his father Patrick, brother James and two sisters, who had moved to the town when Patrick was transferred to Longford station as the maintenance supervisor.

However, Michael was back in hospital again on 30 December 1886, where he was treated for a penile ulcer until 18 January 1887. Further health problems had him back in care one month later with serious bronchitis on 22 February 1887,and obliged him to spend another two weeks in hospital until he was discharged on 7 March 1887. Then on 29 March 1887, he was transferred to Athlone Barracks on the Shannon for a six-month spell, from where he was transferred to Birr Barracks in King's County (now Offaly).[26]

During that period, his army records had monitored the status of his health; he had already contacted gonorrhoea and then chancre in autumn 1885 while in Aldershot. During the following summer, he had developed a throat condition that persisted for two months, until finally treated with K.I. and mercury. In spring 1888, copper-coloured spots appeared, later developing 'a little matter in the centre' which eventually healed up spontaneously.[27] These military health files show that Michael was very sexually active in his early twenties, visiting brothels and, with no protection, contracted the venereal diseases rampant in garrison towns at that time – and these infections were undermining his health.

In spite of his health problems, his conduct was appreciated having been awarded 'Good Conduct' pay of 1d. per day from 29 October 1886. He also took his first step up the ranks, being promoted Lance-Corporal, the first level rank of NCOs, on 16 June 1887. Six months later, on 1 January 1888, he was affected to A Reserve, C&T Corps; his character was noted as 'Very Good'.

Inspite of this promotion, Michael's army days were coming to an end. He was reported 'Absent on day of discharge' when Quartermaster Capt. R.W. Phillips officially discharged him from the army on 1 April 1888.[28]

Unusually, he had been discharged from the army having only served three and a half years service of a normal seven-year short-service period – from 29 October 1884 until 1 April 1888. It was strange that he had chosen to leave just after being promoted Lance-Corporal. However, it is unclear if he was discharged on medical grounds or had he bought his way out. Or whether or not he had just gone absent without leave six weeks before his official discharge.

As researcher Robert O'Hara remarked, 'There was a major distinction between the offences of 'being absent' and 'desertion', and punishments were equally distinct. 'Absence' meant there was an intention to return and was not regarded so seriously, while 'desertion' at one time was literally a 'hanging' offence, often commuted to transportation. Michael appears to have gone 'absent' but we don't know the rest of the story.'[29]

The evidence suggests that Michael was given an early discharge due to his recurring health problems, although he certainly appears to have 'jumped the gun'. At that point, he had been made part of the Reserve, and was only required to report for further duty when needed, during the remaining two and a half years of his service. Whatever the exact circumstances, Lance-Corporal Michael J. Mongan, was not at his post in Birr Barracks when he was officially discharged from the British army on 1 April 1888 – he was already in America.

6

'Southie'. Michael's home away from home

On 25 January 1888, Michael boarded the 3489-ton Cunard steamship SS *Cephalonia* under the command of Captain Henry Walker for the ten-day journey to the New World. The passenger list showed Michael 'Morgan' (a common misspelling), a clerk, travelling in No. 2 compartment with English and Swedish emigrants.[1]

Lance-Corporal Michael J. Mongan sailed from Queenstown (Cobh), Cork on 24 January 1888 on board the Cunard steamship SS *Celphalonia*, under the command of Capt. T. Walker. After a ten-day Atlantic crossing, he stepped ashore at Commonwealth Quay South Boston on 4 February 1888 to begin a new life in America. (*Courtesy National Maritime Museum, Greenwich, London*)

As the *Cephalonia* slowly made its way into Boston Harbour, Michael watched as it slipped past Deer Island, a low rocky prominence located five miles offshore. He could not have failed to notice the mammoth silhouette of the Deer Island House of Industry building, established as a quarantine station by city officials in 1849 to cope with the huge influx of sick and destitute Irish emigrants. Designed by architect Gridley J.F. Bryant at a cost $150,000, it could accommodate 1,500 inmates. The huge complex contained a slate-roofed almshouse, eight circular water towers, hospital, nursery, chapel and 'carriageway for receiving paupers'.[2]

Deer Island, five miles out in Boston Harbour, was established as a quarantine station and temporary hospital to cope with a large influx of sick and impoverished Irish emigrants. In 1849, the mammoth Deer Island House of Industry, designed by architect Gridley J.F. Bryant and costing $150,000, had been built. Accomodating 1,500 inmates, the almshouse had a slate roof, eight circular water towers, workshops, hospital, nursery, chapel and 'carriageway for receiving paupers'. (*Courtesy Boston Public Library, Print Dept*)

During his ten stormy days at sea, buffeted by winter gales, Michael had spent most of the voyage retching over the starboard side of the rolling vessel. Finally, the Mullingar-born, twenty-four-year-old, ex-British army lance-corporal stepped on to American soil on Thursday, 4 February 1888 at East Wharf in South Boston.

I imagine Michael was met dockside by his sister Catherine, who had emigrated four years previously in 1884, aged sixteen, and was living with her new husband, in Abington, twenty kilometres south of Boston. He travelled with her by train down to the small rural town where Catherine was employed in the burgeoning shoe industry.

After a whirlwind romance, Catherine, aged just eighteen, had married a burly, fellow Irish emigrant, David Aherne, twelve years her senior, at St Bridget's Church, Abington, on 7 January 1886. David was employed as a lumber foreman at E.P. Reed's lumberyard and building supplies firm in the town.[3] He was one of four Aherne brothers from Fermoy, County Cork – the others were Francis, Cornelius and Patrick – who were all also working at the local lumberyard and shared a house on Birch Street. Michael told them stories of growing up in Mullingar and working in the MGWR Freight Department at the station. There is some confusion surrounding Michael's early days in America. One version says that he spent time in Abington where, with Catherine's help, he quickly found employment in a local shoe factory where he would work for a year, as he found his feet in the strange new surroundings.[4] He regaled them with stories of his army days dealing with horse-drawn transport wagons and army logistics. He may even have added a few embellished tales of his time in the sweltering heat and scorching sands of Suakin. He spent his weekends trying his hand at baseball with his Aherne brothers-in-law in the local park. However, he again became restless with life in the small rural community and decided to move up to Boston, where he felt sure he would find employment with his Irish railway and British army experience.

Confusingly, in his medical records, Michael later said he didn't spend time in Abington. In this other version of his early days in Boston, he says that he settled amongst fellow Irish emigrants in the Irish-dominated enclave of South Boston, where he first found employment in a glass-bottle-making plant for a month before seeking work with the West End Street Railways.[5]

In July 1898, Michael J. Mongan, employed as a conductor on a West End Street Railway electric tramcar, slipped on the wet running board of his trolley, violently knocking his head against the iron fender; an accident that was to change his life. (*Courtesy Boston Public Libraary*)

He was definitely living at 41 O Street, on 14 April 1888, when he applied for United States citizenship, though it was 15 February 1893 before he took the US Oath of Allegiance. He stated 'his bona fide intention to reside in and become a citizen of the United States, and to renounce all allegiance and fidelity to every

Prince, State, Potentate and Sovereignty whatsoever – moreover to Victoria, Queen of the United Kingdom of Great Britain and Ireland, whose subject he has heretofore been'.[6]

He signed his naturalisation papers: 'Michael J. Mongan'. I was totally fascinated to receive a copy of this document from my researcher Ed Hines in November 1984.

The sight of Michael's strong, elegant copperplate signature made me feel closer to him; its stylish flourish and tall, flowing, slanted hand seemed to reveal much about the writer of a century before. It suggested a man who, with only a solid, third-class education, still revealed a certain sense of style in his character. His years as a clerk had left him with a clear, legible hand.

Michael was 'admitted to become a citizen of the United States of America' when he received his naturalisation papers on that February day in 1893. The twenty-nine-year-old Westmeath man from Mullingar had become an American citizen. [7]

The document was witnessed and countersigned by John J. Peak, 201 N Street, and Henry L. Bates, 898 Broadway, in South Boston; both probable work colleagues from the West End Street Railways, who vouched that they had known the petitioner for five years. It further stated that he had 'resided within the State of Massachusetts one year at least; and has conducted himself and behaved as a man of good moral character; attached to the principles of the Constitution of the United States, and well disposed towards the good order and happiness of the same'.[8] This document was the first tangible evidence of Michael's early days in South Boston and confirmed his initial success in finding steady work in the familiar transport sector of the West End Street Railways.

'By the 1880s, Irish docility in political matters,' Thomas O'Connor remarked, in his admirable study *The Boston Irish – A Political History*, 'was fast becoming a thing of the past.'[9] As the Irish-American population increased in size, income and social status, it was now in a strong position to challenge the hegemony of the Yankee minority in city government. Joseph D. Fallon had been appointed the first Irish-Catholic judge to the South Boston District Court in 1880. Hugh O'Brien was elected as first Irish-born Mayor of Boston in January 1885. In the city's twenty-five wards, new political leaders, or 'ward bosses', were taking control of their own territories.

In the West End's Ward 8 in 1885, Martin Lomasney, son of Cork parents, nicknamed 'The Mahatma' founded the Hendrick's Club, near North Station, where men could gather to talk politics, play cards and gossip. Nearby in North End, John F. Fitzgerald became new boss of the ward in February 1892 and, at twenty-nine, one of the youngest State senators on Beacon Hill. He ran for the United States Congress and was duly elected on 6 November 1894. Across the harbour in East Boston, thirty-year-old Patrick J. Kennedy, tall and lean, with a fine head of dark hair and black moustache, had acquired, through hard work and savings, his own liquor-importing company. He emerged as the local ward boss at that point, his saloon serving as a place for Irish immigrants to gather, to hear news from back home and talk politics. Other ward bosses followed Lomasney's example by setting up their own political clubs. By 1888, Thomas W. Flood had established the Somerset Associates in South Boston's Ward 14 and, in 1901, the Tammany Club of Roxbury's Ward 17 had been organised to advance the political career of a young Michael J. Curley.[10]

Boston historian Thomas O'Connor emphatically underlined the herculean task facing the Irish who emigrated: 'If there was one city in the entire world to which the Irish should have never gone – the Irish Catholics particularly – it was Boston…Through sheer stubbornness, determination, they came here despite the problems, because they came to the one city that was the most anti-Irish… If this were a different forum, I would call it racism, among the Anglo-Irish Saxon Bramhin Yankees who lived here…They regarded the Irish as violent, as uncontrollable, as wastrels.'[11]

On 5 January 1885, the Irish had registered a historic breakthrough when Hugh O'Brien became the first Irish-born Catholic Mayor of Boston.[12] After enduring decades of Protestant-Yankee ridicule and scorn, the number of Irish-Americans Democrats increased sufficiently to tip the political scales in their favour and they were delighted to finally have one of their own in high office. In his first term of office, Mayor O'Brien proved to be a man of ability and integrity, and, notably, he cut back taxes. He had presided at the laying of the cornerstone for the new Boston Public Library on 28 November 1888, promising that the fine building on Copley Square would be a monument 'to our intelligence and culture'. Businesslike, cautious and sober, even the Yankee Bostonian elite were pleasantly surprised; O'Brien was considered as a 'good' and 'acceptable' Irishman.[13]

Another Irishman held in high regard by the Yankees was Patrick Collins. Coming from modest immigrant beginnings, through perseverance, hard work and innate talent, he graduated from Harvard Law School.

A successful, wealthy lawyer, he became a rising star in the Democratic Party and, by 1884, he had become immersed in US politics, actively supporting Grover Cleveland. Speaking to Irish supporters in Albany, New York, during the 1884 campaign, Collins argued that: 'Those of us born in Ireland or who sprang from the Irish race are here to stay. We and our children and our children's children are here merged in this great, free, composite nationality, true and loyal citizens of the state and federal systems, sharing in the burdens and blessings of the freest people on earth.'[14]

In 1892, Collins had given the seconding speech for the nomination of Grover Cleveland for the presidency. He accepted the lucrative post of Consul-General in London and spent four years there.

When Republican William McKinley from Ohio won the race to the White House in 1896, Collins returned from London. In 1897, back in his Boston law practice, he was nominated as mayor, accepting somewhat reluctantly. Although he won the primary elections by defeating fellow Democrat John H. Murphy, he lost the race in November to Republican Thomas N. Hart, by 2,281 votes. Undismayed, Collins worked tirelessly and over the next two years brought unity to the party[15]

Michael had chosen to live in one of the fastest developing cities in America. Boston was the first city in America to build a subway – only the fourth in the world after London, Budapest, Glasgow and Paris. In fact, during the planning and construction stage of Boston's first, comparisons had been made with the line in the Hungarian capital. The subway had been conceived to reduce overwhelming traffic congestion.[16]

By 1885, the main form of transport was the horse-car and due to their phenomenal success, by 1885 seven operating companies dominated the urban transport system, with almost 232 miles of tracks, 1,716 cars and a staggering 8,374 horses.[17] Freezing in winter, sweltering in summer, travel on horse railways was slow and crowded. However, with an average speed of around six miles an hour, they provided reliable and inexpensive transport for the average Bostonian. Passenger numbers increased to in excess of 62 million a year by 1879, as the horse-car network continued to grow. By the time Michael arrived in Boston in 1888, annual passenger numbers had topped the 100-million mark. With a great demand for staff with railway transport experience, Michael quickly found employment with the West End.

If horse-cars were profitable, they were costly to run and had many disadvantages. Teams needed to be changed frequently, extensive feed and stable facilities were required, horses were prone to catch diseases, and the disposal of manure was an endless problem. Severe congestion was created when different lines came together in the downtown Boston business district. Consolidation was needed and this is exactly what occurred in November 1887, three months before Michael arrived in America. A Boston entrepreneur, Henry M. Whitney, brought together the major horse-car companies serving the city, into a giant consolidation known as the West End Street Railway Company. Incorporated on 22 January 1887, it became the largest public transportation system in the world at the time.[18]

With the disadvantages of equine propulsion being increasingly obvious throughtout the 1880s, alternatives were being sought. Cable and steam-powered streetcars had been tested and, by 1885, the electric trolley looked the most promising. The West End Street Railway introduced its first electric trolley to Boston on 3 January 1889, with a line from Aliston railroad depot to Park Square, and on to Chestnut Hill Reservoir. A second electric line was launched from Harvard Square in Cambridge to downtown Boston a month later on 16 February 1889.[19] After this tentative start, electrification of horse-car lines expanded rapidly. In 1889, the West End had 7,728 horses, 1,794 horse-cars and forty-seven electric trolley cars. A year later, only 857 horses and 541 horse-cars were still in service, while the electric trolleys had multiplied to 1,714. That year 94 per cent of the entire track network was electrified. The last horse-car, however, survived until 24 December 1900 when it was retired from Marlborough Street in Boston.

Despite their greater speed, trolley cars still experienced street delays. Once again, passenger numbers rose exponentially and severe congestion was a daily occurrence along downtown Tremont Street. With the growing crisis, a radical plan was needed; proposals included a subway and two elevated routes. The subway line was to run under Tremont Street and Boston Common while the elevated lines were to run from South Boston to Charlestown and from Roxbury to Cambridge. Construction work proceeded at a fast pace, with the first section from Park to Arlington and Boylston streets completed on 1 September 1897. A new Boston Elevated Railway Company, established in 1894, proposed to purchase the West End Railway Company. Although initially hostile, the West End did agree to sign a twenty-five-year lease running from October 1897 to June 1922.[20] This agreement facilitated a single fare throughout their lines. Later known as the 'El', the Boston Elevated took over West End trolley-car system, and went on to operate Boston public transit until 1947. Public transport in Boston had been transformed in less than fifteen years, during which time Michael worked with the West End Street Railway Company.

Like a homing pigeon, Michael had been atavistically drawn to 'Southie' as South Boston was affectionately known by its inhabitants. It was as much a state of mind as a geographic location. In the early 1800s, South Boston, or Dorchester Neck as it was then known, was part of the town of Dorchester, a relatively underdeveloped rural strip of land, with a few rutted tracks, one of which later became Broadway. On 4 March 1804, Dorchester Neck, on becoming part of Boston, adopted the name South Boston. Boston authorities quickly laid out the streets employing the grid system – with east-west streets being numbered and north-south streets lettered, except for Broadway and Dorchester Street, both of which were named in 1805.[21]

The first horse-cars had appeared in the 'Lower End', the industrialised part of South Boston, in November 1856. Ten years later, the Broadway Railroad was running twelve cars from its new carhouse and stables located north of Broadway at H Street. Enjoying high passenger numbers, the company went from success to success. On 24 June 1868, having become the South Boston Railroad Company, it continued developing its system during the 1870s.

A larger horse-car barn was constructed on East Sixth Street near P Street, with a second erected across the street on the northside.[22]

By the early 1880s, City Point, overlooking the ocean, had become a very popular beach and recreation area known as Marine Park. Along with its grassy, tree-shaded picnic areas, Marine Park had a large bathing area, a pier extending out into the bay, and popular restaurants offering seafood dishes. In 1886, the South Boston Railroad inaugurated its last horse-car route, running a line along Dorchester Street from Broadway to Andrew Square.

The company then merged into the huge West End Street Railway Company in 1887. This move benefited South Boston. Several routes now had connections with Roxbury, Cambridge and Charlestown, attracting increasingly huge crowds of visitors to Marine Park at City Point by 1889. Electric trolley cars were introduced in spring of 1892 running from Harvard Square via downtown Boston along Broadway to City Point.[23]

Patrick J. Loftus Jr, in his classic work, *That Old Gang of Mine*, spoke of South Boston being misconstrued as, 'Irish-America's spiritual home'. He also showed that this idea, only partially true, had led to the myth of a totally Irish enclave. The demographics showed that the Irish were spread all over Boston. In the 1905 census, when their relative numbers were gradually declining, they were still the largest immigrant group in twenty-three of Boston's twenty -five wards. In South Boston's Lower End, (Dorchester Street to D Point Channel) with 62 per cent of inhabitants, they constituted the highest proportion of Irish, whereas South Boston in general was only 45 per cent Irish. Other areas of the city could have equally laid claim to being the 'spiritual home'; Charlestown, with 48 per cent or Roxbury with 14,247 first- and second-generation Irish, when compared to 'Lower' Southie's 13,625, might also have made a similar claim.[24]

Loftus pointed out that, while the Irish were predominant, there were at least eleven other immigrant groups residing in South Boston based on the 1905 census. They ranged from 6,463 Canadians to 161 Dutch, and included many divergent nationalities as Germans, Poles, English, Scots, Russians, Lithuanians, Swedes, Italians, Belgians and Austrians. By 1910, Norwegians, Portugese, Turks, Greeks and Armenians had added further layers to the residential immigrant mix, bringing the population to an all-time high of 71,703 in the peninsular wards.

The first great 19th century immigrant waves had been dominated by the Irish and the Germans. Initially the Famine Irish settled in the teeming tenements of Fort Hill waterfront area, until the great fire of 1872 when large numbers settled in South Boston. The post-Famine wave of immigration, mostly female, were also attracted to the area by the largest 'industry' of all, domestic service.

The Irish were split between the east 'Lower End' around Dorchester, a warren of small industries, and the 'Upper End' from Telegraph Hill to City Point, essentially a residential area near the beaches.[25]

Carney Hospital, which had been established in 1863, stood on Telegraph Hill in the former Howe mansion. Generous citizens had established a free hospital there, subsequently endowed with funds by Cavan-born Andrew Carney, after whom it was named. Through his successful clothing store, Carney and Sleeper, in Boston's North End, he had amassed a fortune and became a leading philanthropist. Considered the founder of the Carney Hospital, he became known as 'one of Boston's great Irishmen', having donated a total of $75,000 by the time of his death.[26]

The 'Lower End', with its numerous small mills and foundries, was the single most important source of employment. Many companies employed more than 500 men; like R. Estabrook's Sons City Iron Foundry, established in 1874, located at West First and C Street. Its moulding shop had a vast area where machinery, boiler and building castings, soil pipes and fittings, bathtubs and plumbing supplies, brass and copper work, were manufactured.[27] Alongside the foundries other industries flourished – the South Boston Sugar Refinery, glass-making establishments, shipyards, and numerous dockside activities, where longshoremen and teamsters were in much demand.

In its 1890s heyday, Southie was a place of residence for immigrants in transition. In the 1905 census, the first- and second-generation Irish ethnic group comprised some 30,803 people, or 70 per cent of the inhabitants of South Boston, by far in excess of the next most numerous Canadian group with just 6,463 members.

By 1900, South Boston, as Thomas O'Connor in his engrossing study *South Boston – My Home Town*, underlined, the peninsula had become a most desirable residential quarter. Homes of politicians, judges, well-to-do businessmen, merchants and physicians lined Dorchester Avenue. Increased number of middle-class professionals were making their homes in the area and lawyers, merchants, real-estate agents and insurance salesmen, lived side by side along East Broadway right out to City Point.

On the corner of M Street stood the impressive former residence of hardware business tycoon Otis D. Dana while, just opposite, was the exceptional home of Joseph D. Fallon, judge of the South Boston Municipal Court, with its panoramic view of Boston Harbour. Yet, while there were some doctors, dentists, pharmacists, lawyers and real estate agents in the City Point area, most 'Southie' residents perceived themselves as working-class people.[28]

If the Lower End was home to day labourers, longshoremen, pub owners, grocers and industrial workers, the City Point area was inhabited by carpenters, plumbers, electricians, streetcar conductors, policemen, firemen and letter carriers. As Thomas O'Connor emphasises, 'Southie' was truly separate, distinctive and unique. 'Whatever their occupation, parents were hardworking, proud of their jobs, and raised their children to admire the working-class values of hard work and determination despite their modest homes and meagre incomes.'[29]

During his early years in South Boston, Michael found romance. On weekends, he spent his leisure time with fellow-streetcar men and Southie neighbours out on City Point beaches, they enjoyed hotdogs and fried clams, washed down with chilled beers, whilst they admired the demure girls strolling along the boardwalk in their long white dresses. Eventually, he became smitten by a particularly vivacious visitor from Cambridge. The object of his attentions was a first generation seventeen-year-old Irish-American, Maria Hurd, whose parents Elisha Hurd and Hannah McCarthy, had come to America in the post-Famine period. Elisha worked as a watchman at the River Street stables nearby on the Charles river.[30] As a fellow-street railwayman, there was an immediate entente between the two men.

By 1892, the couple were courting seriously. Then Michael proposed and was accepted. With her parents' blessing, Maria and the twenty-eight-year-old Westmeath man became engaged.

Michael's had signed his naturalisation papers on 15 February 1893 and wasted no time in setting a date for his wedding. His vivacious young sweetheart, at twenty, was eight years his junior. Barely six weeks later, after receiving his citizenship papers, Michael and Maria tied the knot at the First Universalist Church (St Mary's), on Inman Street, next to Cambridge City Hall, on 5 April 1893. The ceremony was celebrated by the distinguished, well-known local First Universalist clergyman, Rev. Dr George W. Bicknell.[31]

Interestingly, on his marriage certificate, Michael gave his father's name as 'Herbert' P. Mongan, most likely an attempt to mask his Irish roots as the Irish were then at the bottom of the social ladder. The choice of venue was strange for two people raised as Catholics though Michael claimed to have become an Episcopalian during his time with the British army. Whether this was based on a sincerely held theological conviction, or more an attempt to assimilate into Boston Yankee-dominated society is not clear.

Ed Hines remarked on the 'anglicisation' of Michael's father name: 'The Irish were not entirely welcome in Boston at that time. They had been coming in by the thousands and disrupted the otherwise ordered lifestyle of the native Anglo-Saxon Protestant stock who liked their cheap labour but little else. Around the

St Mary's Syrian Church (formerly First Universalist Church) at 8 Inman St, next to Cambridge Town Hall, where Michael J. Mongan and Marie Hurd were married by prominent First Universalist minister Rev Dr George W. Bicknell, on 5 April, 1893. The newlyweds rented a apartment at 112 Second St in South Boston, close to where his sister Mary Anne and her foundry-worker husband James Keough were living. (*Courtesy First Universalist Church Archives*)

time of Michael's marriage the Immigration Restrictive League was in full swing and many Irish tried to hide their ethnicity, they also came from poor beginnings and strove to assimilate thus turning their back on Ireland and their past. I have researched many Irish families here, where the census taker was told that they had been born in Massachusetts but had actually been born in Ireland. The very Irish name 'Patrick' was many times concealed.'[32]

In spite of Michael's newly acquired citizenship, many second-generation Irish-American families still had an innate negative preconception of marriage to a recently arrived Irish immigrant as a possible retrograde step, as Edward Hines emphasised: 'I always wondered about the fact that Michael J. Mongan married the American-born 'Hurd' woman. To do this in the 1940s and 1950s was a trauma, so I can only imagine that this only added to Michael's burden.'[33]

Michael's siblings were amongst the guests of honour at the ceremony: his oldest sister Elizabeth, with her carpenter-husband, Charles Edgerly; Mary Anne with her husband, James Keough, a brass moulder in South Boston; Catherine, up from Abington with her husband David Aherne; along with Delia and Maria Theresa, recent arrivals in Boston. The Hurds were represented by the bride's parents, Elisha and Hannah; her uncle, Jimmy McCarthy; her sister, Anne; and brother, John, all delighted with the first marriage in the family. Daffodills blooming in the gardens announced that spring was already in the air.

I imagined that, after the ceremony, the wedding party celebrated at nearby Old Hovey Tavern on Lafayette Square with a typical Boston dinner of salt cod with baked beans, washed down with Pickwick beers – then a few whiskeys, lots of chat about future plans and stories of the 'Ould Sod'. The Mongan sisters sang Irish songs and laughingly recalled their schooldays in Mullingar. It was a day of joy, celebration and hope – three sisters were already married in America, and now Michael had tied the knot with a lovely Irish-American girl. It was an auspicious day and augured well for the future.

The newly married couple rented an apartment in a typical three-storey clapper-board house at 112 Second Street, South Boston, in Michael's familiar neighbourhood near the P Street streetcar barn.[34] They were only a few minutes walk away from Michael's sister Mary Anne, and her husband James 'Jimmy' Keough, living at 15 M Street near the beaches. On a sunny 28 June 1893, the two newlywed couples were among the milling South Boston crowds, assembled to celebrate Faragut Day. The unveiling of the Admiral Faragut statue at Marine Park was performed by Annie Flood, daughter of Irish-born Alderman Thomas Flood.[35]

However, as Michael and Maria embarked on their new life together, there was a growing sense of concern across America in the financial sector. The 1880s had seen strong growth of industrial securities on the New York Stock Exchange. As Lee Niedringhaus in his work, *The Panic of 1893*, explained, on 4 May National Cordage, the darling of the industrial stocks and one of the most widely traded, suddenly collapsed. The panic was on. Nationwide banks began to fail, with 128 going under in June alone. A run on world silver prices saw America's great silver mining industry collapse overnight. During 1893, almost 15,000 companies failed, 500 banks went to the wall and nearly 30 per cent of the country's rapidly expanding railway system became financially insolvent. Violent strikes became rampant throughout the country with increased personal hardship everywhere. [36]

Recently elected president, Grover Cleveland, was confronted with a plummeting gold reserve heading precariously close to the statutory $100 million mark. The country slid into its worst depression, and the economy was put under huge pressure over the next three years. Unemployment soared to over 10 per cent and immigration, which had averaged over 500,000 annually, dropped by 50 per cent from 1894-1898. Even fortunately employed street railway men like Michael J. Mongan felt the increased pressure and strain of holding down their jobs.

The triple-decker house at 15 M Street, South Boston, where Mary Anne (Mongan) Keough and her husband James, were living in May 1900

In this atmosphere in 1893 on City Point beach, Maria announced to her delighted husband that she was pregnant. Their first child, a girl baptised Annie in memory of Michael's mother, was born at home on 15 March 1894. Their joy, however, was short-lived. Baby Annie caught cholera and died aged only four months and two weeks in July, at an infectious disease centre in Malden just north of Boston.[37] (Curiously, on Annie's death certificate, Michael's profession was listed as 'policeman'. Had he been training to join the force?) The couple were heartbroken and inconsolable. The death of their first child was to mark Michael indelibly, and years later he still mourned his lost daughter.

Happily, two other children arrived to console them: Charles Joseph, born on 12 May 1895, and another girl, Mary Elizabeth, on 29 May 1896; both delivered at home after the family had moved to another triple-decker at 21 M Street, next to Michael's sister Mary Anne Keough, at 15 M Street.

As Michael celebrated his daughter Mary's birth, there was further uplifting news on the sporting front. James Brendan Connolly, a member of the Suffolk

21 M Street, South Boston, where Michael J. Mongan shared this triple-decker house with his elder sister Mary (Mongan) Keough and her family from 1893 TO 1898. These typical emigrant residences provided an entire floor for each family. Today these properties are highly desirable South Boston residences. (*Courtesy Jake Manning*)

Athletic Club in South Boston, had become Southie's greatest athlete. In 1896, in his freshman year, he had left Harvard after being refused permission to take part in the Olympic Games in Athens. Borrowing money to pay his travel expenses, he went out to join the American Olympic team at the Games. By winning the first event, the triple jump (then called the hop-skip-and-jump), Connolly became the first South Boston native to win an Olympic gold medal in modern times when he soared forty-five feet to beat his nearest rival by three feet three inches. He also collected a silver medal in the high jump and a bronze for the broad jump. Michael and Maria joined with the Southie population, and other Bostonians, in their delight at the determined young Irish-American's inspirational sporting achievements.[38]

Michael had settled well into a daily routine as conductor on the new-fangled West End electric trolley cars. He left home at 5.a.m. for the early shift transporting Bostonians to their place of work. A proud father, he even had a costly studio photo portrait taken of his baby daughter to send back to his younger brother, James, in Longford. On the reverse of the sepia print, his proud wife Maria pencilled a caption: 'Mary Mongan, Boston, USA'.

Working the street cars was hard and demanding, with an exacting timetable and tiring schedule to respect, but steady employment was vital to support his wife and growing family. David Fouhey's early 1880s poem *The Famous Conductor* captures the constant company pressures on an Irish streetcar conductor.

> The famous conductor from the Bay State
> Always on time and he never was late
> He attended the bell and he pulled down the rope
> And put all the change then into his coat
>
> When his fares were collected
> He could sit or could stand
> And salute all the passengers as they came along
> But now he is hunched with his hand on the brake
> Afraid of his life not one word to spake
>
> Twenty per cent he was cut in his pay
> He must grin and bear sure every day
> His stripes cut no figure when it comes to the dime
> The company wants it every time [39]

Ed Hines emphasised the abrasive nature of employment on the street railways. 'The US at the turn of the century was a "raw-boned" and crude social state and the many new arrivals competed fiercely for survival; a job was essential to one's ability to live and, like land, one would kill to retain it. The Irish took control of the transit system. I have read how they were feared by other ethnic groups and ran their trains with an iron hand. Unlike today, if an Irishman was in charge of the coach, there would be little "cutting up" at the risk of being thrown bodily off the train. My own grandfather Edward Quinn from Arboe, County Tyrone, was a railway conductor. He had arrived here in 1907. He was a hard man but worked the Boston Elevated up through the 1930s when he lost his job due to "drink".'[40]

On sunny weekends, Michael and Maria would stroll from M Street to Marine Park, with their two babies and were often joined by Michael's sister, Mary Anne and her husband, Jimmy.

Mary Anne had married her Irish-born sweetheart, an immigrant like herself, around 1885, and started a family in 1887, with the birth of her first daughter, Josephine Frances, at 7 P Street in South Boston. The child was baptised at the Gate of Heaven Church on 18 September with her aunt, Delia Mongan, as sponsor. The family were traced in the archives as they changed address around the area. A second child, James, was born on 14 July 1889, when the family was living at Second Street, with the baptism held at the Gate of Heaven and Michael Dowling and Margaret as sponsors. A second boy, Hubert, came along on 4 November 1892, when the Keoughs were living 8 Kemble Place, close to M Street. The fourth child, Mary Helene, was born – most patriotically – on 4 July 1898 at 21 M Street, where the family were then installed in a triple-decker apartment. Again the baptism took place at the Gate of Heaven with Martin Greeley and Anne Hurd as sponsors.[41]

As these births dates showed, the Keoughs moved around various addresses in the neighbourhood during those years, probably changing apartments in order to find more space for their growing family, or less expensive accommodation each time they relocated. Every morning, Maria and Mary Anne would walk over to St Eulalia's kindergarten where their young children began their education.

The young families would avail of the various other recreational amenities too. The Great Pier, long and wide, projected from Head House, with a covered roof deck where dances were often held during the summer season. At Marine Park, a wide lawn extended from Colombia Road to East First Street where great crowds of Southies and visitors held their picnics. The popular L Street Bath House on Colombia Road had bathing and swimming facilities for men and boys; K Street Bath House, provided similar services for women and girls. The Wave Cottage Café served chilled Pickwick ales, wine and liquors to accompany fish dinners or barbecued chicken to the milling throngs.

Mesmerised children were entertained by travelling Punch and Judy shows sponsored by the city authorities. Head House, with its soaring copper cupola and weather vane, based on the design of a north-German *rathhaus* (municipal building) was a landmark at City Point. At its rear, 500 lockers catered for a multitude of bathers who flocked to the beaches during the summer months. Brass bands entertained visitors with free concerts as they enjoyed the sunshine.[42]

This was a halcyon period for the Mongan and Keough families in South Boston. Life was reasonably good and hopes were high for the future. Michael and Maria were living in marital bliss with their young family in a nice neighbourhood. However, their tranquil days were not to last.

In July 1896, Michael had barely had time to rejoice at the birth of his daughter Mary, when disaster struck. On a showery summer day, while working as a conductor, he slipped of the wet running board. His head collided violently with the metal fender and he also received a nasty gash to his leg. Momentarily stunned, he recovered and, though still dizzy, was able to run his car back to the trolley barn. Due to the severity of his leg wound and his concussion, Michael was out of work for four days, through he suffered no paralytic consequences. The resulting ulcer on his leg was to take a very long time to heal, with the wound reopening on seven different occasions.[43]

Due to the shock of the accident, a shaken Michael decided to transfer to driving electric trolley cars as a motorman shortly afterwards, rather than taking any further risks on slippery running boards. With the demands and cost of supporting and rearing a growing family, Michael made a crucial and ultimately fateful decision when he decided to acquiesce to Maria's pleadings and moved his family to live with his Hurd in-laws at their 86 Kinnaird Street, Cambridge, apartment, in the industrial part of the city.

The Boston City directories at the time traced Michael's change of addresses. In 1894, Michael J. Mongan, 'Conductor', was listed as living at 112 Second Street in South Boston; in the 1895 edition, he was still listed as 'Conductor' but then living at 21 M Street and then, in 1897, his entry read 'Removed to Cambridge'.[44]

With its delightful rural character, Old Cambridge had grown up around Harvard until 1846, when it was united with its two rival villages, Cambridgeport and East Cambridge. From 1809, with the completion of the Canal Bridge, East Cambridge had developed into the city's major industrial centre until the 1880s. Glass and furniture factories were the industries attracted by cheap land, water transportation and proximity to Boston. Thousands of sick, destitute Irish immigrants had landed in Boston and Cambridge following the Great Famine in the late 1840s. Crowded into worker's cottages, they laboured in the clay pits and brickyards of North Cambridge. Toiling at unskilled jobs in the local glass and furniture factories, the majority of these immigrants lived in East Cambridge where 22 per cent of the population were Irish-born by 1855.[45]

The Hurd family had arrived in Cambridge with the immediate post-Famine wave of immigrants.[46] Elisha Hurd, Maria's father, had been employed as a watchman at the huge Bennett Street Stables and at River Street Car Station. Maria's brother, John, had also been working as a streetcar conductor, and was later employed at Murray Street Stables.[47] The family home at 86 Kinnaird Street was a typical wooden, two-storey house, originally built as a single-storey worker's cottage in the 1870s and later converted into a two-storey duplex building with a low slanted roof.[48]

Sited on the corner of Kinnaird and Bay streets, the Hurds – Elisha, his wife Hannah, and children John and Anne – lived on the upper floor of the building, with a separate right-hand ground-floor entrance. Michael and Maria moved into the ground-floor apartment, with its own separate entrance round the corner at 32 Bay Street. The Christmas holiday season of 1898 was warm and joyful with both families sharing the festivities.

However, as research has revealed, shortly after this tensions began to surface in Michael and Maria's marriage, especially when Michael discovered that his wife was handing over his hard-earned, precious savings to her mother to safeguard. Trouble was brewing. He protested on and off at the injustice of the situation and Maria did ask for the money to be returned but did not receive it until further dramatic events befell the family.

Back in Ireland in 1888, Michael's father, Patrick, now a widower, had received the news that Michael had found employment with the West End Street Railways with relief, although he noticed that Michael was working as a trolley conductor, rather then his original position as clerk. Patrick had been living at Railway Terrace and, working as permanent way supervisor when, in 1886, the MGWR transferred him as maintenance foreman at Longford station.

Patrick's second son, James, then seventeen, and his youngest daughter, Maria Theresa, only seven, moved to Longford with him. After his transfer, he leased two houses at 16-17 Dublin Street, off Main Street, near St Mel's Cathedral. Evidence from the Valuation Office books shows that he had leased the premises at £14 per year from the Earl of Longford, the Packenham family of Tullynally Castle.[49] He was subletting the adjoining property at 17 Dublin Street to tenants. Then, in 1891, further tragedy struck when Patrick, aged sixty-one, passed away suddenly. James, at twenty-two, and his remaining sister, Maria Theresa, only twelve, were now totally alone in the world. They had the sad ordeal of organising the funeral, and accompanying their father's coffin to his final resting place at Ballymacormack cemetery outside the town. Now James and Maria Theresa had to choose where their futures would take them.

Cupid was to decide James' destiny. On one of his regular trips to the MGWR Broadstone terminal in Dublin, James met a petite, dark-haired young woman called Mary O'Toole. There was an immediate chemistry between them, However, Mary, daughter of Dublin jeweller Frederick O'Toole, was preparing to emigrate to Canada. She left for Montreal promising to write to James in Longford. In spite of being separated by the vast Atlantic, letters travelled back and forth with Mary writing from Montreal where she was working as a domestic servant. Eventually, love won out and Mary returned to marry her suitor. Prior to the wedding day, she stayed for two weeks at the Midland Hotel in Dominick Street, Dublin. On 6 May 1896, James, twenty-seven, married his twenty-year-old Montreal housemaid, at St Saviour's Church in Upper Dominick Street, Dublin. It was an intimate ceremony with a few of Mary's Dublin friends, and James' young sister, seventeen-year-old Maria Theresa, who had travelled up from Longford for the special day. The witnesses were Mary's mother, her sister, Kate, and friends Eliza Shanley, who lived at Parkgate Street, near Phoenix Park, and James O'Neill of Temple Cottages off Upper Dominick Street. A small reception was held at the Midland Hotel, and a few days later the couple took the train back to Longford.

James, now had to decide what to do about his young sister Maria Theresa. Everything seemed to suggest that she would be better off with her sisters in

America. She had finished her schooling in Longford and, with both her parents deceased, she now had less attachment to the town. She continued to share the family home at 16 Dublin Street, as her sister-in-law Mary became pregnant. On 29 April 1897, Mary gave birth to a boy, Michael Reginald, who was baptised at St Mel's Cathedral at the end of Dublin Street. Maria Theresa finally sailed for Boston in 1898, where she would live out the rest of her days.

7

Michael's sisters. Exodus to America

Oh brave, brave Irish girls,
We well might call you brave
Should the least of all your perils
The Stormy ocean waves.
                    James Conolly, *Labour in Ireland*

Parnell's Ireland was a land overwhelmed by a sense of doom, decay, and 'the moribund quiet of a society in decline'.[1] By the last decades of the 19th century, the country offered little hope for women, few of whom could find any reason to remain in the agricultural towns of the country; realistic chances for employment or marriage looked bleak. To foster any chance of attaining either, women felt forced to flee Ireland, which became one of Europe's most acute and heart-wrenching examples of the demographic change linked with the shift from traditional to modern societies.

The havoc wreaked by the Famine on the Irish landholding system led to a radical change in Irish marriage patterns. For over sixty years, single young Irishwomen left Ireland in droves, fleeing from the dismal and depressing prospects offered in their native land. Their flight also corresponded with the era of rapid industrialisation in America, leading to mammoth changes in urban employment. By the 1870s, Ireland had become the nation with the latest age of marriage. Because of the bleak economic prospects, a greater percentage of young Irish men and women were coerced into bypassing marriage and choosing single lives. In 1864, about 18 per cent of Irish women who married were under twenty-one; by the early 1900s little more than 5 per cent had married by that age.

The women who emigrated kept alive links with other female family members back home, particularly with sisters. A stream of letters sent from America were filled with stories of how women could earn good money and take part in the exciting possibilities and challenges of an expanding society and they fired the imaginations of those who received them. The letters also contained money, enabling younger siblings to travel to America. Sisters aided sisters, as Hasia Diner in her wide-ranging study, *Erin's Daughters in America*, explains:

Women actively promoted migration and travelled along what might be seen as female chains. They made trips together. They helped finance one another, and they met and greeted one another. Although they certainly assisted male kin as well, particularly brothers, the primary emphasis focused on their sisters and other female relatives.[2]

Curiously, although they came from a rural or small-town background, Irish women absolutely rejected the farming possibilities offered on the wide plains of the American midwest. Instead, they chose the cities and large industrial towns in the north, which offered the widest choice of economic opportunities. Factory and mill work and, especially, domestic service were the preferred choices. By 1860, Irish women had become the single largest immigrant group in Boston, New York and Philadelphia, and the second most important in Baltimore and Cincinnati. Nine years later, they also led the way in Providence, New Haven, Albany and Pittsburgh, while ranking second most numerous in Buffalo, Milwaukee, Chicago and St Louis. Other important Irish communities developed in San Francisco, Omaha, Memphis, New Orleans, Cleveland, Detroit and Denver. As an ethnic group, Irish women dominated the domestic service industry in America in the late 19th century.[3]

With such a large female migration, it was a natural consequence that many of the Irish communities had a female majority, especially in New York, Boston, Baltimore, Philadelphia, Providence and Worcester.

Interestingly, whilst Irish women saw domestic service as the best way to fulfil their economic goals, it was a profession largely scorned by native-born Protestant, Italian, Jewish and French-Canadian women, as being the most demeaning of all types of work. Hasia Diner stressed the distaste with which the native population held domestic service:

> Young American women basically refused to do this kind of work. Native-born Protestant girls... found the notion of domestic work so odious, so demeaning, so beneath their sense of self that they often in fact took lower paid jobs in mills and in factories and even willingly accepted less pay as seamstresses and needle women rather than humiliate themselves in somebody else's home.[4]

The main reason why so many Irish women flooded the domestic service industry was the incessant demand for household help. From the 1850s, as the daughters of American families availed of the increased educational opportunities, young Irish women stepped into the resultant labour vacuum.

In fact, Irish women had greater job security than Irish men. In 1887, when almost 20 per cent of all Irish-born men in Massachusetts found themselves out of work, only 13 per cent of Irish-born women were unemployed.[5]

As Diner argues, ingrained Protestant Yankee prejudice against these Catholic Irish girls was a constant theme:

Many considered that the Irish colleens could not cook, had standards of cleanliness judged inappropriate for middle-class homes and had religious beliefs that might contaminate their Protestant children. Probably the best attribute of the Irish domestic was her availability. If employers gave any praise, it was usually that the women were chaste. Critics pointed them out as lazy, poor housekeepers, terrible cooks, sometimes temperamental or even violent, and either clumsy or awkward with the family's precious china. Despite all these real or alleged failings, middle-class America came to depend heavily on this major source of domestic help. Whatever the scorn and mockery poured on the young Irish girls, they remained steadfastly impervious to the brickbats. Domestic service was to become the overriding life choice for women of Irish origin in America. In 1900, some 60 per cent of all Irish-born women in America were still working as domestic servants.

Financially, the rewards for such work could vary from city to city. In Massachusetts, around 1906, only female teachers earned more than domestic servants. The state average for domestics was $9.08 per week, while overworked textile workers only managed to earn $7.15 and salesgirls just $6.21. Most domestics were live-in servants in their employer's homes and, as such, had the bonus of no food, rent or transport costs.

As employers generally provided them with liveried uniforms, they also avoided clothing expenses, something that was often costly for salesgirls. Other natural advantages came from living in far more healthy environments in the most desirable neighbourhoods of the city, compared to their sisters labouring in the dirty, accident-prone mills and factories. They also shared the same good quality food – albeit leftovers – as their employers, and usually had their own private rooms in the house. With these in-built perks, domestic servants could save their earnings, to spend on themselves, send home, invest or donate to their favourite charities. It became their individual choice, freed from the requirements of basic survival. These monetary rewards of domestic work became a strongly persuasive reason for postponing, or even foregoing, marriage.[6]

Irish communal leaders had mixed opinions about Irish servant girls. One Irish priest in Memphis in the 1880s, found them to be 'the most faithful specimens of womanhood that ever crossed from the shores of Europe'.[7] Others expressed their dissatisfaction with their sacrificed lives not being properly recognised and many believed that the Irish would do better in the West, away from the congestion of big city life. One founder of an Irish community in Iowa wrote back to fellow immigrants on the east coast, exhorting them:

> To every single man I would say… with or without money, move westward. Your labour is ample security for your living… marry some of those fine girls buried alive in the basement kitchens… and bring her west.[8]

Some also felt that the persistence of Irish women in domestic service symbolised their failure to rise above their menial positions in urban society.

> Service work was not an easy choice by any means, particularly for live-in staff. They lived at the beck and call of their employers around the clock, as they cooked, dusted, cleaned, ironed, laundered, scrubbed and cared for children. Middle-class American homes varied in size, family numbers and the amount of socialising the family undertook; all aspects that that influenced servant routine and schedule.[9]

Legendary long-time mayor of Boston, James Michael Curley, whose Galway-born mother had worked as a domestic, recalled one particular story of the Back Bay maid who served a Thanksgiving turkey with one leg missing.

> She was fired when she explained that she gave it to a cop on the beat, in response, she picked the turkey by the other leg and threw it at the dowager who had called her a 'dirty Irish pig'. 'I'm not fired,' she said, 'I quit.'[10]

Yet American middle-class homes also provided an education for young Irish girls, a place where they could learn the lessons that would guarantee a upward social mobility into the ranks of white-collar and semi-professional work. The kitchens and parlours of Protestant America exposed Irish girls to an exciting 'modern' world of Boston society.

The daughters of the Irish-born female emigrants were to seize the opportunities offered in other fields like nursing, office work and teaching, as they climbed the social ladder. In the early 1900s, sociologist E.A. Ross commented on the spectacular economic-professional rise of Irish women:

> 'Of the first generation of Irish, 54 per cent are servants and waitresses; of the second generation, only 16 per cent. Whither have these daughters gone? Out of the kitchen into the factory, the store, the office and the school.'[11]

To take advantage of these opportunities, undreamed of in small towns in Ireland, Irish women in America were able to achieve greatly improved incomes and status. Not all the women married but those that did found that, by postponing marriage for years, they were able to build a financial nestegg that eventually gave them a better start to married life.

The destinies of the Mongan sisters followed the general pattern of Irish women who emigrated to America. They may have also been influenced by the example of their aunt Mary Duignam, who had found long-term employment as housekeeper at Belvedere House.

Mary Anne Mongan, born in 1858, emigrated to America in 1874 when she was just sixteen years old. She had left to join her older sister Elizabeth who was already settled in Boston. They were just two of the 2 million Irish women who emigrated from Ireland between 1851 and 1901 – 90 per cent of whom chose domestic service as their preferred option for survival in their strange new land.

Through the help of Ed Hines in Boston, I was gradually able to learn something of their lives from the archives. Elizabeth, born in 1864 was the first to flee the misery of the post-Famine Ireland around 1883, aged nineteen. She headed for the strong Irish enclave in Boston, where she was to spend many years in domestic service. We found her marriage certificate which showed that she was working as a seamstress in Boston when she married in 1894, aged thirty.

Her fiancé, like her father and younger brother James, was a carpenter by trade and a country boy. Three years her senior, Charles A. Edgerly, was a native of Barnstead, New Hampshire, a thickly wooded mountainous wilderness region, 80 miles north of Boston. The proposed union was problematic as Charles was a member of the Congregational Church, which created difficulties for Elizabeth's staunch Catholic beliefs. Another fact further envenomed the situation for the couple – Charles was divorced.[12]

These two complications must have strained relations with Elizabeth's sisters and recently married brother, Michael; the Catholic Church also frowned on such inter-denominational unions and the couple had to obtain an official dispensation in order to marry. Timothy J. Meagher, in his *Inventing Irish America*, remarked on the prevailing official conservative Irish Catholic attitude to mixed marriages at the time:

> 'The Catholic Messenger frequently contended that Catholic women who married Protestants or non-Catholics usually lost their faith and easily fell into sinful practises of birth control or abortion, or ended their marriages in divorce.'[13]

Elizabeth's marriage certificate revealed her poignant attempts to cover up her Irish origins, which she still perceived as a liability. She gave her name as 'Morgan' and stated that she was born in 'London, England'. She even changed her father Patrick's name to a more English-sounding 'William'. The ceremony was celebrated at the vast Cathedral of the Holy Cross, with its capped towers and elegant rose windows, on Washington Street by Rev. H.A. Sullivan on 19 July 1894. The witnesses were Charles' friend Willard Hardy, and a fellow Irish emigrant Mary Kelly. Charles gave an address in Cambridge, Mass, as his residence, while Elizabeth was residing in Boston. The radiant couple walked down the aisle as the 5,000 pipes of the cathedral's huge organ, one of the largest in America, resonated to the strains of 'The Wedding March' with 'unsurpassed purity of tone and remarkable power'.[14]

The couple celebrated their wedding surrounded by family members and a few close friends at a local hotel; Elizabeth's sister Mary Anne and husband Jimmy

Keough, a foundry worker, already proud parents of three children, Josephine, seven, James, and Hubert two; Catherine, married eight years to Corkman, David Aherne from Fermoy and still childless. Her brother Michael, took time off from his job as conductor on the West End Railway trolleys to attend with his young Irish-American wife, Maria, then pregnant with their first child. Charles' parents, Sylvester and Sarah Edgerly, were also on hand to take part in the festivities.

It was a rare chance for a family reunion in their demanding, stressful new lives in America. Speeches were made, glasses were lifted to toast the bride and groom, and absent friends; maudlin, sentimental old Irish songs brought on a touch of homesickness, and a tear to some eyes. They fondly remembered their loving mother, Annie, already dead ten years, and their widowed father Patrick, then fifty-seven and living in Longford, with their nineteen-year-old brother James, and youngest sister Maria Theresa, then fifteen. The sisters intended to bring her over to America as soon as she finished her schooling.

The couple then set off on a short honeymoon near Charles' hometown of Barnstead, and enjoyed long lakeside walks in the tranquil New Hampshire backwoods. On their return, they set about finding suitable accommodation to start their new life together.

An 1894 Arlington town directory indicated that the couple set up their first home at 31 Lowell Street, in Arlington, a small northern suburb of Boston, close to where Charles had been living in Cambridge.[15]

The town, originally known as West Cambridge, with less then 1,000 inhabitants, had been only incorporated as a separate town in 1807. By the 1890s, horse-drawn trolleys had been replaced by electrics, leading to an influx of new residents. The local shipbuilding industry on the Mystic river, along with house construction, attracted shipwrights and carpenters like Charles Edgerly to the area. Local historian Denis Ahern recalled:

'There was, at one point, quite a lot of shipyards, and the Mystic river was tidal right up to Arlington, into the end of the 19th and early 20th centuries. "Goat's Acre", along one side of North Union Street, was where the Irish lived primarily, and Arlington had a sizeable Irish population.'[16]

Milling was another activity well established on the Lower Mystic Lake, where hydraulic energy powered such diverse businesses as shoemaking, calico printing, saw making, wood turning and grain-meal production.[17]

Catholics had been settling in the area for some time; their first house of worship was St Malachy's, built as a mission church built of St Peter's Church, Cambridge, in 1870.[18] With growing Catholic prosperity and influence in the town, St Malachy's, located on the corner of Medford and Chestnut streets, was later restored, enlarged and rededicated, in 1900, as St Agnes', while St Agnes' Grammar School, had been built next to the enlarged church in 1888.[19]

During the winter months, ice cutting at Spy Pond was a profitable business, with a harvest estimated around 62,000 tons in a good season. Much of the production, packed in saw-dust, was carried by rail to Charlestown docks for export around the world. Market gardening was another vast operation, with the density of glass hothouses to produce fruit and vegetables the highest in America.[20] On the northeast (Cambridge) edge of the town, lay St Paul's Catholic Cemetery, along the Alewife Brook, a small river that periodically flooded the area.[21]

Elizabeth 'Lizzie' Edgerly gave birth to her first child, a daughter called Eliza, at home on 27 November 1895, who was baptised at St Malachy's Catholic church nearby.[22] Eighteen ninety-five had been a prolific year for the Mongan family, as Mary Anne had given birth to her first son Hubert, on 4 November, and Michael had welcomed his son Charles into the world on 12 May. Messages of congratulations flew between family members, as the news of the happy events was sent back to brother James in Longford. Two years later, Elizabeth gave birth to a son, Charles William, on 1 September 1897, by which time she and her family had moved home from 51 Mystic Street in Arlington to 45 Arlington Street in nearby leafy Medford.[23]

Elizabeth was followed to America by Mary Anne, born in 1858, who left Railway Terrace in 1874. She quickly found employment in domestic service and continued for the next twenty obscure years in this profession. She only emerged in the archives at the time her marriage to foundry-worker and fellow-Irish immigrant, James Keough, around 1890, when she was living in South Boston.

Catherine, born in 1865, headed for America around 1884, and chose to settle in Abington, a small rural town 16 miles south of Boston. The town was famous as part of the shoemaking industry, as well as having its roots in lumber and agriculture. There, Catherine found employment initially as a domestic servant and then as a worker in the burgeoning shoe sector. The regional towns of Abington, Rockland, Holbrook, Weymouth and Brockton in Plymouth county, were all part of the widespread shoe-manufacturing industry located throughout the South Shore Old Colony region.

Shoemaking was a long established tradition on the South Shore area. One of the earliest industries was the tannery of Experience Mitchell, built in 1680 – through father and sons the business continued for 171 years. The first settlers were drawn by the rich woodlands of pine and oak and the first mill was opened by the Thayer family in 1703. Abington, founded in 1712, was to grow in prosperity through the shoe and boot manufacturing.[24]

Abington was the first town in Plymouth county to gather a number of shoemakers under one roof. These shops were called 'ten-footers' because of their usual 10'x10' dimensions. The first enterprising manufacturers hauled their products by wagon to Boston and returned with loads of leather for further production.

During the Civil War era, 1,850 Abington workers produced 1,250,000 pairs of boots and shoes each year. It is said that half the Union Army wore Abington-made shoes. By 1885, when Catherine Mongan started working in the industry in Abington, there were 97 shoes factories operating in Brockton.

Although she was the third sister to emigrate to America, after Mary Anne and Elizabeth, Catherine was the first to marry when she wed David Aherne on 15 February 1886 at St Bridget's Church in Abington.[25] Located at 455 Plymouth Street, near the railways tracks, St Bridget's was the oldest wooden Catholic building on the South Shore. David, a tall, burly, thirty-year-old Irish-born worker from Kilworth, near Fermoy, County Cork, had come to America with his three brothers, Cornelius, Francis and Patrick. After a spell working on the railways, the Aherne brothers found work in Abington at the local E.P. Reed Lumberyard and Building Supplies Company. The wedding reception was probably held at the well-known Keene's Hotel, located at the intersection of Walnut and Cherry Streets.[26] Catherine's sisters took the train down from Boston; Mary Anne and her fiancé, James Keough; Delia, who had got a day off from her Yankee Brahmin family in Boston; Elizabeth and her boyfriend Charles Edgerly.

E.P. Reed's Lumber and Building materials yards, c. 1913, in Abington, MA, where the four emigrant Aherne brothers from Fermoy, Co. Cork – Cornelius, Francis, Patrick and David – found employment around 1880. David eventually became lumber supervisor and married Catherine Mongan in 1886. (*Courtesy Abington Public Library*)

David's brothers and friends were present for the joyous occasion. They feasted on a New England boiled dinner, with tender, succulent beef brisket, carrots, onions, cabbage and halved potatoes, washed down with cranberry juice for the ladies and Pickwick beers for the men. A modest wedding cake was cut by the happy couple. More immigrant songs were sung, as the sisters remembered their late mother Annie, and posted a copy of the wedding invitation back to their father Patrick, brother James, and youngest sister Maria Theresa in Longford.

With the sisters now all gainfully employed and enjoying their new-found economic independence, they were able to send money back to their father so that Maria Theresa could join them. They had been out of touch with their other brother, Michael, who, at that time, was still serving with the Commisiariat and Transport Corps in the British army, then based at Portobello Barracks in Dublin.

The Aherne brothers had been sharing a wooden frame house on Birch Street, so Catherine and David set up home nearby in a similar house at 33 Charles Street, only a five-minute walk from her husband's employment at E.P. Reed Lumber Company, where he later became lumber supervisor, as noted in the 1889 Abington Directory.[27]

David Aherne and his wife Catherine (Mongan) Aherne lived at 33 Charles St in Abington, MA, where David died on 21 December 1921. Catherine had worked with her young sister Maria-Theresa in the burgeoning shoe factories. She was later joined by her sister Delia in 1923, after she had left Groton School, who lived with her until her death in 1932. The three sisters now lie buried in St Patrick's Cemetery, Rockland, MA.

Catherine was among the hundreds of Irish women who found employment in Abington's shoe factories. Contemporary photos showing lines of female workers sitting at long tables with heaps of shoes placed in front of them gives an idea of working conditions. Noise from many chattering voices, constant

From 1880 Catherine Mongan and her young sister Maria-Theresa, were employed in the shoe factories in Abington, MA. This c.1900 photo shows how Irish female immigrants worked at long tables assembling shoes at that time. *(Courtesy Weymouth Historical Museum)*

hammering and under constant pressure to speed up production, made the factory a stressful and draining environment to spend ten hours a day for minimal piece-work pay.

Abington boasted several major shoe factories. The Crossett Shoe factory, just built in 1888 by Lewis A. Crosett, produced about 300 cases of boots and shoes each week. The Alden Shoe Company was located on Lake Street on the shore of Island Grove Lake. Moses Arnold had built his redbrick plant in 1875 on a site at 200 Wales Street, and business was booming. He became the first to have electricity installed in his factory and in his home in 1903 by the Edison Electric Light Company.

Nearby Gilman's Restaurant, opposite the Rail Depot at 94 Railroad Street, was a popular spot for town residents and a much frequented lunch spot for Arnold factory employees. The William S. O'Brien Heel Factory, employing some seventy-five people, stood at the intersection of Rockland Street and Brockton Avenue from 1880 until it was destroyed by fire in 1905.[28]

The Mongan sisters were familiar with a highly visible figure around town – retired world heavy-weight bare-knuckle boxing champion, John L. Sullivan, known across America as the 'Boston Strong Boy'. After defending his title thirty times, he finally lost to James 'Gentleman Jim' Corbett on 6 September 1892 and retired to live in Abington where he resided at 704 Hancock Street and was frequently seen riding around the streets on his horse-drawn Irish jaunting car until his death on 2 February 1918.[29]

These were the Abington streetscapes where Catherine, and later her young regally named sister Maria-Theresa Josephine, knew in the heyday of the shoe-making industry in the late 19th century.

Mary Theresa, born in 1879 at Railway Terrace was only five years old when her mother Annie died. In 1888, she moved to Longford with her father, Patrick, and her brother, James, and went to school locally. She was only twelve when Patrick died, aged sixty-one, in the family home on Dublin Street. She probably left for America around 1898 as a nineteen-year-old and joined her sister, Catherine, working in the shoe-making factories.

On summer weekends, Catherine and Maria-Theresa spent their leisure time with Aherne relatives strolling along the lake shore through Island Grove, with its tall stands of pine, elm and oak. In winter, they skated on the frozen water of the lake, and watched the workers cut the ice with large handsaws. Ireland, with its misery and gloom, and political upheavals, seemed far away, if not forgotten.

We were only able to find minimal information on the life of Maria Theresa in the archives. Had she been unlucky in love? She was the first to pass away – unmarried – maybe overwhelmed by the relentless production demands of the shoe factories. After twenty years in America, she died in February 1916, aged only thirty-six, from chronic endocanditis and was laid to rest at St Patrick's Cemetery in Rockland, near her Aherne relatives.

I was able to resurrect information from the archives about Delia, born in 1872, who was brought out to America around 1892 to join her sisters. Like a generation of emigrant young Irish women, Delia was to remain single due to her restricted social life. At the time of the 1900 US census, twenty-nine-year-old Delia was employed as a domestic maid with the William H. Partridge family at 23 Pembroke Street, Newton, just north of Boston.[30]

In 1912, Delia went on to become part of the staff at the exclusive Ivy League college, Groton School, founded in 1884 just 45 kilometres northwest of Boston. Groton School was the brainchild of Cambridge graduate and famed American headmaster Endicott Peabody (1857–1944), scion of an immensely wealthy Puritan trading family from Salem, Massachusetts. The school became the first choice for Boston Brahmin families over generations. Names like Auchinloss, Biddle, Adams, Whitney, Saltonstall, Coolidge, Thayer and Roosevelt filled its classrooms. Future president, Franklin D. Roosevelt had graduated in 1900 and his four sons all attended the school in the early 1920s when Delia was employed there. She arrived there as a mature, experienced forty-one-year-old, and was appointed a member of the catering staff in the dining hall, under Mrs McMurray's stern matronship.[31]

Delia was hired by the stubborn, intractable martinet, Mrs McMurray. Former pupil F.D. Asburn in his *Fifty Years On*, published in 1934, remembered the impressive presence of Mrs McMurray:

> If Mrs Whitney defied Mr Peabody, and Mr Peabody defied President Roosevelt, all three walked circumspectly before Mrs McMurray, the formid-able matron at the School for thirty years where she ruled with an iron hand, or so School tradition recalls. She was one of the real founders of the school. She came at the very start, having kept a boarding house in Denver and in Buffalo. The Groton tradition of cleanliness was laid by her. Under her regime, the food was always good, always nourishing, but her mind 'was not full of nimble changes'. It was frequently possible to be sure on Wednesday what one would have for lunch the following Tuesday.[32]

Delia worked under Mrs McMurray until Mrs Edna Cram became matron in 1915. Mrs Cram introduced a decided improvement in food quality and choice, becoming a much admired figure at the school. Another of Delia's contempo-raries, Miss Burnett, a loveable little Scotswoman, presided over the infirmary for twenty-seven years, before retiring in 1922.

> 'Smaller than most first form pupils,' recalled Ashburn, '[Miss Burnett] was a martinet, if a kindly one, and there was never any nonsense in her kingdom. She was an excellent nurse, and sick boys were well cared for. She had two amiable weaknesses, Democrats in general, and [President] Wilson in partic-ular... unfortunate indeed was the small or big boy who went into the Infirmary a Republican at election time'.[33]

Life at Groton ran in a well-organised routine. Wake-up on weekdays was at 6:55 a.m. with breakfast at 7:25, which implied an even earlier rise for the catering staff. Morning school started at 8:30. Lunch was served at 1:30 p.m. Supper was at 6:05; with stiff collars de rigeur. Faculty supper came at 9:30 and lights out at 10:30 p.m. The staff quarters were located close to Hundred House, where the dining room was located.[34]

An 1895 photo shows the then new school dining room. The vast oak-panelled room, with a traditional beam ceiling, imposing open hearth, raised dais for the rector's table, had wooden floors that resonated with waitresses' scurrying feet. From the dais, Endicott Peabody would supervise the white tablecloth laid tables for all the assembled pupils. In these august surroundings, Delia spent a twelve-year period serving in the dining room from 1912 until 1923.[35]

Groton School archivist David Brown found Delia's employment file card in the archives and confirmed that:

Evidently she was a waitress and or a maid at the at the school. Mrs McMurray was the lady in charge of all the indoor staff from 1884 until 1914 or so. Her staff report card noted Delia as 'a very nice lady, good waitress. Left to be with her sister'.[36]

Her file indicated the salary she received started at $5, rose to $25 dollars, $6 dollars per week from December 1916 and then, from October 1918, in the dining room at $30 per week. Finally, in September 1919, she had a raise to $35 dollars per week and an extra $10 in 1920. Delia left Groton School in 1923 to live with her recently widowed sister Catherine in Abington.

Delia lived with Catherine for a decade. No doubt, they made regular trips by trolley over to Holbrook to visit their sister Mary Anne and her family. They attended the joyous occasion of their neice Helene's marriage to local master mechanic Bob Burns in January 1925, in South Weymouth. The Mongan sisters had looked on with pride as Mary Anne's first-generation, Irish-American daughter walked down the aisle with her new husband.

Delia eventually returned to domestic service with a Boston Brahmin family on Clarendon Street, in Boston's exclusive Back Bay area. Finally, worn out by a life of constant service, she died from arterio-sclerosis at Massachusetts General Hospital in May 1932.[37] She was only fifty-five years old. Catherine buried Delia with their younger sister Maria-Theresa at St Patrick's Cemetery, Rockland.[38]

Catherine had become a registered nurse and was operating from her new address at 75 Central Steet in Rockland in 1937.[39] She died in July 1942 at the Lonergan Rest Home on Water Street in Abington.[40] Her ever faithful neice Helene Burns stepped in to take care of her funeral arrangements, having kept up contact with last surviving aunt in Abington over the years. In turn, Catherine was laid to rest with Maria-Theresa and Delia at St Patrick's Cemetery, where the grave was to remain unmarked for over sixty years. In 2004, I had a small marker stone erected over the grave in memory of the three Mongan sisters, which reads:

AHERNE – MONGAN
David – 1921 = Catherine – 1942
Delia – 1932
Maria T. – 1916

8

Michael. A first descent into Hell

The intensity of the research I undertook from 1980 to 1985 meant that I was in regular correspondence with Ed Hines in Boston, with letters flying back and forth across the Atlantic. Following my first letter to him in September 1980, he had methodically trawled through the Massachusetts State Vital Records archives, bringing to light information of the destinies of the Mongan family in America. I was impressed by the speed and accuracy with which he came up with birth, marriage and death records for Elizabeth, Mary Anne, Catherine, Delia and Maria-Theresa.

He had also quickly located Michael's son and daughters, Charles, Mary and Annie, enabling me to begin reconstructing the story of their lives. I was grateful that he was even able to locate tragic little Annie, who died an infant from cholera. However, their father Michael's later life was still shrouded in mystery.

Despite intense historical detective work, Ed had no luck in locating him in any of the archives. He had traced him to his addresses in South Boston at the time of his children's births, and his 1898 move to 86 Kinnaird Street, to live with his in-laws. Cambridge City directories listed him living there, as a 'Motorman', from 1898 until 1901. Frustratingly, the microfilms for 1901-03 were missing. Michael seemed to vanish from the records completely. From 1904 to 1909 there was no reference to him at all and, in 1904, only his father-in-law, Elisha, and his brother-in-law, John Hurd, were listed as living at Kinnaird Street. Then, from 1908, a clue surfaced, Hannah Hurd, was listed as 'widow', while her daughter, Maria Mongan, was entered as 'widow of Michael'. What had happened?

As an experienced researcher, Ed found it quite uncanny and mystifying.

Initially, I had wondered if Michael might have returned to Ireland. We also discussed whether or not he might have abandoned his family and drifted off into obscurity elsewhere on the American continent. Now it seemed he had died – perhaps in a streetcar accident. It was proving very difficult to find any information, it was as though he had something to hide.

I was not sure what to do next and Ed was feeling stumped. Nevertheless, with a true investigative reporter's persistence, he never gave up hope and he kept looking for other angles, other sources, that might reveal Michael's destiny.

I contacted the Boston State Transportation Library archives in the hope of possibly finding whether Maria Mongan might have been granted a pension, but drew a blank. The paper trail through the archives seemed to have hit a brick wall. Was this a dead end to the quest? Was it all a wild goose chase after shadows? Ed rechecked death registers for 1902–07 in vain.

A few 'Michael Mongans' did emerge but from other parts of Ireland or the wrong age. He ran another search through the Cambridge and Boston City directories right up to 1937, tracing the Hurd family right through to that period and found that they had lived out their lives on Kinnaird Street. However, there was still no sign of Michael. Was there a jinx on the search? We persisted with the research from 1981 until 5 October 1985. I knew there was never any guarantee of results from even the most intensive research but I was still frustrated and disappointed. On a hunch, Ed decided to try the City Clerk's Office in Cambridge, who had custody of the local birth, marriage and death records. His instinct proved to be right.

On Thursday evening, 5 May 1983, Ed posted me a letter that arrived in Paris a week later. I remember holding the airmail envelope from Boston, noting the colourful American stamps that brought new information.

As I tore open the envelope, I had a premonitory flash that it contained something important. The long-awaited discovery was short, stark and to-the-point, it gave the details of Michael's final days. Ed spelled out how he had come across my elusive grand-uncle in the archives:

> At last I can report to you that I have found the death entry and burial location for your grand-uncle Michael J. Mongan!! Today I took a few moments away from the office and went to the City Clerk's office for the City of Cambridge. The City Clerk is the custodian of birth, marriage and death records at local level. Copies of all these records are forwarded to State level which is where I have been doing my research on Michael J.
>
> I thought possibly the death record of Michael J. Mongan may not have been forwarded to the State through some administrative oversight. I asked the attendant at the City Clerk's office for the Index Book covering the deaths in Cambridge between 1901 and 1908. They were busy so they let me look at the Index Books directly, a stroke of luck. I checked each name until the entry in 1903...MICHAEL J. MORGAN... caught my eye. It was entered in longhand and one had to look twice to see if it said 'MONGAN' or 'MORGAN'.
>
> I asked to see the entry identified as Volume No 3, line 221.[1] Right away, I knew he was ours as his residence was Kinnaird Street, Cambridge, and his mother's name was listed as 'Annie Murray'. Curiously, his father was listed as 'Hubert Mongan'. You remember that early in our search I found Michael J. marriage certificate and he listed his father as 'Herbert Mongan'. At the time, I speculated why he may have done that. In any event, he

continued with this name rather than 'Patrick', on whatever documents that were used to fill out his death certificate. Curiously, his wife's name is not entered, possibly because of the circumstances surrounding his tragic death. She may have asked that her name not appear. Another thought, his wife may not have known that Michael's father was named 'Patrick'. Michael may have told her from the outset that his father was 'Herbert'.

In any event, you will see by the attached that Michael J. died at the Insane Hospital, Worcester, Massachusetts. The cause of death tragically tells us that it was from 'Constitutional Inferiority – Suicide by Hanging'. I have no idea what 'Constitutional Inferiority' means, possibly some sort of nervous breakdown. He died on October 5, 1903 and was buried at St Paul's Cemetery, Arlington, Massachusetts. Arlington abuts Cambridge but I have no idea why he was buried there, no other Mongan was buried there. Shall I check the cemetery to see if others are interred there with Michael? His age is listed as thirty-six years, which is a little off the data you furnished. I believe you thought he had been born in 1863. If he was thirty-six when he died, then he was born in 1867, and with this his birth certificate could be located in Dublin. I'm confident we have the right man.

Unfortunately, the clerk at the time's penmanship was such that the 'N' in Mongan became an 'R', and he was listed in the State records as MORGAN which I did not check. I would guess that the Insane Hospital in Worchester is the present Worcester State Hospital but I would not know if they maintained the records of patients of eighty years ago.[2]

I sat in my Paris apartment, staring unbelievingly at the letter. I read the stark words 'Suicide by Hanging' uncomprehendingly. I re-read it several times, my mouth dry, my heart pounding, the paper trembling in my hands.

I gulped, swallowed hard but would allow no tears. Too late for that now. Unwilling to absorb the harsh, obscene nature of the unadorned words, I didn't want to believe what I was reading. There had to be some mistake. The horror of the discovery slowly dawned on my reeling brain.

Deep inside me somewhere, the young boy I had been at my grandfather's knee was sad, yet wryly smiling at the tragic news. Somehow, his unrelenting demand that the search for the truth to continue had been vindicated. Instinctively, he had always sensed that something was amiss. Now, through the discovery of the his grand-uncle's achingly sad demise, he had proved himself right to insist on seeking out the truth, however hard to bear. He had screamed and stamped his feet, bawling for an explanation for those missing paternal aunts, uncles, cousins and relations. Now, frighteningly, here was the answer in black on white. He suddenly felt calm and serene, knowing he had been right to question the silence from the very start. Ed's letter contained an official Commonwealth of Massachusetts, Cambridge City Clerk's copy of Michael's death certificate. There was no mistake. It repeated the official cause of death: 'Constitutional Inferiority – Suicide by Hanging'.

During his search in the Cambridge Chronicle newspaper archives between 1902–03 to find the elusive Michael, Ed Hines had unearthed many other dramatic tales of woe.

> I came across many stories of people deemed insane; several suicides by drowning after jumping from bridges or by gun-shot or poison; stories having to do with 'runaway' horses and subsequent severe accidents, the runaways many times being under the control of a 'Conductor' of a street railway. Periodically there was news coverage of those sentenced at both the District Court and the Police Court. Drunkardness seems to have been a rampant problem. There were corresponding news articles calling for the establishment of an institution to care for the mentally disturbed and those suffering from 'delerium Tremor', which I believe is the after-effect of prolonged heavy drinking of alcohol. Irish surnames were commonly found through many of these news coverages.[3] I'm sorry to have delivered such a sad tale concerning Michael J. Mongan.[4]

As a Boston native and experienced researcher, Ed Hines had penetrating insights into the Yankee attitudes of the time.

> Worcester State Hospital, is the present-day name of the place once called the Lunatic Asylum back around the turn of the [20th] century. Although the name of the place suggests all sorts of horrible implications, institutions such as this were used to house people that the 'courts' found to be, in their opinion, rabble-rousers. Many of the inmates back then would in 'no-way' pass for a present day person suffering from mental illness. A convenient tool used years ago to get rid of a person [was to] send him to the Insane Asylum.[5]
>
> The tragic ending of the life of Michael J.Mongan has bothered me. I discussed the entry on his death certificate, Constitutional Inferiority, with a lawyer friend of mine. The condition 'Constitutional Inferiority' is no longer used to describe a condition of a resident of the US. Basically, constitutional inferiority means that the individual who is described as such had no rights within the US. This discription was struck down by the Supreme Court in recent years… Remember, in 1903, the Irish were at the very bottom of the socially accepted ladder. At that time, there were militant movements to stop immigration into the US, demonstrations, etc. No doubt, the local magistrate was an upstanding true 'American' so when poor Michael shows up he is sent off to the Insane Asylum at Worcester. Once in, never out in those days. His wife most likely had no influence. God knows what went on in Worcester or in Michael's head, possibly he went insane, then choosing what he thought to be his only option, took his life.[6]

In spite of the shock of the news, I began to realise why there had been so much silence surrounding my father's family in America. I deduced that my grandfather knew the horrific truth by mid-October 1903 and I wondered if my father was aware of the dark family secret, though I sensed he must have known about his uncle Michael's tragic destiny at some point. There must have been a reason why he was baptised 'Michael Reginald', but was known as Reginald.[7] Now, I wanted to find out all the dramatic circumstances surrounding Michael's last days on earth. I wanted to remove the 'family skeleton' from the cupboard and finally lay it to rest. I decided I would contact Worcester State Hospital to learn if any medical records had survived the eighty-year interval. From a dilettante's dabbling into the family past, it was now becoming a compelling obsession that would dominate my life. Yet the necessities of life took over as I was swept back into the pressurised turmoil of the Parisian advertising world.

In between a helter-skelter career in advertising in Paris, I managed to find a few moments to contact Worcester State Hospital to find out if they still held Michael J. Mongan's medical records might still be on file there.

I wrote to the Hospital Administrator, Mr Edward Riquier, outlining my quest for missing family relatives in the United States, and how I had finally discovered my grand-uncle's tragic demise at Worchester.

He replied on 5 December 1984, stating that:

Due to the time lapse of time and without more specific information as to admittance date, it is impossible to track down any record if it still exists on Mr Mongan. I regret that we cannot assist you in your request.[8]

It sounded very much like another dead end, yet I was now determined to leave no stone unturned. After all the time and effort expended in locating Michael, I had to get to the heart of the sad story. I knew there still had to be some way around this apparently insurmountable obstacle. I sensed that the young boy inside would not be stopped in his tracks by some bureaucratic barrier. He was determined to find a path to the truth. Nothing was going to stop him from extracting the full story. There had to be a way forward.

He was convinced he would find one.

Research on the Worcester aspect of the search was to remain blocked for almost fourteen years. During that time, it hovered constantly at the back of my mind, challenging me to forget. I wrote to the Cambridge City Police Department and the Clerk Magistrate's Court without finding any way through the bureaucratic red tape. Then, in November 1998, I decided to write to Worcester State Hospital again and contacted the Chief Operating officer Mr Raymond Robinson, who passed on my letter to the Director of Medical Records, Ms Carole A. Persia. She replied on 2 November 1998.

> Our confidentiality law (Mass Gen.Law c123 d36) does not permit the disclosure of this information to individuals unless they are the legal representative of the deceased individual's estate or have a court order authorizing the department to make disclosure. I appreciate your interest in obtaining information about your grand-uncle but, under law, mental health records are afforded substantial legal protection. I am certain that you can understand the need for the Department to be careful about the release of such records. To provide you with some basic information, I did ask our Chief of Psychiatry, Chris Kennedy MD to review the record. He felt that the documentation did corroborate a diagnosis of depression, possibly exacerbated by alcohol abuse. He did not see evidence to suggest a primary psychotic disorder such as schizophrenia. If you wish to pursue obtaining a copy of the actual record, it will be necessary to procure an order from the Worcester County Probate Court. We do not, by the way, have a picture of your grand-uncle.[9]

Straight away, I was ecstatic. Now I had confirmation that Michael's medical records were still on file – after ninety-five years of gathering dust; miraculously they had survived the passage of time. That news even further reinforced my determination to find a means of obtaining a copy of Michael's file, to bring completion to the whole tragic event. Now I had to deal with Massachusetts courts for access to what I considered was an essential and primordial part of the family heritage.

I followed up by contacting Cambridge City Hall, where all the required legal requirements began to fall into place. After several months of transatlantic correspondence, with Ed Hines acting as my agent in Boston, various legal transactions were completed. I had to go through a complicated court procedure to prove that I was the only surviving relative of my grand-uncle. After much form filling and forwarding the required payments, I awaited a court decision that would allow me to be sent a copy of Michael's medical records. Progress appeared to be blocked by bureaucracy and the lack of any living family members in Boston to give me the necessary permission to access Michael's medical records. Then, suddenly, eureka! I received a positive answer. I became acknowledged as Michael's nearest surviving next-of-kin. Permission was finally granted by the Probate Court allowing me to obtain a copy of Michael's medical records from Worcester State Hospital. At last I'd made the breakthrough.

Some eights months later, on 29 July 1999,[10] a large brown paper envelope arrived from Worcester containing the ninety-six-year-old records. Reading through the depressing account of Michael's descent into the living hell of asylum incarceration made for grim, yet compelling, reading. There was no turning back now. I had to face up to the raw truth of the tragedy. Typed on specially laid-out 'Worcester Insane Hospital' case history form, it traced Michael's entire period of involuntary incarceration at Worcester. I read the verbatim transcripts of Michael's words in awe – he was speaking from beyond the grave. The harrowing circumstances surrounding Michael's initial incarceration at Worcester were specified in his detailed case history, a innovative development then established under Swiss-born director Dr Adolph Meyer.

Worcester, in central Massachusetts, stood on a series of hills overlooking the Blackstone river, some 65 kilometres west of Boston, or one hour by train. Lake Quinsigamond, named by the indigenous Nipmuc people, marked the eastern boundary of the town. Major industrial development had begun after the opening of the Blackstone Canal in 1828, linking Worcester with Providence. Rhode Island, leading to the city's incorporation in 1848.

It rapidly became the second-largest city in Massachusetts. Industrial innovation, in textiles, wheel grinding, wire making and envelopes, led to increased prosperity. It became noted for its outstanding educational and cultural facilities and several institutions of higher education, like Clark University in 1887, were founded there in the 19th century. The Worcester Art Museum had an extensive collection of Asian and Western art and the Worcester Historical Museum chronicled the city's industrial achievements.[11]

Harold Mann, at the outset of a distinguished career as an educational reformer, had first proposed that the Massachusetts State establish an asylum for the insane in 1830. Initially, located on Summer Street in Worcester city centre, the hospital opened in 1833, under the direction of its first superintendent Samuel B. Woodward. Unlike other mental institutions, it acquired a national profile by admitting relatively large number of patients; by 1847 it counted 359 inmates.[12]

Its patient numbers continued to grow from 400 to 500 leading to the decision by the trustees to build a larger facility outside the city. They purchased a 300-acre estate on the eastern outskirts at Belmont Street, near Bell Pond Lake. Completed in 1877, the new Worcester Hospital was modelled on guidelines laid down by eminent hospital architect Thomas S. Kirkbride. He believed that no hospital should care for more than 250 patients, and should conform to his plan of a main central building with wings. Kirkbride's propositions were based on the prevalent assumption that insanity was a curable disease. However, the large hospitals, built to accommodate 500 to 1,000 patients, began to take on the appearance of huge prisons, apart from society.[13]

Worcester State Hospital, *c.* 1905, a massive, gothic, prison-like building, completed in 1877, that symbolised the increasing therapeutic despondency that dominated American psychiatry from the 1890s. *(Courtesy Worcester Public Library)*

Worcester Insane Asylum, with its prison-like architecture, reflected the growing therapeutic nihilism that overran American psychiatry in the late 19th century. Leading psychiatric historian Gerald Grob, in this wide-ranging study *The State and the Mentally Ill*, describes the hospital layout:

> It consisted of a central administration builing with 500-foot long wards on either side... Each of the four-storey wings was divided intor wards, the same plan being followed on each floor... Suites of rooms were available for well-to-do private patients. Rooms in the wards were about 8½ feet by 12½ feet, and each ward was a separate and distinct establishment, having dining and dressing rooms, bath and lavatory [facilities] and an exercising corridor.[14]

A massive fire engulfed the Kirkbride Building on 22 July 1991, destroying almost all of the roof and floors, save for the right side wing and the main administration building. the burned-out shells of the other areas were bulldozed and the extra stone was used to seal up the gaping holes left by the connections to the remaining sections.

> In spite of the new facilities, Worcester Hospital quickly faced the old familiar problems – overcrowding, lack of patient occupational facilities and a high turnover rate amongst the non-professional staff.[15] During the 1870s and 1880s, the mindset of the American psychiatric profession remained wedded to the thesis of incurability of the insane, often in the face of evidence to the contrary.[16]
>
> Constant pressures of an ever-rising patient population continued unabated; in its early years the average number of inmates was 496; by 1890 numbers had risen to 811, while assistant physicians had been only increased from three to six.[17] Attendants and nurses also rose to a ratio of one attendant to every ten patients. In 1885, of a total of eighty attendants – thirty-five female and twenty-eight male – had left under the strain, while another nine females and eighteen males were dismissed as unsuitable.[18]

The original 1877 Worcester State Hospital building had survived since closure in 1991, when it was gutted by a major fire. Preservationists had fought to save the historic building as one of the oldest and historically most significant state hospital in the country. However in 2008 demolition continued leaving only the main Clock Tower (left) and Hoover turret building standing, This will prepare the way for a new $278 million psychiatric facility.

For the inmates, incarceration at the hospital was monotonous and dreary, with space limitations and lack of occupational facilities as acute as before. Out of 780 patients, only 38 per cent (102 men and 218 women) were given employment. Restraints were regularly employed. One visitor to Worcester reported sixteen patients under restraint while three criminal inmates were locked away in seclusion. Restraints became a substitute for therapy, a way of enforcing discipline and order. Gradually, medical men had retrograded into being mere administrators of detention centres for the insane.[19] In the 1880s, drugs were also still used to calm violent patients, if less frequently.

In 1894, S. Weir Mitchell, a renowned neurologist, unleashed a blistering critical attack on mental hospital superintendents. He pointed out their numerous shortcomings: a lack of interest in research; erratic hospital management; limited use of qualified medical personnel; and a general indifferent attitude.[20] Much of the criticism of the state hospital was totally justified. With the United States being transformed into an urban–industrial nation in the 1880s, traditional methods could no longer handle the many new emerging health problems.[21] In Europe, psychiatry was being influenced by the intellectual and social upheavals of the period. In Vienna, Sigmund Freud was embarking on a career that would create a whole new understanding of human behaviour.[22]

In 1896, Swiss-born psychiatrist Dr Adolph Meyer arrived at Worcester. He was appointed with a mission to carry out much-needed reforms at the hospital. Although brief, his period at Worcester was to leave an enduring legacy on the future functioning of the hospital and its medical staff and, as Director of Clinics and Pathologist from 1896 to 1902, he transformed Worcester Hospital into one of America's leading centres for scientific research and training in psychiatry.[23]

Meyer believed that physicians needed to be trained to keep satisfactory observations and records. To help with this directive, clerical tasks were to be reduced to a bare minimum by hiring several stenographers. On top of this, each physician was supplied with an intern earning $20 a month. The purpose of these new measures, especially examination and case histories, was to enable them to be used for clinical investigations.[24]

> All patients on first admission would be examined. One or two hours would be spent on learning about the history of the individual and his family. It was planned that records had to be written by dictation with several persons present; avoiding any lapse of memory in compiling the case history, while maintaining a degree of control. These rules had contributed to the high standards in German hospitals in Europe.[25]

One of Meyer's first innovations was to change the method of classifying patients. All recent admission cases were put on the first two floors of the hospital to facilitate observation, while the third and fourth floors were allotted to those not requiring continual observation.[26] As Gerald Grob explained:

Swiss-born Dr Adolph Meyer was Director of Clinics and Pathologist at Worcester State Hospital from 1896 to 1902. He was responsible for transforming the institution into one of America's foremost centres scientific research and training. He also established the practice of making files on each individual patient. Michael J. Mongan's medical records survived in the archives for almost a hundred years before being brought to light in 1998. *(Courtesy Alan Mason Chesney Medical archives)*

... a physician assisted by a junior assistant, gave each patient a total mental and physical examination on admission. Previously, the medical history had been collated by an assistant directly from the patient, or from his family, friends or by correspondence. A one-hour daily meeting was held, often with the recently admitted patient present, or those about to be discharged, where the physician discussed his findings along with a provisional diagnosis. Eventual treatment was then discussed.[27]

During the ward rounds, notes were taken and later typed up by a stenographer. To ensure uniform and complete records, Meyer shaped the extent and order of the patient history and case record. He also saw the patient, along with the senior physician, on alternate mornings and supervised the accuracy and standards of the record.[28] When Meyer left Worcester in 1901, no replacement was found until 1903, when Dr Theodore A. Hoch, one of Meyer's students, was appointed. Hoch remained in the post until 1906.

Meyer left a legacy of of innovative case histories. Instead of being handwritten in large volumes, the new case histories were kept on individual sheets in a single folder, ensuring all patient material was easily accessible. Once dictated, all entries were typed on the permanent record. The first page was a standard printed sheet, recording such basic facts as name, age place of birth, residence, education, religion, habits, occupation (of both patient and family) civil condition, previous record of insanity, causes, diagnosis and condition when discharged.[29] With the physician's Certificate of Commitment, providing basic outline of the patient's behavioural pattern. Next was a description of the patient's previous history, generally based on contacts with as many relatives and friends as feasible. In the days following admission, the physician examined the patient every few days, recording his assessments.

Although such procedures sound normal now, in Meyer's time it was a radical innovation.[30] This case history was the exact document I now had in my hands after ninety-nine years obscurity in the archives and a long, frustrating search.

The circumstances of Michael's downward spiral came to a head in spring 1900 after many months when relations between Michael and Maria had deteriorated. Arguments, money worries, rearing the children, while keeping a steely grip on his all-important motorman job must have made life, with interfering in-laws upstairs, almost impossible. On top of all that, ever since his street-car accident, Michael had recurring headaches, dizzy spells and eye complaints. On Wednesday evening of 16 May, Michael cracked. Two days later, he found himself travelling west by train from South Station, escorted by an officer from Cambridge District Court, having been committed to Worcester Insane Asylum. For any family to agree to having a family member interned was a terrifying responsibility. Grob examined the exact process in having an individual committed to an asylum.

> In theory commitment was a complex legal process designed to safeguard against wrongful confinement and at the same time to ensure that insane persons threatened neither the safety of themselves or others. In practise commitment was an informed process that involved human decisions rather than strictly legal ones. The decision to commit was largely made by the family of the mentally ill person…Those involved with the criminal justice system also played a peripheral if not inconsequential role.[31]

On arrival at Worcester on 18 May, feeling nervous, bewildered and full of dread, Michael was interviewed by a doctor and his assistant, who noted down his biographical information, according to Dr Adolph Meyer's new guidelines. Michael's case was given a Worcester Insane Asylum reference number 20 965, and entered under the title 'Homocidal and Suicidal' – he was now imbedded in the system. His personal details were typed on the standard form.

> Michael J. Mongan; Sex: Male; Birthplace: Ireland. Year of Birth: 1866. Address of Correspondent: Sister, Mrs Keough, 15 M Street, So Boston. Applicant: Maria E. Mongan, Cambridge. Name and Birthplace of Father: Hubert Mongan, Ireland: Name and Birthplace of Mother: Annie Murray, Ireland; Education: Common-school; Religion (Denomination): Episcopalian; Habits: Temperate; Occupation: Motorman; Occupation of Father: Carpenter; Civil condition (Date of Marriage): Married; Number of Children: Male: 1; Female: 2; Assigned Cause of Insanity: Four years ago (1898), thrown from board of street-car, leg hurt. This is supposed to be the cause in great part. Date of Onset: Nov 1899; Date of Admission: May 18, 1900; Committed by: District Court of Cambridge. Physicians: L.L. Bryant – J.L. Hildreth; Diagnosis: Neurasthenic irritability (syphilis-trauma) Varicose ulcer in place of injury.[32]

The second page, under 'Anamnesis', outlined of Michael's background.

> Family History: Negative, except father a rather hard drinker; Personal History: Patient was strong and healthy as a child. His only sickness was measles. At school till 14. He stood at the head of his class. At sports he would hold his own. After leaving school, he worked up, in six years, to head freight clerk. At 20 he enlisted, and served three years in England and at Suakine. No alcoholism or illness. Sexual History: Little masturbation ('A dozen times or so'). One gonorrhoea, and in Fall of '85, chancre. Summer of '86, sore throat lasting two months, treated by K.I. and mercury. Spring of '88, copper-coloured spots appeared, with later 'matter in the center', healing up spontaneously. Patient was married April 5, 1893. Had three children; the first died at four and a half months of cholera infantum. Occupation:

February 1888, patient came to America, and after a month's work at bot-tling, he had worked for West End ever since. July '98, while conductor, on a wet day, patient slipped from the car, the running board rasping his left shin severely. He was momentarily unconscious but ran the car home. He was out of work four days. No paralytic sequelae, but the resulting ulcer on the leg has broken out about seven times. After the accident, he got work as motor-man rather than take chances on a running board. November 1898, patient and family went to live with wife's mother. Six or eight months later, patient's wife began giving her mother their savings to keep. On and off since, patient has protested. Wife has asked for it back but did not get it till day of commitment. After the accident, patient thinks he was probably more cross and irritable when his leg got sore, and he felt blue, but he denies abus-ing his family ('Wordy quarrel, that would be all').

The evening of 16 May '00, one child came in crying, and he told wife, 'If you can't take better care of them, I'll blow your bloody head off.' Patient denies meaning anything by it. His revolver (which he purchased two years before), on account of having to return late at night through a tough neigh-bourhood) was not on his person. His wife, on the threat, immediately went next door to her mother's for the night. She had been after him to get rid of the pistol for a long time, so next day he tried to sell it to a conductor, telling him he had had some words with his wife the night before, and threatened to blow her head off. 'I thought he was my friend, but he proved to be nothing but a police spy.' The conductor complained to the police. The officer questioned the wife, and she admitted they had a little trouble, and he arrested patient.

Michael's sister, Mary Anne Keough, also gave a statement to the doctors.

Cause: Unhappy married life. No change in patient's manner. He has always been quick tempered, and threatening, but not dangerous. She says he has not been different in any way of late. Says his married life has always been unhappy; that his wife is a spendthrift, and she never stays at home; and she looks like a woman that drinks. That he has always had a quick temper, and often threatens but never executes. She does not think that there was any danger or intention on his part to shoot his wife.

Michael's wife, Maria, was also questioned and confirmed Mary Anne's statement.

Patient always quick tempered, but not violent. She became afraid lately. He threatened to kill whole family. Nailed coffin-plate over front door, and she had him arrested and sent here. He has a habit of threatening to shoot her, and would often say it even when in good humor. About two weeks after Bergen killed his entire family, the patient said (to a fellow-labourer) that he was 'going to the Bergen act some day', and that his family would be the act.

He was all right till Wednesday, when he was angered by his sister's actions when he was coming home. He came in the house Wednesday evening, and the children were playing outside and making some noise. He at once went out and kicked the little girl in the stomach twice. She cried some ('though the mother is evidently lying to secure the release of her husband').

She picked up the child when he struck her on the arm. She went to her mother that night, (mother lives in the same flat) because she was frightened. The next morning when she went back, he had during the night taken the coffin-plate of their dead child, and tacked it up over the front door.

She thought it was a sign of death, but he refused to give her any explanation, laughing at her when she asked. He told the officer he did it to make her feel bad. She was frightened and sent for an officer.

The doctor's assessment of the various statements was summed up in a Physicians' Certificate dated 18 May 1900.

Onset gradual, present attack May 16, 1900. Violent, destruction, depressed, carries revolver, threatened his family. Patient denies all the statements of wife, brother-in-law, and T.E. Frawley, that he ever threatened his wife's life, or anyone's life with a revolver. He said that his wife drank liquor, and paid more attention to what her mother said than what he wanted; that his brother motormen were down on him, calling him names, and laughed at him because he did not join the strike of three years ago.[33] Appearance is morose, with scowling features, and shifting gaze. According to his wife and T.E. Frawley, he was injured in the head four years ago, and during the last two years, he has been growing gradually more irritated, and has uncontrolled attacks of violent anger, during which he breaks furniture, kicks the children, and this has culminated in personal violence to wife and threats of shooting his wife, children and himself; a loaded revolver was taken from him by the police.

The following day, Michael was again assessed by the doctors.

Mental Status, May 19. Attitude and Manner: Normal. Patient spoke freely, but rather loudly. He gave a full account of the psychosis, admitting he threatened his wife, but said he never intended to execute it. Orientation: Perfect for time and place.

Q: 'What is the date?' A: '19th of May 1900.' Q: 'What day?' A: 'Saturday. (Correct.)' Patient's Account of Psychosis: Q: 'Why are you here?' A: 'I have enemies like other people. I'm a motorman on West End R. R. and did not strike three years ago, and the strikers are mad at me. Some time ago he had some trouble with his wife, and threatened to shoot his wife, and threatened to shoot her because she had given money to her mother which he had saved. He worked Wednesday, and asked for excuse for Thursday. On that morning, he was walking along when arrested by policeman. He was then carrying a revolver, because he was going to sell it. He does not think that he has been 'worried over his leg' which was injured then. Alcoholism denied. Traumata: Four years ago, momentary unconsciousness. Struck on the forehead; did not quit but for four day; no paralysis. Since then he has had pain in his eyes. No hallucinations: Headache: Since the accident he had had headache with dizziness in the morning, which he attributes to his stomach or his eyes. Syphillis: He admits an infection of syphilis eighteen years ago.

Michael was given a complete physical check-up by doctors. They took note of his physical appearance:

Well developed and nourished. He had a symmetrical skull and ears, with adherent lobules. His complexion was fair, with blues eyes, dark brown hair, and a light brown moustache.

They remarked that he had brown patches on both his legs, noted as 'syphilis' as well as two dime-sized ulcers, an 'old injury'. Michael also voluntarily brought to their attention a 'dubious scar on foreskin'. He also underwent muscular, knee-jerk, hearing, lungs, stomach and eye tests which revealed nothing abnormal. Among other tests, Michael also wrote out his signature, and the phrase 'God Save the Commonwealth of Massachusetts'. His writing in pencil; strong, slanted, fluid and flowing, gave no suggestion of any mental instability whatsoever.

At Worcester two days later, on 21 May 1900, Michael was reported to be quiet, and had showed nothing abnormal, except that he said he was 'nervous'. His immediate main anxiety seemed to be about the healing of his leg injury. He admitted the threat to his wife, but again said that he meant nothing by it.

He spent his time reading quietly on the ward, and had made the acquaintance of two inmate 'Odd Fellows'. 'He answered freely, rationally, and to the point, volunteering nothing beyond the questions posed.'

He carried out mental arithmetic easily, subtracting sevens from 100 correctly in forty seconds. The doctors noted that his memory 'remote and recent was unimpaired and exact'. They found no evidence of any delusions, although they believed that his statement of the 'men being down on him for not joining the strike' as likely to be true enough, while he rejected any accusations 'of unfaithfulness'. They noted that Michael had written to his wife, saying that he was first 'among the loonies' on the S.1. ward, and went on to give an accurate pen-portrait, which the doctors noted 'characterises the patients there quiet well', and the same on T.1. ward.

On 31 May, Michael's chart showed 'an irregular sleep curve and temperature over 100'.

Three weeks later, on 23 June, the doctors reported a 'considerable rather coarse hand tremor of his hands, at rest or on rotation'. They noted that Michael had said 'that this will be a lesson for him that will be of note'.

He was given a temporary release, and 'goes on visit in care of his sister' Mary Anne, with whom he probably travelled back to her home at 15 M Street in his old haunt of South Boston.

Doctors G.F. and A.C. Jelly believed that his alleged mental instability had been a 'constitutional defect' along with other causes; traumatism, opium and alcoholism. They diagnosed 'constitutional inferiority, with a liability to depression with suicidal following trauma'. Michael received an official release from Worcester on 21 August 1900, with the note that 'patient is today discharged from visit of June 23', with the added note, 'Much Improved'.

He had been involuntarily incarcerated at Worcester Insane Asylum from 18 May until 12 August 1900 – a total of three months and two days.

At the instigation of his scared wife, Maria, and her family and friends, Michael had been coerced onto a relentless treadmill that would require a monumental battle to escape from. As Grob remarked:

'The decision to commit was normally undertaken with a great deal of reluctance. Indeed, most families did everything within their power to find alternative means of dealing with mentally disordered members. The final decision generally came after prolonged tensions had created a crisis, and forced a choice between institutionalisation and the very destruction of the family unit. A variety of behavioural patterns often precipitated family action, especially the threat or actual use of violence and possible suicidal behaviour.'[34]

Maria, probably reluctantly but encouraged and supported by her parents and friends, had taken the traumatic decision to have her husband, and her children's father, committed to Worcester. At the same time, Michael's sisters, led by Mary Anne, must have protested vehemently against the decision. They felt that Michael's marital problems and family strife were as much Maria's and her parents' problem as well. They felt that the whole affair had been blown up out of all proportion and their brother had been brutally removed from his loving family circle for the horrors of internment with the insane. Tension between the Mongan sisters and their Hurd in-laws had reached breaking point.

Upon his release on 21 August, Michael must have felt that now his life was looking distinctly better. He had come through a frightening, stressful, and sobering experience with the 'Odd Fellows' reasonably well considering the trauma, and now, with the help and support of his sisters, he could get on with his life. Above all, he wanted to be reunited with his wife and children, Charles, by then an energetic six-year-old, and his darling little five-year-old daughter, 'Minnie' Mary Elizabeth.

9

Michael. 'Living with the Loonies'

Back in Ireland, James was alerted by a letter from Mary Anne informing him of Michael's woes. He passed the worrying news on to his aunt Mary Duignam at Belvedere. As the younger brother, he was very worried by developing crisis in Boston but he now also had the responsibility of his wife and their three-year-old son, Reginald Michael. He wondered what to do, discussing the situation with his wife, Mary. During Michael's three-month incarceration, they made their decision – they were going to America. Both James and Mary felt bound to help Michael in his darkest hour.

Years later, Reginald recalled, with some pride, the trip the family made to America. He remembered that they had visited Springfield in the west of Massachusetts, most probably to visit his Aunt Bridget. They also travelled to Montreal in Canada where Mary had worked before her marriage.

Michael Reginald was born in April 1897 and so was three years and six months old when they arrived in South Boston in late August 1900.

The Mongans held a family gathering at 15 M Street to assess how they might move things forward. Elizabeth and her carpenter husband Charles Edgerly, along with Eliza, now three, and Charles Junior, just two, joined them on weekends, and played with their Irish cousin Reginald in M Street Park just opposite the house. They were joined in their games by the four Keough toddlers – Josephine, five, James Junior, four, Hubert, three, while little Helene, just two, cradled in her mother's arms, googled with delight. James and Charles immediately found a common interest, exchanging banter about their respective carpentry skills and their experiences in the building trade. The families shared walks along L Street Beach, watching the bathers frolicking in the waves, the children building sand castles with their spades, enjoying ice cream and fizzy pop drinks, paddling in the shallows, while the concerned parents attempted to appear light-hearted, although the shadow of Michael's commitment hung over them like a pall. Catherine and Maria-Theresa took the train up from Abington, while Delia, working as a live-in domestic with a Boston Bramhin family, used her day off to join them, all were aware of Michael's worrying situation.

James and Michael spent days together mulling things over, discussing how the rift between Michael and his wife might be healed.

James most likely acted as an intermediary between his sisters and Michael's wife, Maria, and the Hurd family over in Cambridge. On meeting the Hurds for the first time, James, tense and suspicious, was unable to help himself from thinking Maria was to blame for having had Michael committed to Worcester. He talked with Maria's parents, Elisha and Hannah, and the children, Charles and Mary, remarking on how much Mary resembled her father, with her pale blue eyes, fair skin and dark brown curls. Reginald and his American cousins went outside to play in the garden at Kinnaird Street in the bright sunlight with that natural disposition of children to just have fun and leave their parents to deal with their adult problems. James spent much time with his shaken brother, encouraging him to attempt to find a truce with Maria, for the children's sake. He tried to reassure Michael that things would work out and said that he would talk to Maria for him.

Since his release from Worcester in August, Michael had had trouble finding work and had become discouraged, believing that people were laughing at him because of his internment. And there is little doubt that the stigma of incarceration at Worcester did work against his employment prospects. Could a company put someone with alleged mental instability in charge of a streetcar carrying fare-paying passengers? The uncertainty of his situation made Michael so grateful that James had come over to help him resolve marriage crisis and the worrying accusations over his mental health. The brothers went over and over the details of the events leading up to his incarceration – Michael felt that Maria had been neglecting the children's upbringing, listened far too much to her mother, to whom she was handing over his hard-earned savings, and generally spent far too much money rather than staying at home to look after the children. She regularly left Charles and Mary with their grandparents upstairs.

After a month's enjoyable hospitality, with his sister Mary Anne and her foundry-worker husband Jimmy Keough at 15 M Street, James and his family left to continue their trip. Stopping at Springfield, they probably stayed with James' elder sister, Bridget, before heading on to Montreal in Canada. Four months later, James and his family had returned to Ireland, where the 1901 Census (taken in March) showed him listed as 'House Carpenter', with his wife Mary and son, Reginald, aged almost four, living in a new two-storey house at 11 Fee's (later Ward's) Terrace, on the outskirts of Longford.[1] James had found employment on the various new housing projects being developed in the town at that time.

Meanwhile over in Boston, Michael was increasingly worried and anxious, as he had no income to support his wife and family. He had finally returned to live with Maria and the children at 32 Bay Street in late September. Then, after three months unemployment, and increasingly desperate, he took a menial job washing

James Mongan's wife
Mary, with son Reginald,
aged 4, and baby sister
Ester Mary 'Dolly', in
Longford, on their return
from Boston in 1901.

streetcars at the P Street car barn in October 1900. For a former MGWR Head Freight Clerk, ex-British army lance-corporal and West End Street Railway motorman, it was a demeaning and humiliating fall from grace.

Michael was still plagued by recurring dizzy spells and severe headaches. He eventually had to give up the work at the P Street car barn after Christmas. Being stuck at home unemployed, he spent days lying on his bed, saying nothing, eating little and suffering from headaches.

In March 1901, Boston was hit by a severe blizzard. Michael, imagining that he was snowbound, appeared disorientated, asked where he was and demanded to know why he was being kept in the house. The situation was serious. In 1900s Boston, a job was vital for survival and Michael felt his commitment at Worcester was working against him, stopping him from getting more work. Sick with worry, he stood in the corner, often saying, 'I'm doomed.'

Michael was now feeling increasingly vulnerable.[2]

At the family home at 32 Bay Street in Cambridge, Michael had spent an icy March 1901, prostrated on his bed with shivering spells and a general tremor that lasted anything from a few hours to a whole day. He constantly rubbed his face and picked his eyebrows. He was not feeling cold, but slept poorly, although his appetite was good, and he had all he wanted to eat. He also complained of severe headaches. These recurring health symptoms went unattended, apparently ignored by his wife's family, and he received no medical attention. The next crisis began on 27 March when events began a dramatic downward turn. On 1 April, Michael left the house at 4.45 a.m., believing it was 7.a.m. He was discovered in the street in a dazed state, without coat or hat, by a young Cambridge police officer, and brought to the police station nearby on Western Avenue. Agitated and confused, Michael told the police that he had left the house under the impression that he had drowned four members of his wife's family in the cellar, by letting the water tap run. He had left the house early to escape arrest for his crime. Maria was called to the police station where Michael did not seem to know why he had done this or just how it had happened. It would seem to have either been a nightmare or he somehow imagined the whole episode.

This latest developments suggested a deeply felt anger towards his Hurd in-laws and a subconscious reaction to the pressures of sharing the house with them. Inwardly, he probably regretted leaving South Boston.

That Thursday morning, 1 April, Michael had been picked up 100 yards from his house at 32 Bay Street and taken to the local Cambridge Police Station on Western Avenue, where he was held from 7 a.m. until 1 a.m. the next day, 2 April. The police officer told Dr Bevan, a Cambridge physician, that he believed that Michael was going to nearby Fresh Water Pond Reservoir 'to jump overboard', although Michael vehemently denied this allegation. Alerted by the police, Maria hurried to the Western Avenue station.

On Dr Bevan's recommendation, Maria gave her consent for the Cambridge District Court to have Michael recommitted to Worcester. His second period in hell had begun. He left Cambridge under the escort of a court officer from Cambridge District Court at 12.30 p.m. on 2 April, and took the train from South Station, arriving at Worcester Insane Asylum at 2.30 p.m.

Michael was readmitted to the hospital that afternoon. As the doors of Worcester State Hospital's grim, Gothic, main entrance building closed behind him, Michael felt an icy hand of terror run down his spine. He was trapped again. Stepping across the threshold at Worcester, he had re-entered the deranged, surreal, dysfunctional world of the mentally ill. Most contemporary observers had long been critical of their terrifying internal environment.

'In the wards, rooms of one of our state psychiatric hospitals,' John M. Gessell wrote in outrage, 'the beginning of each day is marked by the resurgence of a giant throbbing tempo of life, as much felt as heard... All too often one finds every sort and condition of patients locked together in the same ward, milling about and bruising one another. The noise and the filth, the crying, swearing, laughter, and inarticulate mumbling drive the depressed into deeper chasms of oblivion and the maniacs up ever more dizzy precipices of exaltation. Few are ever helped to break out of the fog of illusion that envelops them and to grasp some little part of reality which might lead toward mental health again… Violent patients are kept on the floors above. The silence of the night is often rent by their cries of insane rage.'[3]

This was the world in which Michael found himself. He underwent the Meyerian standard admission procedures, was given a bath and was fed. He was again part of a cold, confining, custodial regime, as defined by the Massachusetts State public institutional policy of caring for the insane since the 1870s.

Confinement itself for many patients was a major traumatic experience. Deprived of personal freedom, uprooted from a friendly, familiar environment, and compelled to mix with individuals from multifarious backgrounds who acted in most eccentric ways, not surprisingly resulted it in a deeply negative attitude to the hospital.[4]

Michael's medical records gave the doctors assessment of his condition after interviewing him. On admission, on 2 April 1901, the Physicians' Certificate spelled out their tersely worded viewpoint, in damning detail.

Onset gradual. Present attack began about a week ago. He received an injury to his head five years ago. Excited and depressed. Patient said that he had lost his position in the employ of the Boston Elevated R. R. last December, because of increasing inefficiency. Since then he has made no effort to obtain work. Has been low-spirited and says that he has attacks of temporary unconsciousness; that he went out on the street at seven o'clock this morning, when in fact he was found in a dazed condition about 4.45 a.m. and has since been at the Police Station. He sat immovably, staring into vacancy and answering questions slowly and with tremulous lips. Appearance and manner depressed and stupid. He was committed to the Worcester Insane Hospital May 18th, 1900 and was discharged on writ of Habeas Corpus June 21st, 1900. He had exhibited an increasing stupor since then, is now sleepless at night, stands staring fixedly for some time at different periods, makes no effort towards self support and exhibits loss of sense of time. He takes no interest in his wife or children.[5]

Michael's mental status, attitude and manner, were also noted.

Since admission patient has been quiet and well-behaved on the ward. He shows a disposition to be left alone. He is usually sitting on the settee or window seat, with his head bowed down with a sad, dejected expression. He does not mingle with other patients and does not busy himself.

Occasionally, he picks up a paper for a few minutes. When approached by a physician he is pleasant. He slept about five hours the first night, but had eaten little. In reacting to questions, he showed some initial retardation, and usually paused in the midst of a sentence or even a word, and after a long time completes the sentence. Repetition of the question is often necessary.

He opens his mouth to speak often half a minute before he said anything and then speaks with trembling lips. Usual test words show no speech defect. The stream of thought is interrupted by frequent pauses before or during a sentence. The intellect is little if any impaired.[6]

Michael had a good grasp on occurrences in his surroundings, although he mistakenly believed the date was 27 March 1901 when it was actually 2 April. He recognised patients, attendants and physicians and his grasp on the immediate past and memory for recent events was only slightly impaired.

Michael responded to the doctors' questions:

Q: 'When did you arrive?' A: 'Today about 2.30'. Q: 'Where were you before coming here?' A: 'Cambridge.' Q: 'When did you leave Cambridge?' A: 'Today 12:30.' Q: 'Give an account of admission?' A: 'They searched my clothing, took my name, etc.' Q: 'Were you ever here before?' A: 'Yes, I came on May 18th, 1900 and left on June 21st, 1900.' Q: 'Business?' A: 'Motorman before I was here first, and was in the repair shops since. I haven't worked since Christmas, but was at home since doing nothing.' Q: 'Are you married?' A: 'Yes. I had three children, one died.'[7]

Questioned on the remote past, Michael 's memory was good. He remembered dates and events quite accurately. 'Age 37, born in 1864. [1863] I was married in '93, the 5th of April. My last child was born in Ireland[?] and came to America in 1888. In 1894, I fell off an electric car and hurt my head. I have been nervous and irritable since. I hurt my leg at the same time. I was unconscious for a moment or two. In 1882, I had syphilis, but got over it all right.'[8]

Was the error about Mary's birth Michael's or was it a typographical error? The doctors assessed the patient's psychosis.

'[He] claimed to have drowned four people by turning on the water. He could not explain why he did it or how it was possible. He said he was a physical and mental wreck. He had micro-manic ideas, believed he weighed 57lbs, [that] his brain had collapsed and organs [had] shrivelled up. He left his house this A.M. to escape arrest, and his appreciation of lapse of time was faulty. He was worried and felt depressed and said he often lapsed into apathy but had no fear.'[9]

Michael answered a further set of probing questions.

Q: 'Why are you here?' A: 'I turned on the water and drowned four people. They were in their rooms, they were my wife's father, mother, one sister and one brother. They were in a cellar at the time and I flooded the cellar.' Q: 'Why did you turn on the water?' A: 'Just to have it run and see how it worked. I let it run for half an hour.' Q: 'That wasn't enough to drown those people?' A: 'No, I don't know where the rest of the water came from.' Q: 'When was this?' A: 'Saturday evening.' Q: 'When was the funeral?' A: 'They're not buried yet. I don't know when they will be. I'm here for having caused the death of those four people, also because I'm a physical and mental wreck. I am all run down now and weigh 57lbs. I am strong enough to lift double my own weight. Sometimes I say things that I don't know afterwards that I said them. I worry because I'm down as far as I can go physically. I feel depressed for the same reason. I always think of what the outcome of this will be. Since I left home, I have only eaten occasionally in a few weeks, and the rest of the time only ate very little. The first time I came here I made a threat to shoot my wife because of a family trouble and money matters. She spent too much.'

Michael claimed he had not been unconscious and had no amnesiac periods.

'I left the house at 7 a.m. yesterday morning (4.45 a.m.) because I killed those four people and wanted to escape arrest and to go away as far as possible. A policeman met me 100 yards from the house and arrested me and took me to jail. They didn't try me for murder, but said I was mentally weak and sent me here. I was there from yesterday A.M. till 1 o'clock today.' [10]

Michael underwent another handwriting test similar to that on his previous incarceration. He wrote his signature rapidly and without effort, in keeping with the experience of a former MGWR Head Freight Clerk: *Michael J. Mongan – God Save the Commonweatlh of Massachusetts'*. The doctors noted that he had a good grasp of things he had acquired at school and from general experience. He had a good knowledge of geography, historical events and their dates, along with a good conception of current events. In mental arithmetic, he showed no impairment and could work simple and complex problems with ease and rapidity, counting from one to twenty in five seconds.

The doctors believed that Michael showed he had some insight into his mental weakness, through not his delusions:

'I am completely upset in my mind and often lapse into apathy and feel as though I didn't care how anything went. There isn't much of my brain left. It seems to have collapsed and I feel a vacancy in my head. All my organs seem to have shrunk away.' He took a deep breath and said his lungs were still there and felt his pulse and said his heart was still there but weak. 'My stomach and intestines are still intact but shrivelled up and I always have a hungry feeling. It's no imagination but a fact that I drowned those people.' [11]

The next day, 3 April 1901, the doctors noted that Michael seemed duller than the previous day, and was slower to answer. During this day's questions, he knew that he was picked up at 5.a.m. More questions were posed.

Q: 'How is your head?' A: 'Not quite clear.' Q: 'How?' A: 'Dizzy.' Q: 'Ever unconscious?' A: 'No, sir.' Q: 'Why here?' A: 'Dr Bevan of Cambridge sent me here.' Q: 'What for?' A: 'For being in the street.' Q: 'What did you do?' A: 'Walking around.' Q: 'What else?' A: 'An officer told the Doctor that I was going to Fresh Pond Reservoir to jump overboard, but that was not true.' Q: 'How about the drowning affair?' A: 'I mentioned that. I did it.' Q: 'What time were you picked up in the street?' A: '5 a.m. day before yesterday.'

Later on the same day, the doctors added a further note that Michael claimed to have a dull feeling in his stomach. He was weighed (150½lbs) and measured (5ft 9¾inches).

Two days later, Michael was again interrogated. Doctors noted that he now said that the drowning episode was untrue, that he weighed 150lbs, and his viscera did not seem shrivelled up. He felt better and was occupying himself.

Q: 'How are you?' A: 'Feeling better, thank you.' Q: 'How about the drowning episode?' A: 'That wasn't true. I thought so at the time, but see now that it was impossible. I can't account for it now.' Q: 'How much do you weigh?' A: '150lbs.'[12] Michael said that he still had the sensation of the shrivelling of viscera but to less extent. He had been reading and assisting in the ward work.

Seven weeks slipped by. On 20 May, Michael was interviewed again by the doctors, who noted that he no longer retained his former delusions. However, they found his appreciation for the lapse of time was slightly faulty, and he worried a lot, but thought his mind was all right. He had no speech defect, though he showed a slight tremor of his tongue and hands, and his knee-jerk reactions were exaggerated. Michael responded to further interrogation.

Q: 'When did you come?' A: 'About a month ago.' [2 April] Q: 'How long were you on T.1. [ward]?' A: 'Nine days.' [thirteen] Q: 'Why are you here?' A: 'Because I was on the street early in the morning.' Q: 'How about the drowning episode?' A: 'I believed it at the time, but know now it wasn't.' Q: 'Why did you think so?' A: 'I don't know.' Q: 'How much do you weigh?' A: '150lbs.' Q: 'How old?' A: '35.' Q: 'When born?' A: '1863. I'm 38 years old.' Q: 'What is the date?' A: 'May 21st, 1901.' [20th] Q: 'Do you worry?' A: 'Yes, sir.' Q: 'About what?' A: 'About the way things went.' Q: 'What did you do?' A: 'Getting sent here the first time. There is something to worry about all the time.' Q: 'What worries you just now?' A: 'Being sick in here.' Q: 'How are you sick?' A: 'My strength is gone.' Q: 'How is your head?' A: 'My mind is alright only I worry a little.' Q: 'Any reason to complain?' A: 'No, sir.' Q: 'Does you head still feel vacant?' A: 'No, sir.' Q: 'Have you any peculiar thoughts?' A: 'No, I haven't.'[13]

Six days later, on 26 May, Michael developed a small red spot on his right cheek, well defined by an 'indurated and slightly elevated border' and he ran a high temperature of 104°F. The physicians reported it as an 'attack of facial erysipelas'. Michael was sent to bed and ichthyol ointment was applied to the sore. The following day, the inflammation had spread to cover most of the right side of his head. By 1 June, he had recovered as the inflammation gradually disappeared and the skin was 'desquamating [exfoliating] dry and flaky'. Michael's temperature had been normal for two days and he was allowed to sit up in bed.[14] On 10 June, the monotonous, dreary routine of the hospital was suddenly shattered. The Doctors typed a report in Michael's file.

'Escape by jumping from T.1 [ward] window. This evening about 9 o'clock the patient watched his chance and when the attendants were busy putting the patients to bed, Mongan pried a cleat from on of the T.1. bay-windows which have no screens, raised the window and jumped to the ground. He ran off leaving his slippers where he jumped. He had no hat.'[15]

The next day, 11 June, the doctors made the following entry:

Return from escape. Found loafing around the lake. Admitted suicidal intent. The patient was returned to the hospital this after noon by two men who saw him loafing around the lake and acting suspiciously. He admitted to them that he had contemplated suicide, but said that he didn't do it last night because he had heard that drowning was a slow death. He had, however, decided to do it today. He came back without resistance, but asked not to taken to the hospital as they would abuse him for running away.[16]

On 12 June, another entry was added:

Regrets escape. Says something came over him, admits that he was more despondent and was thinking of suicide. Claims that he was on his way back to the hospital when taken up. The patient's ankles and left leg are badly swollen from walking. He says this morning: 'I am sorry, Doctor, for the way I acted.' Q: 'Why did you go away?' A: 'It came over me, Doctor, I didn't premeditate it.' Q: 'What was it that came upon you?' A: 'My place was at home and I ought to be there.' Q: 'Where did you go?' A: 'I went to Union Station, but I didn't have any money.' Q: 'Then where did you go?' A: 'I went to the lake near the boat house.' Q: 'What for?' A: 'Well, I didn't have any particular reason for going there.'[17]

Michael claimed that he was on the road coming back to the hospital when he was taken up by two men. He admitted telling the men that he had thoughts of suicide, but denied that they saw him hanging around the lake. He said he did not ask them not to take him back to the hospital. He also admitted he was more despondent and had thought of making away with himself just before he escaped.

On 5 July, as Michael's desperation to be discharged grew, the doctors reported that he had written a letter which he tried to smuggle out to his sister Mary Anne, in South Boston.

He had given a letter to one of the parole patients and asked that it be mailed on the outside. In it, he begged Mary Anne to please bring laudanum or chloroform in order that he might end his life. He also wrote that he was kicked and abused by the attendants. When questioned he said he did not want to die, and admitted he had been lying about being abused.

When questioned the next morning about the letter, Michael admitted having written it, and said:

'I am guilty of lying, Doctor, and I have acted like a cur.'

Q: 'Do you wish to end your life?' A: 'No sir. I have plenty of chances and I didn't. I felt discouraged.' Q: 'Have you been ill-treated?' A: 'No, sir, you have treated me like a gentleman.' Q: 'Have the attendants abused you?' A: 'No, Doctor, they have not.' Q: 'Why did you write such a letter?' A: 'Well, I don't know. Doctor, I lied. I was wrong.'[18]

On 7 July, in spite of his answers to the doctor, Michael tried to send another letter secretly to his wife, again asking for poison, and also claiming abuse at Worcester. [Letter was filed and then later removed from file]

Around 10 July, Michael's wife Maria travelled out from South Station by train to visit him at the hospital. She gave him news about the children, Charles, and Mary, now aged six and five, and attending playschool near Kinnaird Street. The Hurds sent their best wishes. Encouraged and with high hopes for their future together, Michael desperately wanted to have an imminent discharge date set by the doctors.

An eternal month later, 9 August, Michael told his doctors that he thought he was all right now. He denied any hallucinations of sight or hearing, and said his other ideas were imaginary. The doctors noted that he was quite anxious for a discharge. He frequently said to the physician:

'Well, Doctor, what are my chances for getting another trial?' Q: 'Where do you get these ideas?' A: 'I don't know, but I had them for a day. It seemed real at the time and think now it was imagination.'[19]

He denied any hallucinations of sight or hearing. The doctors carried out reaction tests on Michael, his left knee-jerk was considerably more marked than the right, while his left Achilles heel was also a little more marked.

At Worcester on 18 September 1901, the doctors reported that Michael had '... worked some and maintained a fairly cheerful attitude, though he often gazed at the floor as if in study. He claimed to not having the "blues" now and had no thoughts of suicide.'

The doctors probed him for any insight into his former delusions.

Q: 'How are you now?' A: 'I am getting along all right now, sir, got through with all these notions I had.' Q: 'When did you give them up?' A: 'Well, after my wife came to see me, a few days after I wrote that letter.' [7 July] [He referred to his talk of suicide.] Q: 'Why did you have these thoughts?' A: 'Well, Dr G[elly] said to me when he was going that I would be here for life, that preyed on me.' Q: 'What was your condition when you came here?' A: 'Well, I had run away with the idea that by turning on a faucet, I had drowned four people in the house (laughing), but I was over it in a day. He said this was the only idea he had.' Q: 'Did you think you were shrivelled up?' A: 'Oh, yes, I thought I only weighed 57lbs when I came here.'[20]

On 11 October 1901, Michael's doctors reported that he was 'a good worker'.

On the ward, the doctors reported that Michael was quiet and that his spirits were lifting:

'Good worker. Appears cheerful. Anxious for discharge. Good insight into previous delusions. Attributes his first commitment to a family quarrel and say he had no imaginations. Denies ever seriously considering suicide. Admits he had the blues here. On the wards, the patient frequently asks about his discharge. He wants one more chance to make his living out in the world. Today when questioned, he thinks his idea of drowning the people was imagination, and doesn't know why he should have had such a thought.

He explains his saying that he only weighed 57lbs. Because when he was weighed it was 157, and he only heard the attendant say 57. He says he only had the idea about drowning the people for about 24 hours.

He says that the morning after he got here, he was perfectly well and he realised it was imagination. When questioned, about his first commitment, he says his mind was not affected and that he had no imaginations. He thinks he was sent here as a result of a family quarrel. His wife told the police he was not acting right and they found a revolver on him. This he carried chiefly for target practise. He says that he was now on the best of terms with his wife. He admits quarrelling with her, but denies ever threatening her or himself. When asked about the letters he wrote here of suicidal content, he says, "I had a touch of the blues, did it more to get them to come to see me more than anything else."[21] He denies that he ever thought seriously of suicide.'

On 8 November, the doctors reported no further change and Michael was discharged. He was cheerful and denied he had the 'blues' now. The doctors reported. 'At the request of his sister and wife, he was allowed to go home with them today.' They noted him as 'Much improved'.[22]

Michael was ecstatic, relieved and elated to be free again. He was ready to take on the world. Smiling and happy, he headed back home to Boston with his wife Maria and sister Mary Anne, the two women who counted most in his life. He was impatient to see his children, Charles and Mary – he had spent far too long away from them. Now things would be different. He was determined to find regular work no matter what it took. Interned from 2 April until 8 November 1901, he had passed a harrowing, traumatic seven months and six days as an inmate of Worcester Insane Hospital and he never wanted to experience such an horrific ordeal ever again. Surely life could now only get better.

10

1900s Boston. Yankees versus Irish

Life in the outside world had continued in Boston. The city, and the nation, had gone into shock on 6 September 1901, when President William McKinley was assassinated while attending Pan American Exposition at Buffalo, NY. His assassin, the anarchist Leon Czolgosz, had approached the president in the Temple of Music. In spite of tight security, Czolgosz, who had been waiting in line to shake the president's hand, shot him twice in the stomach with a pistol hidden under a bandage. Rushed to the Exposition Hospital, McKinley succumbed to his wounds and died next day.[1]

In contrast, the political fortunes of the Boston Irish continued to improve when, in November 1901, Irish immigrant Patrick Collins had his political revenge, by defeating Republican Thomas N. Hart in the election for mayor. He won by the largest majority in the city's history, polling 52,038 votes to Hart's 33,173, to become Boston's second Irish-born mayor. The inauguration ceremony took place in the Council Chambers on 4 January 1902. The Irish were beginning to claw their way up from the bottom of the social ladder.[2]

Since his discharge from Worcester in 8 November 1901, Michael had been boarding with his sister Mary Anne and her husband Jimmy Keough at 15 M Street. Totally determined, he had travelled far and wide to find employment. He worked at three different places and was regularly sending money to his wife Maria in Cambridge. However, he was easily discouraged and discontented, and suffered periodic depression. During the winter months of 1901-02, he was taking morphine to help him sleep and had begun drinking to some extent. Shortly after his discharge, he went to Pennsylvania, where he worked firing a steam engine in November and December. There had been a strike and he was taking the place of one of the strikers but, when the strike was settled, he was let go.[3]

He then went to New Jersey where he worked as a motorman until April. However, he got into trouble when he struck a horse team and was discharged. He returned to South Boston and went to work at Estabrook & Sons, Iron Foundry on Q Street. He had worked steadily there from April until July, but became increasingly discouraged with his work as he was paid low wages. He was sending $5 dollars every second week to his wife and was paying $3.75 for his board – and he only earned $8.50 per week. After hours, he spent time with Mary

Anne and Jimmy Keough. Mary Anne had told Maria that he had been taking morphine pills and, on some days, he would be fairly stupid.

Then on 26 June 1902, Michael stayed home from work, complaining that his stomach troubled him and he appeared to have taken some drug. When he visited Mary Anne at 15 M Street, he fairly staggered on leaving. By that point, Michael was lodging at Whitehead's Boarding House, at 856 East Broadway, which was just 400 yards away from where Mary Anne lived. On 27 June, he was found unconscious on the floor of the bathroom at Whitehead's. He had gone into the bathroom early in the morning and had, allegedly, turned on the gas with suicidal intent, as the room was full of gas and the door was locked. He was found at 7 a.m. slumped unconscious on the bathroom floor and was rushed by horse-drawn ambulance to nearby Carney Hospital on Telegraph Hill. Michael vehemently denied that he had tried to commit suicide, though he admitted that he had been drinking quite heavily during the previous two weeks (14-27 June 1902), something he had never done before. Michael was low-spirited at times, and Maria had stated that, at the new moon, he had a hypochondriacal attack lasting for several days at a time. He seemed to be brooding over something and would hardly speak to his family.[4]

With his growing reputation as being allegedly mentally unstable, Michael was recommitted to Worcester on 1 July 1902, by the Cambridge Probate Court. Leaving on the 2 p.m. express train from South Station, Michael, escorted by Court Officer Hennessy, travelled through the increasingly familiar countryside, arriving at Worcester at 4 p.m. On admission, it was found that he had large blisters on his legs due to molten metal burns received while working at the Estabrook & Sons foundry on West First and C Streets in South Boston. He stated the he earned $10 a week at the foundry.

At Worcester, the doctors noted his habits – 'uses opium to excess' – on the standard form and while the cause of his alleged insanity was 'unknown', they believed that the probable cause was 'constitutional defect, Opium, Traumatism, and alcohol'. The onset of the attack was dated to 26 June 1902.[5]

Again with Maria's agreement, Michael was recommitted by the Probate Court of Boston, on the recommendations of Doctors G.F. and A.C. Gelly. They gave their diagnostic as: 'Consitutional Inferiority. Liability to depression with suicidal impulses following trauma.' (A hand-written gloss in his medical case history noted 'Diff. of N.J.')

The increasingly familiar admission procedures were strictly adhered to by the doctors. The Physician's Certificate, drawn up on his admission, noted his recurring decline:

'Onset gradual. Present attack began two months ago. Depressed, suicidal. Patient said that he went to the bath-room in the house where he boards, was sick at his stomach and fell; that he knew nothing till he found himself at the Carney Hospital. He admits that he sometimes takes some morphia when he cannot sleep. He was committed from Cambridge to this hospital in 1900 and 1901. He talked in a depressed and suspicious manner. His appearance and manner are somewhat demented and as if under the influence of delusions which he does not express. It is probable that drugs have little to do with his conduct. He is said to have been depressed and more so of late. The occurrence in the bath-room on the 27th was undoubtedly a suicidal attempt. He tries very hard to conceal his mental condition.'[6]

Continuing their examination of Michael, the doctors noted that he was quiet and orderly on admission. When addressed, he answered freely, admitting alcoholism but denying any suicide attempt.

He is perfectly aware of his surroundings and is well-oriented. He denies the charge of attempted suicide and says that it was accidental and that if he wanted to commit suicide, he could have done it in his own room. He says that he had been drinking heavily before coming here and tries to conceal the true mental condition. There is no evidence of depression, no retardation, no hallucinations elicited. Slight tremor of hands and tongue.[7]

Michael was submitted to more intensive questioning.

Q: 'When did you come?' A: 'I just arrived this afternoon.' Q: 'Have you been here before?' A: 'Yes, I was here five weeks before.' Q: 'When was that?' A: 'May, two years ago.' Q: 'When did you leave?' A: 'Twenty-third of June.' Q: 'Weren't you here only that time?' A: 'I was here a year later and left last October. I got up last Friday and went to the bath-room and the gas was escaping and overcome me while I was on the stool and I was unconscious and they sent me to the Carney Hospital. The doctors believed my story. I didn't do it on purpose for I could have done it if I had wanted to commit suicide.' Q: 'Have you any cause for committing suicide?' A: 'No, sir. I was making good money and had back pay coming to me.' Q: 'Had you been drinking some?' A: 'Yes, I was drinking some.' Q: 'Had you any trouble outside?' A: 'No, no trouble at all.' Q: 'Why were you sent here before?' A: 'I worked on the electrics and there was a couple of electric conductors trumped up a charge that I had threatened to kill my wife and so got rid of me in that way.' Q: 'Anyone been using you mean since you came here?' A: 'No, not at all.' Q: 'How long were you in Carney Hospital?' A: 'One day.' Q: 'What day?' A: 'Tuesday, July 1.' Q: 'How much had you been drinking?' A: 'Quite a good deal in the past two weeks. I had all I could carry sometimes.'[8]

The doctors applied zinc oxide to the affected parts of his leg burns. The following day, they also noted his mental status, attitude and manner.

The patient since admission has been quiet and orderly and is inclined to be sociable with the other patients. His facial expression is slightly sad, but he smiles frequently and occasionally jokes and laughs heartily. On the ward, he spends most of his time sitting by the window, but occasionally gets up and moves around the ward in a rather restless manner. When addressed, he speaks freely and often takes the initiative in conversation. His trend of thought is that he wishes to get out as quickly as possible and says that there is nothing wrong with him except his stomach feels badly and he has been excessive drinking considerably. His speech and actions are normal in time, showing no retardation.

About his former terms at the hospital, he at first gives rather evasive answers and appeared not to care to discuss or rather conceal their nature, but afterwards he tells of them freely. He is neat about his person and shows by his hands that he has done some hard work recently and upon his legs there are several blisters, the results of burns from hot metal, according to the patient's statement, which he received while at his work in the galvanised pipe factory. He sleeps well and eats well but very fast and complains of much fermentation in his stomach. When questioned he answers promptly and the reaction is very sharp and to the point.[9]

The doctors found Michael's orientation perfect, and knew the place and date, and recognised people.

Q: 'What day is this?' A: 'July 2, 1902.' Q: 'What place?' A: 'Worcester Insane Hospital.' Q: 'Who am I?' A: 'Dr C.' Q: 'Who are these people?' A: 'Patients.'

Michael's comprehension of occurrences in the surroundings was good. They noted his hand grasp was very good, and he had been sent here twice on suspicion of having attempted suicide, that he has been here twice before and knows all about the place. His memory was good, especially his memory for recent and remote events was very accurate, and he was able to give dates and all the details. They posed even more personal questions on his background.

Q: 'When did you come?' A: 'Yesterday afternoon and left Boston at 2 o'clock.' Q: 'How did you come?' A: 'In an express train.' Q: 'Was anyone with you?' A: 'A court officer named Hennessy.' Q: 'Give and account of your admission?' A: 'He brought me into the office and told me to sit on the chair and then the other doctor came in and they gave him an envelope of the things they took out of my pocket, and then Mr C came in and I saw Dr H.' Q: 'Did you know Dr H?' A: 'Yes.' Q: 'Was he here when you were here last?' A: 'Yes, I guess he got moved to the female side before I left.' Q: 'Who was here when you were here the first time?' A: 'Dr G and Dr H.' Q: 'When were you here the first time?' A: 'May, two years ago.' Q: 'And when did you leave?' A: 'June 23.' Q: 'When the second time?' A: 'April last year and left in October.' Q: 'When were you born?' A: 'Thirty-five years ago.' Q: 'When was that?' A: 'August, 1867.' [actually it was 1863] Q: 'Where?' A: 'Belfast, Ireland.'

[actually Mullingar] Q: 'When did you come to this country?' A: 'February, 1888.' Q: 'Did you get your education in Ireland?' A: 'Some in Ireland and some in England and Hampshire.' Q: 'Remember your teachers' names?' A: 'Kartin [Curtin?] in Ireland and Mr Foster in the army school in Aldershot.' Q: 'Did you go in the army?' A: 'Yes, I was there three and a half years.' Q: 'When were you married?' A: 'April, 1893.' Q: 'Have you any children?' A: 'Two.' Q: 'How old are they?' A: 'One was born in 1895 and the other in 1896, both in May.' Q: 'How old is the oldest?' A: 'Seven years [Charles] and the youngest six [Mary].'[10]

Michael spent many of his long days of incarceration at Worcester State Hospital in the Hoover Hall day room sitting on a sofa or window seat pondering his fate. (*Courtesy Worcester Public Library*)

Michael was also quizzed on his education and general experience. He showed a good knowledge of history and geography, and his reactions were prompt and to the point. He carried out mental arithmetic calculations, with responses sharp and accurate in simple as well as combined forms. He showed no retardation and made no mistakes. He subtracted successive sevens from 100 so rapidly that the doctor found it 'nearly impossible to keep up with the pencil'. Michael's writing showed no deterioration, made without hesitation and showed a knowledge of capitalisation and orthography. His speech showed no slurring of test words, and he spoke freely on matters of his life.

Then the doctors went over the characteristics of Michael's alleged psychosis:

The patient has been in this hospital twice before with doubtful diagnosis. Admits syphilis and alcoholism, denies morphineism. There is no evidence of hallucinations and the patient will admit no delusions. He says he has been the victim of circumstances. At first, committed through persecution of a fellow-workman, the next through the hasty conclusions of a policeman, and at present on account of accidental gas poisoning. He denies the apparent attempt at suicide and states with tears in his eyes that he cares too much for his family to think of such as thing. There is an apparent attempt to conceal his true mental condition. No retardation. No mental deterioration.

Later in the day, there was another question and answer session.

Q: 'How are you?' A: 'My stomach seems to be knocked out this morning. I have belching wind.' Q: 'How did you happen to come here this time?' A: 'Friday morning about 4 o'clock in the morning I went to the bath-room and had a movement from my bowels and the gas was turned on and I didn't notice it. I had a cramp and was in a hurry and after about ten minutes I was overcome and fell on the floor and began to vomit and I don't remember any more after that.' Q: 'When did you come to your senses?' A: 'In the Carney Hospital in the afternoon about 4 o'clock. When they went to wake me up they missed me and found me there.' Q: 'Didn't you smell the gas?' A: 'No, I didn't. I didn't know what the trouble was, I began to get weak and fell.' Q: 'You are sure you had no idea of suicide?' A: 'No, I had gas in the room, if I wanted to use it for suicidal purposes.' Q: 'What is your business?' A: 'In a foundry in the galvanized room.' Q: 'Have you been having any trouble lately?' A: 'No, I used to pay my way and give my wife $5 dollars a week.'[11] [Here Michael contradicts his previous statement that he sent Maria $5 every second week.]

Q: 'Everyone use you well?' A: 'Yes, sir.' Q: 'Have they always?' A: 'Yes, generally.' Q: 'Do you get discouraged at times?' A: 'No, not often.' Q: 'Sometimes?' A: 'I got drinking a little for the past two weeks.' Q: 'Your habits good?' A: 'Yes sir. I never had anything to do with any other women since I was married.' Q: 'Do you take any morphine?' A: 'No. sir.' Q: 'Did you ever?' A: 'No, well, a year ago I took a few ¼ gram pills. I took one each night for three or four nights.' Q: 'Have you been working?' A: 'Right along each day.' Q: 'Sleeping good at night?' A: 'Yes, sir. If I hadn't been for this unfortunate accident I would have been working yet.' Q: 'Have you had any peculiar experiences lately?' A: 'No, sir, I haven't had.' Q: 'When you were drinking did you ever see things?' A: 'No, sir.' Q: 'Or hear voices?' A: 'No, sir.' Q: 'Why were you here the first time?' A: 'There was a Conductor I was on with who was always trying to make trouble between me and my wife and one day he told the policeman that I had threatened to shoot her and all this business.' Q: 'And they took his word for it?' A: 'Dr Bryant sent me down here on observation and I was discharged in five weeks and since then none of the other men would speak to this man. It was a regular put-up job. He seemed bent on making trouble for me.' Q: 'Why did he do this?' A: 'Well, we differed on religious subjects sometimes, some of the other men would make remarks and he didn't like me siding in with them.' Q: 'What was his name?' A: 'Tom Frankley.' Q: 'Was he after your wife?' A: 'No, but he cast reflections on her, but she is above reproach. He said she used to romp around with the boys and all this.' Q: 'Did you see this man after you went out?' A: 'No, I never spoke to him afterwards.' Q: 'Wasn't you acting a little peculiar at the time?' A: 'No, I worked every day.' Q: 'At home?' A: 'No, not at home. I got along all right there.' Q: 'Why did you have to come last year?' A: 'Well, I went out on the street one morning. I wasn't fully dressed. I didn't have a coat or hat on and I wanted to see a motorman before he left and a police-man saw me and took me to the station.' Q: 'Wasn't that a peculiar thing to do?' A: 'Yes, it was but any man that has the name of being here they try to impose on him.' Q: 'They tried to impose on you?' A: 'In that case they did.' Q: 'Is that the only time?' A: 'Yes, it was.' Q: 'Then you have always been all right?' A: 'Yes, I never attempted my life and it was only an accident that brought me here.' Q: 'Couldn't you have been a little off temporarily at these times from drink?' A: 'No, sir. I never drank enough for that.' Q: 'Don't it strike you as being peculiar that you should be here three times and nothing the trouble?' A: 'The first time it was a put-up job, and the next time it was the police that was too fresh and this time it was an accident.' Q: 'You used to have blue spells?' A: 'No, never. I was always of an even temperament. I always try to look on the bright side.' Q: 'Will you admit that it looked suspicious?' A: 'Well, yes. I will admit it did look so, but I went in there to attend the call of nature and if I had wanted to commit suicide, I could have done so in the bed room, there's a gas jet there.'[12]

Michael was then administered Nux vomica and Gentian, a dosage of one teaspoonful with water before meals. He had another physical examination on 3 July 1902, which showed that his condition had remained the same as in his previ-ous commitment. They noted the sores on both legs, which Michael claimed were burns he suffered on 25 June 1902. The doctors reported on the scars:

There remains now, on right leg, a sharply defined area on shin, 3 x 1½ cm. Just below this is a large sized blister, which resembles a burn very much, several other suspicious areas on the same leg. On the left leg, inner side, similar blisters some of them broken, a large area of pigmented tissue, due to previous trauma. [13]

On 4 July, Michael was reported quiet and orderly as usual, still denying any intention of suicide. The penetrating scrutiny continued.

Q: You get on better here?' A: 'No, I have worked every day.' Q: 'You got through rather sudden?' A: 'Well, I didn't turn the gas on.' Q: 'How much did you earn a day?' A: 'Ten dollars a week.' Q: 'Well, you are glad to get back here among your friends?' A: 'No, I ain't glad to get back here. I never turned on the gas. I could have committed suicide in my own room if I had wanted do so.[14]

Days dragged by. On 7 July, Michael was in bed for treatment of the burns on his legs. He continued to deny taking drugs and insisted that there was no suicidal intent.

Q: 'How is everything going?' A: 'I could start working if my legs were better.' Q: 'How is your head?' A: 'All right. I didn't turn on the gas.' Q: 'Do you sometimes do things you are not aware of?' A: 'No, I didn't.' Q: 'Who were you living with?' A: 'Whitehead's Boarding House.' Q: 'How much did you make?' A: 'Ten dollars.' Q: 'Did she [Maria] ask you to give her so much?' A: 'No, but I thought she needed it.' Q: 'Did you get full?' A: 'Sometimes I drank beer, but it seemed to affect me pretty quick.' Q: 'How much did you drink?' A: 'Oh. Sometimes I would drink a glass twice a day.' Q: 'Not any more than that?' A: 'No, sir.' Q: 'You claim that you didn't want to [commit] suicide?' A: 'No, sir. I did not. I went in the bath-room and the gas was turned on and I got sick and began to vomit and became unconscious and when I woke up I was in Carney Hospital.' Q: 'Had you been taking any drug?' A: 'No, sir.' Q: 'Do you feel sad?' A: 'Well, I don't feel elated over this accident.' Q: 'Did you ever wear glasses?' A: 'I used to when I was on the car, blue glasses.'

On 10 July, Michael was given 1 ounce of Lanolin and 20 grams of Boric acid to be used on his burns. Four days later, the doctors reported him 'as usual, admitting nothing. Emphatically denies any attempt at suicide'. Michael said his legs were feeling better and that otherwise he felt all right.

Q: 'Have you any pain in the head?' A: 'No, I haven't.' Q: 'What did your wife say?' A: 'Said that she went and got what money was due to me and give me a better job when I came back.'[15]

On 18 July, Michael again denied any desire to commit suicide, but gave a different cause for the episode of the bathroom.

Says today that the pains in his legs caused him to faint in the bath-room. He is still in bed in T.1. [ward] and his legs are healing finely.

By 1 August, Michael's burns were nearly healed and he was pressing for release.

Q: 'Do you feel troubled?' A: 'I don't feel as though I ought to be here. My leg is about healed and that is what brought me here.'

On 11 August, the doctors reported him as improved and anxious to go home. There was no formal disorder and no insight into the alleged suicidal episode, claiming it was all an accident.

The long days of summer passed slowly. He was held at Worcester Insane Hospital for another agonising three months until 21 November 1902, when the doctors considered him much improved. He again admitted to depression, but still denied suicidal intent, and he had a normal attitude. He had remained quiet, orderly and pleasant. The doctors held a final session with Michael.

Q: 'Are you feeling better?' A: 'Yes, sir.' Q: 'How are you feeling better?' A: 'Well, I've got away with those despondent spells of mine.' Q: 'You don't feel so depressed?' A: 'No, I don't.' Q: 'What brings them on?' A: 'Well, I attribute it to the injury I received in the foundry – the burn.' Q: 'You have had them before?' A: 'That is the only time I remember of being depressed when I got burned with the metal. It was very painful.' Q: 'Wasn't you before when you were here?' A: 'No, only on account of being here.' Q: 'Didn't you have the injuries the other time?' A: 'Well, I got hit with the fender and the cut wasn't healed up. That is the only injury I had.' Q: 'Were you a little upset mentally?' A: 'Well, I felt a little depressed.' Q: 'Didn't feel as if you didn't care to live?' A: 'No, I never felt that way at all. The gas was turned on when I went in.' Q: 'You feel depressed now at all?' A: 'No, sir.' Q: 'What is you explanation of getting in here so many times?' A: 'Well, the first time I had a little misunderstanding between myself and wife and I made a threat or two, but never meant anything by it.' Q: 'And the next time?' A: 'I was on my way one morning to see a motorman and I went out on the street without my coat and just because I went out that way, the policeman took me.' Q: 'You must have been upset each time?' A: 'Well, I shouldn't have been sent here. I was working up to the day they took me and this time I was caught under compromising circumstances.' Q: 'You think you have never been out of your head?' A: 'No, I've never been so, but what I thought I knew what I was doing.' Q: 'How about taking drugs?' A: 'Well, I have been taking a few morphine pills, a few when I couldn't sleep well. I never took more than a dozen in all.' Q: 'Do you think drink had anything to do with it?' A: 'Well, I drank some this last time.' Q: 'How long have you been here?' A: 'About three months.' Q: 'What day did you come?' A: 'I came about the 20th of June.' Q: 'What month is this?' A: 'November 20th.' Q: 'Sure you came in June?' A: 'Yes, sometime at the end of June.' Q: 'What are you going to do?' A: 'I will see the parties I worked for before: I'll see if they will give me work.'[16]

The doctors noted: 'Patient is discharged today into care of his wife as "Much Improved".' Michael was discharged on 21 November 1902, into the care of Maria who had come out to collect him at the hospital. He had survived a third incarceration from 1 July, a total of five months and three weeks in Hell. Now he had work awaiting him outside. His relationship with Maria was back on track and he looked forward eagerly to seeing little Charles and Mary. He was convinced his life had turned the corner and a better future beckoned. On the train back from Worcester with Maria, they silently held hands as they watched the russet colours of the Massachusetts landscape glide by.

11

Michael. Slipping back into Hell

As Boston Democrats celebrated the inauguration of Patrick Collins on 4 November 1902,[1] Michael returned home with Maria to a excited welcome from his darling Charles and Mary, visibly grown since he had left them almost five months before. Now he was ready to take on the world and determined to hold his family together.

He was brimming over with hope for their future in America. Thanksgiving was being celebrated across New England, and the whole family sat down to enjoy their turkey dinner. Michael's spirits were buoyant, almost light-hearted, and he felt he had come through his horrific ordeal with a surprisingly positive attitude. He had turned a corner in his life. Charles and 'Minnie' sat on his lap as he read them stories.

The family passed a peaceful festive season. Winter blizzards engulfed Boston, yet the family were warm and dry in their Cambridge home. Michael had found more congenial work as a coachman, just like his aunt Mary Duignam's husband back in Ireland. Every morning, he took the train to Roxbury, where he was taking care of the horse and carriage for a wealthy Peters family. He drove family members around the town on their errands and visits, and he had a regular wage of $10 dollars a week, so he could support his family. Then, in April 1903, things began to unravel.

Maria, again frightened by Michael's unprecedented two-day drinking binge and subsequent hallucinations, had become increasingly worried about her husband. She felt he had slipped back into an unstable mental condition. Events came to a head on 25 April.

Michael had met some friends on Washington Street, in downtown Boston, and they had bought him a few drinks in a local bar. Leaving afterwards, Michael was found staggering unsteadily on the street by two policemen, who apparently knew of his past reputation of mental instability. Public drunkenness was a minor offence, but Michael was taken to Dr Jelly's office, where the physician recommended that he be sent for observation to the dreaded Deer Island Hospital in Boston Harbour. There, his case was discussed and, with his previous record of alleged mental instability, Michael was recommitted to Worcester Insane Hospital. Fate was working relentlessly against him.

Michael was brought back to Worcester Insane Hospital where he arrived on 30 April 1903. A new standard printed form of his case history was filled out with his now familiar biographical details. Under the line 'Habits', the doctors added in the words 'Drinks some'. His diagnostic was again given as 'Constitutional Inferiority'. The Physician's Certificate completed on his admission spelled out the reasons for his return to Worcester:

Onset gradual, has threatened suicide, demented, confused and he has hallu-cinations of sight and hearing. April 25, he said that there was a man follow-ing him who told him that he would be obliged to do anything he suggested. He told him to strike. [On] April 30, he denied this, saying that he had been drinking for two days. He claimed that he had been living with his wife, had been working steadily; had not behaved peculiarly, did not own a revolver and had made no threats of suicide. Patient did nothing peculiar, insisting on the truth of what his friends claimed is not so. His appearance and manner are demented. Probably has hallucinations and delusions which he tries to conceal, is confused. He was sent to Worcester Insane Hospital July 1, 1902, where he remained for several months. He has been peculiar since. Has done little work, does not support or live with his wife. Acts very peculiarly and has put a loaded pistol to mouth threatening suicide. He was arrested on April 25, for insane conduct and sent to The Observation Hospital on Deer Island.'[2]

On 30 April, Michael was reported as quiet, orderly and well-oriented on admission. He freely admitted to excessive drinking, but denied all the statements recorded in the Physician's Certificate. He thought he was all right and that his only trouble was a little too much beer. He responded to questioning.

Q: 'When did you come?' A: 'This afternoon.' Q: 'Where from?' A: 'Boston.' Q: 'What did you come here for?' A: 'I got drunk and they sent me here.' Q: 'Did you do anything strange?' A: 'No, sir, I didn't.' Q: 'Didn't you threaten to kill yourself?' A: 'No, sir. I didn't.' Q: 'Didn't you threaten to shoot yourself?' A: 'No, sir. I haven't got a pistol.' Q: 'Has anything strange been said to you?' A: 'No.' Q: 'Seen anything strange?' A: 'No, sir.' Q: 'Have you been treated well?' A: 'Yes, sir.' Q: 'What is your trouble?' A: 'I was getting along all right only I took a little too much beer.' Q: 'What did you do when you got too much beer?' A: 'I was on the street and two policemen came up and took me to Dr Jelly.' Q: 'Has anything been done to you?' A: 'No.' Q: 'Have you been poisoned?' A: 'No, sir.' Q: 'Didn't you say you had to do what someone told you to do?' A: 'I don't remember making those statements.' Q: 'Have you been out of your head?' A: 'No, sir.' Q: 'Is anything wrong with your head?' A: 'I don't know. I am rational all the time.' Q: 'What is the date?' A: '30th of April.' Q: 'What place is this?' A: 'Worcester Insane Asylum.' Q: 'Who am I?'

[Dr K.] A: 'Doctor…' Q: 'Were you ever here before?' A: 'Yes, sir.' Q: 'When?' A: 'Left here last September.' Q: 'What were you here for?' A: 'I was drinking.'³

On 1 May, Michael was again interviewed. The doctors noted that he admitted to alcoholism, although minimising the amount, and total denied the statement on the Physician's Certificate. He said he was sad and recognised that alcohol was the cause.

Q: 'When did you take your first drink?' A: 'Last Friday.' Q: 'How much did you earn?' A: 'Ten dollars.' Q: 'As a coachman?' A: 'Yes.' Q: 'Did you get along well?' A: 'Yes. Q: 'How long after you left did you get a job?' A: 'About a week.' Q: 'How long did you keep the place?' A: 'All the time.' Q: 'What made you go to drinking?' A: 'I met acquaintances on Washington Street and they took me in to give me a couple of glasses of beer and it went to my head.' Q: 'When?' A: 'Last Saturday morning.' Q: 'What happened then?' A: 'A policeman took me down to Dr Jelly's office.' Q: 'What did you do?' A: 'Walked a little unsteady was all.' Q: 'Then what happened?' A: 'They sent me down to Deer Island for observation. They didn't see anything wrong so sent me back.' Q: 'Then what?' A: 'Sent me down here. They said I was carrying a revolver.' Q: 'Were you?' A: 'No.' Q: 'Did you threaten anybody or yourself?' A: 'No.' Q: 'Make any attempt to?' A: 'No.' Q: 'Did you feel cheerful?' A: 'No, sir. I did not.' Q: 'Didn't you drink but two drinks?' A: 'No.' Q: 'You didn't drink anything before that morning?' A: 'No, sir.' Q: 'What is the story about the revolver?' A: 'Didn't have a revolver for some time and I sold it.' Q: 'What did you do with the revolver you put in your mouth?' A: 'I didn't do it.' Q: 'Is that straight?' A: 'Yes, I didn't make an attempt on myself.' Q: 'Were you living with your wife all the time?' A: 'Yes, sir.' Q: 'Anyone complain of your conduct?' A: 'No, sir.' Q: 'What makes you feel sad now?' A: 'My fault of taking a drink.' Q: 'You had a revolver?' A: 'I had one. It was lying in a drawer in the house.' Q: 'I thought you sold it?' A: 'I did.' Q: 'When?' A: 'A week or two ago.'⁴ [15 April 1903]

On 13 May 1903, the doctors reported on Michael's mental status, attitude and manner:

'On admission the patient was quiet and orderly but somewhat confused. He was well orientated and admitted he was sad, recognising alcoholism as the cause of it. Since admission he has remained quiet and orderly, and has continued slightly depressed though at present he denies that he feels sad. He is indolent and spends his time quietly on the settee. He shows very little interest in his surroundings, and has rather an indifferent attitude. He answers questions promptly but shows a marked tendency to conceal mental defect, denying all of the statements in the Physician's Certificate, and trying to show that he was simply sent here for drinking.

He probably has some ideas of persecution through no definite ones could be elicited. He thinks this is not the place for him and that he should have been fined for drinking instead of being sent here. He has a fairly neat and tidy appearance, his habits are good. He does not associate with the other patients and seldom has anything to say to them. Physically he has been in good health, his appetite has been good and he has slept well. [5]

More questioning was carried out.

Q: 'What is the date?' A: 'Wednesday, the 13th of May 1903.' Q: 'What place is this?' A: 'Worcester Insane Hospital.' Q: 'Who am I?' [Dr K.] Q: 'Dr … I don't know your name.' Q: 'Who are the people here?' A: 'Insane people, doctors and attendants.' Q: 'When did you come here?' A: 'I came a week ago Thursday; two weeks tomorrow.' Q: 'Where from?' A: 'Boston.' Q: 'Who came with you?' A: 'An officer.' Q: 'What was done for you when you got here?' A: 'Mr Campbell sent me to G.H. and I was given a bath and I have been here ever since.' Q: 'Where were you born?' A: 'Belfast, Ireland.' [Mullingar] Q: 'When?' A: 'In 1867.' [1863] Q: 'When did you come to this country?' A: 'February 1888.' Q: 'Where did you land?' A: 'Boston.' Q: 'What was the first work you did?' A: 'I worked at North Abington in a shoe factory for a year and then I went on the cars in Boston.' Q: 'What did you study at school?' A: 'I went to grammar school and when I graduated I went to work on a railroad as a freight clerk and then after working there six years, I joined the British Army.' Q: 'Name the five largest cities of the US.' A: 'New York, Chicago, Boston, New Orleans and Philadelphia.' Q: 'The five largest rivers?' A: 'The Mississippi, Hudson, Allegheny, Potomac and Rappahannock.' Q: 'What wars has this country had?' A: 'The War of the Revolution in 1776, the war of 1812 with England, Mexican War, Civil War from 1861 to 1865, the Mexican war in '46, and the Spanish War in '98.'[6]

Michael also carried out arithmetic calculations promptly and accurately and counted from one to twenty in five seconds. They gave him another standard writing test and his writing was slanted, strong and as flowing as ever. His signature gave no indication of any stress and instability.

The doctors assessed his mental attitude again. Michael was found to be clear-headed, denying all of the statements on the Physician's Certificate, with the exception of alcoholism. 'He had a rather sad expression but denied any attacks of depression except at the death of his child ten years earlier. He denied any attempts at suicide and explained away his alleged attempt by saying he intentionally went to the toilet when the gas was turned on. No deterioration was shown in calculation or memory tests even though his expression showed some signs. He recognised alcoholism as the cause of his commitment, although no hallucinations or delusions were elicited, and he still had no insights into his condition.'

He underwent yet more questions.

Q: 'Why are you back this time? A: 'I drank a little too much and they took me down to the house of retention for Dr Jelly to see me. I didn't do anything for them to send me down here or to confine me.' Q: 'Were you arrested for drinking?' A: 'Yes.' Q: 'Were you drunk?' A: 'Yes, sir. I had been drinking.' Q: 'How long had you been drunk?' A: 'I started Saturday morning two weeks ago. I drank two drinks of whiskey and a few glasses of beer and it took effect on me.' Q: 'What effect did it have?' A: 'I didn't walk steady, that was all.' Q: 'Did you do anything strange?' A: 'No, sir.' Q: 'He just arrested you for being drunk?' A: 'Yes, sir.' Q: 'For how long have you been drinking?' A: 'It's the first time I ever took too much.' Q: 'For how many years have you been drinking at all?' A: 'Sometimes take a glass of beer since I came to this country.' Q: 'When did you come?' A: 'In February 1888.' Q: 'Did you ever feel sad from drinking?' A: 'No, I never drank enough for it to affect me only on that occasion.' Q: 'Never felt downhearted?' A: 'Not account of drink.' Q: 'What caused it then?' A: 'I buried a child ten years ago and I worried about that a good deal.' Q: 'Anything else trouble you?' A: 'No. sir.' Q: 'Did you ever attempt your life?' Q: 'No, sir.' Q: 'Never did?' A: 'I went into a bathroom once and the gas was turned on while I was sitting on the closet. I never attempted my life.' Q: 'Who turned the gas on?' A: 'It was turned on before I went to the bathroom, I went in about 4 o'clock in the morning. I got up and started out and fell to the floor. They took me at a quarter to 7 to the Carney Hospital.' Q: 'How long after you fell to the floor before you came to?' A: 'I came to shortly after they got me up to the hospital.' Q: 'Did you know anything about been taken there?' A: 'I got up and started to my room and fell and began to vomit and didn't know anything after that.' Q: 'Didn't you smell the gas?' A: 'No, sir, I had a touch of diarrhoea and went to the water closet. I stayed there about 15 minutes and started to my room and fell.' Q: 'Do you think it probable that the gas would be turned on and you not smell it?' A: 'Well, I didn't dare to smell it. I rushed in there and wasn't thinking about it. I had gas in my room if I wanted to turn it on but didn't feel that way.'

Q: 'Does anyone have any special influence over you?' A: 'No, sir.' Q: 'Didn't you say a man was following you and you would have to do what he said?' A: 'No, sir. I don't remember saying that.' Q: 'Were you unconscious this time?' A: 'No, sir.' Q: 'Have you been working steadily?' A: 'Yes, sir. I have been working for Mr Peters, 20 Gould Street.' [in Roxbury] Q: 'Did you get along well with your work?' A: 'Yes, sir.' Q: 'Did everyone in the shop treat you well?' A: 'I wasn't working in a shop. I was attending to a horse and driving members of the family out.' Q: 'Did they treat you well?' A: 'Yes, sir.' Q: 'Anybody treat you wrongly?' A: 'No, sir.' Q: 'Has anything strange been said to you?' A: 'No, sir.' Q: 'You haven't heard any strange voices?' A: 'No, sir.' Q:

'Were you frightened at anything you saw?' A: 'No, sir.' Q: 'Did you see any-thing strange?' A: 'No, sir.' Q: 'How is your appetite?' A: 'All right.' Q: 'You didn't get any medicine in your food.' A: 'No, sir.' Q: 'Have you felt any strange sensations in your body?' A: 'No, sir, normal all the time.' Q: 'Did you feel sad this time?' A: 'No, sir.' Q: 'When were you here before?' A: 'Over a year ago.' Q: 'What for?' A: 'They claimed I turned on the gas in that water closet, but I didn't do it.' Q: 'Are you sure you didn't?' A: 'Yes, sir.' Q: 'Did you ever feel like taking your life?' A: 'No, sir.' Q: 'Did you ever have the horrors?' A: 'No, sir.' Q: 'Was the time you inhaled the gas the only time you were unconscious?' A: 'Yes, sir.' Q: 'Do you know everything you did when you were drinking?' A: 'Yes, sir.' Q: 'Do you support your wife?' A: 'Yes, sir. I have been sleeping there every night and get up in the morning and take the train for Rocksboro [Roxbury].' Q: 'Did you ever have any trouble with your wife?' A: 'No, sir. I never did.' Q: 'Never any trouble at all?' A: 'There was one time somebody told her I would shoot her and all this business. I never had any such intentions.' Q: 'Why did they tell her so?' A: 'The party who told her – I guess I was getting on along too well to suit him. There was a strike on the Elevated Road [R.R.] and he wanted to get something against me.' Q: 'Why did he wish to do that?' A: 'He lost a car he was running and had to start at the foot again.' Q: 'Why should he blame you for it?' A: 'Because I worked and didn't lose the car I was running?' Q: 'That was no reason why he should want to injure you?' A: 'Ill feeling. There was a strike on and they wanted me to join the strike. I didn't belong to the Union so I kept working.' Q: 'Did you go with bad women?' A: 'No, sir.' Q: 'Do you abuse yourself?' A: 'No, sir.' Q: 'Anything you would like to explain to me?' A: 'I don't know of anything. I would like to get out to work again.' Q: 'Are you troubled about anything?' A: 'I don't like the idea of being sent here from a simple drunk. This is not the proper place. They should have fined me for it and let it go at that.' Q: 'Do you think you have been a little wrong in your head?' A: 'No, sir. I haven't.' Q: 'Do you see any change in yourself?' A: 'No, sir.'[7]

Two months passed in this way as the summer heat and humidity left all the inmates limp and lethargic on the wards. On 22 July 1903, the doctors reported that Michael was quiet and a good worker. He was speaking freely and admitted to suffering from alcoholism, although they suspected he was trying to minimise the amount. He had no insights into his condition and continued to deny any sui-cidal attempts or feeling any depression. They observed that Michael showed no peculiarities, was quiet and was a good worker in the dining room and the dormi-tory. A further questioning session was carried out:

Q: 'Why were you sent here the last time?' A: 'I got drinking.' Q: 'Much?' A: 'A good deal.' Q: 'For how long did you keep it up?' A: 'For a couple of days.'

Q: 'How much did you drink within that time?' A: 'Three or four glasses of whiskey and several beers and that went to my head.' Q: 'How did it affect your head?' A: 'I staggered a little.' Q: 'What did you do within that time?' A: 'Nothing. I knew everything.' Q: 'Didn't you do something you could not be responsible for otherwise?' A: 'Not a thing.' Q: 'Didn't you turn on the gas?' A: 'No, sir.' Q: 'Didn't you have some ideas of suicide?' A: 'No, sir. I went to the water closet one morning about four o'clock and I found the gas turned on. If I wanted to commit suicide, I could have done it in my room, as there was gas there also.' Q: 'Weren't you a little downhearted?' A: 'No, sir, I had a pretty fair job.' Q: 'Was you mind affected?' A: 'No, sir.' Q: 'Was it the other times you were here?' A: 'No, sir.'[8]

On 9 September, the doctors recorded that Michael was given a few grams of Taka-Diastase V. No XII, to treat his indigestion. Autumn winds had begun to blow the leaves from the trees as the spectacular New England reds, golds, and yellow hues announced that October had arrived. The daily routine continued on the wards. The seriously unstable mental patients still stumbled around distractedly, mumbling incoherently, as sudden maniacal piercing screeches rented the air.

On 5 October 1903, the doctors made a brief laconic, almost routine, entry in Michael's case history.

> Nothing unusual in conduct up to this morning. Then found dead in room, having committed suicide by hanging. The patient was as usual last night and during his last few days on Lincoln 1 [ward] had acted normally. The attendant saw him at 8.30 p.m. last night in bed and he spoke pleasantly. This morning, at 6.05 a.m. he was found hanging from the upper grate in his window, by a sheet tied around his neck. There was no sign of life. He was in a half sitting posture, the body and extremities were warm, and there was considerable lividity in the face and extremities. There was no rigor. An autopsy was refused. Inquest by Dr Baker showed death to be due to suicide by hanging.

The report closed with the official words: 'Suicide by hanging. (Body removed by Undertaker Athy).'[9]

I tried to comprehend Michael's last moments at Worcester. The lack of rigor mortis suggested that he had not been dead long – no more than one and a half hours at most, thus having begun his final tragic act around 4 a.m.

Had he spent a sleepless night torturing himself with thought of despair, despondency and anguish? Had he felt that, on his fourth incarceration at Worcester, his luck (of the Irish) had run out? Had he despaired of ever being able to work outside ever again, earning a living to support Maria, and his darling children, Charles and Mary? Had he decided to rejoin his mourned first-born child Annie? He left no note for his wife, nor any of his sisters, particularly Mary Anne, who had stood by his side through his darkest moments. Had his tortured mind snapped and wanted to escape the horror of his surroundings?

The last moments would have been a slow and agonising death. As he lacked the necessary height to actually break his neck from the fall, he in fact died from gradual strangulation as his tortured soul left its earthly envelope. Had his Episcopalian faith failed him, leaving him far too vulnerable to his interior demons? Had he ever tried to contact his clergyman Rev. Dr George Bicknell, who had joined Maria and himself in matrimony? Had his original syphilis infection finally crippled his mind? Alone, isolated and frightened, he only saw a terrifying future imprisoned in a maniacal world of madness and horror. Did the harsh urban-industrial Boston society, with the lowly social status of the struggling Irish immigrants finally take its toll? His spirit broken, had Yankee America robbed him of his will to live?

In the darkest moments of the night, in his own small room pierced by the chilling ravings of other inmates, Michael, tossing and turning, unable to sleep, his mind racing out of control, unwilling to face up to the thought of spending the rest of his life 'living with the loonies', had acted impulsively. He got up, removed the sheets from his bed, and tore them into strips, weaving them into a rope. He then tied it around his neck, stood on his bed and attached the end to the iron window grating. He stepped off the bed and the rope had tightened around his neck, and he gradually suffocated.

It was a prolonged, protracted death. Blood flow was no longer able to reach his brain and he lost consciousness. Then, around 4.30 a.m., his life was finally extinguished. Had his last agonised, delirious thoughts been for the wife and children he was abandoning, for his loving sisters, who strove to save him from his demons, for his brother, James, back in Ireland? Or was it a confused, frightening mental jumble to horrific to continue living with? By 4.30 a.m. it was all over. At last he was at peace.

If Dr Adolph Meyer had left behind a better organised and valid clinical system at Worcester, little had changed in the therapeutic treatment of the inmates. Michael's surviving case history was a revelation about the character of the man. It showed that, apart from periods of deep, black depression, he came across as an alert, rational and quite reasonable individual, who reacted with great forbearance, while, in fact, attempting to convince the inquisitorial interrogations of the well-meaning physicians, of his normality. Many of their questions seemed loaded and invasive, and constantly slanted towards convincing him of alleged suicidal tendencies, accusations he always rejected. American or emigrant, it would have been a totally unnerving, and frightening experience for anyone. For an Irish immigrant in a hostile, anonymous and impersonal surroundings, locked up with some thousand mentally unstable inmates, it was a horrific, nerve-wracking situation of huge stress, anxiety, isolation and loneliness. A 19th-century gulag concentration camp, it was where Michael's worst nightmare had become a reality. He had become another victim of the crude, inhumane, barbaric conditions of the 19th-century American mental hospital system.

Deep inside, the young boy inside me took some pride in his grand-uncle's overall relative composure during his time at Worcester. Michael had exhibited grace under pressure, while subjected to intensely invasive questions from the doctors. Mentally, he had remained alert, whether recalling distant or recent events. The interviews revealed how he had changed the name of his father, Patrick, giving him an English-sounding 'Herbert'. He also gave 'Belfast', as his birthplace, rather then his home town of Mullingar. He had even changed his religious denomination to Episcopalian in order to be more easily accepted by the Boston Yankee mindset. Or had he simply converted to that faith during his time with the Commissariat and Transport Corps in Aldershot in 1885? Throughout his ordeal, Michael's signature and handwriting had never shown the slightest weakness or hesitation. I felt a certain empathy with Michael's life in spite of his sad destiny.

No image of him survived in the archives. He would have to remain faceless. Written descriptions were all that was left of his physical appearance – blue eyes, fair complexion, dark brown hair and light brown moustache.

I felt grateful to Dr Adolph Meyer, whose revolutionary reforms had established a system of individual case studies at Worcester. The surviving verbatim reports of Michael's interviews showed how resilient he had been in the face of tremendous adversity. It had allowed his voice to he heard down the generations, allowing the truth to come out. It had opened a window on a dark family secret. The pain, grief, trauma and sorrow caused by Michael's last tragic act, could now be better understood. They had taken the family 'skeleton out of the cupboard' and laid it to rest.

Strangely, the hospital authorities only officially reported Michael's death a week later, although family members were informed immediately. The body was removed by Athy & Co., Undertakers in Worcester, and brought by horse-drawn carriage and train to Cambridge. In his last days at Worcester, Michael had been in custody from 30 April until 5 October 1903; a total of five months and five days. All his entire purgatory at Worcester Insane Hospital had lasted one year and nine months. His descent into depressive mental instability had begun when he was thirty-seven and, within three short years, he had been swept away by the pressures of survival in a fast-changing, urban-industrial world. He had died at only forty years of age, father of two children, Charles, aged eight, and Mary, just six, husband to Maria, and brother to seven supportive siblings.

As the hearse with his mortal remains passed the russet-leaved trees, and the horses clip-clopped down the avenue towards the main arched entrance, a startled dove winged upwards into the blue yonder.

12

Life after death. Grieving a suicide

Immediately after Michael was found, the State Medical Examiner was called to Worcester Insane Hospital to record the death officially. Ed Hines found the evidence for this information in a less-used source at the Massachusetts State Archives in Boston. The examiner had filed a report (number 132) for Michael J. Mongan, Worcester Insane Hospital, aged thirty-seven, at 10 a.m. on 5 October, at the hospital, stating '*No Autopsy / Suicide by Hanging*'. He reported that:

> [Michael] was an inmate of the Worcester Insane Hospital and was found dead hanging by a sheet attached to a window grating in his room at 6.05 a.m. October 5th, evidently had been dead several hours. One knee was resting on the window sill and the other foot was upon the floor. There was marked pressure indentations ¾ inches wide, with slight abrasions over the front half of the neck.[1]

In a pragmatic routine manner he added: 'Medical Examiner's Expenses: $5.60.'

The next person informed of the horrible news was Michael's wife Maria, in Cambridge. She broke down weeping in front of her uncomprehending children, when she heard the tragic news. Mary Anne, at 15 M Street, also received a telegraph message from the hospital superintendent, Scribner, with a terse note announcing the horrific, disastrous news. The shock and trauma of the event paralysed her into a catatonic state of grief. The news spread like wildfire throughout the family. The first to react was the oldest sister, Elizabeth, then employed as a live-in domestic at 29 Reservoir Street in north Cambridge with her husband Charles Edgerly and their two children. Cambridge City directories indicated that the large 1870-71 structure was the residence of Horatio S. White, professor of German at Harvard from 1902 to 1919. It had an annexe with two separate entrances to house the domestic staff.

On hearing the news, Elizabeth immediately contacted St Paul's Catholic Cemetery, near her old home at 51 Mystic Street in Arlington. Moving quickly, she took charge and purchased a grave plot for her brother. She also made arrangements for the arrival of his body. Athy & Co., Undertakers removed Michael's corpse and transported it by horse-drawn hearse and train the 40 miles east to undertakers J. Ross & Co., funeral home in Cambridge.

Elizabeth, ever resourceful and determined in such harrowing circumstances,

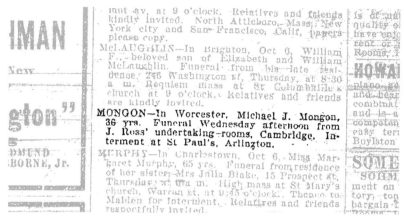

Obituary of Michael J. Mongan (misspelt Mongon) in the *Boston Globe*, October 7, 1903, announcing his funeral from J. Ross, Undertakers, in Cambridge, MA. *(Courtesy Boston Public Library)*

stoically accepted the challenge of organising the funeral arrangements. She acted quickly and efficiently, while her distraught younger sister Mary Anne attempted to comfort her brother's widow, shattered and devastated in her grief. Elizabeth also contacted the Boston newspaper to insert an obituary notice which appeared in the *Boston Globe* on Wednesday, 7 October 1903:

> Mongon – [another misspelling] In Worcester, Michael J. Mongon, 36 years, funeral Wednesday afternoon from J. Ross undertaking rooms, Cambridge. Interment at St Paul's, Arlington.[2]

On a grey, overcast day, the desolate Mongan family group, along with Maria, her parents Elisha and Hannah, brother John and sister Annie, led the cortege for the short journey to St Paul's. A few of Michael's former West End street railway colleagues turned up to commiserate with Maria and Mary Anne. They followed the hearse to St Paul's Cemetery in Arlington, where the coffin was lowered into the ground at the foot of an young American oak.. The discon-solate weeping Mongan sisters, stood side by side, holding each other as the priest read the burial service. At the time, the Church normally forbid suicide victims to be buried in consecrated ground. It appears that, as Michael had been deemed deeply disturbed at the time of his death, a dispensation was granted allowing the religious burial.

After the short service, they all returned to 29 Reservoir Street where Elizabeth, had prepared some refreshments. I imagine that a rift was already dis-cernible between the Hurds and the Mongan sisters; who felt that Maria, by giv-ing her consent to internment, had begun Michael's downward spiral. They parted soon after, their hearts broken by the tragedy.

Elizabeth had the painful task of writing to her brother James back in Ireland

wedding will be a family affair al-
exclusively. The couple will reside
...ding where Mr. Badger has just
him a home.
..n Joseph Evirs, who was knighted
...meeting of the Knights of Pythias,
...day evening, left with his family.
...esday, for Los Angeles, California
...they will in future make their

Mary E. McLeod and family have
...from 8 Centre to 39 Inman street.
...ong the names of tourists register-
...cently at the Paris Reading Rooms
...e American Express company are
Mark Sullivan, Mr. W. M. Russell
...r. A. V. Kidder of this city.
B. Moller has been confined to the
...several days this week owing to
t.

motion last week. His employer, James
Johnson of East Cambridge, opened a
large tea and coffee house on Massachusetts avenue, and his selection for manager was Mr. Aldham, who is receiving
the congratulations of his many friends.

Michael J. Morgan, aged 36, whose home
was in this city, committed suicide by
hanging from an iron window grating at
the Worcester Insane hospital on Monday,
October 5. The hospital authorities did
not report it until compelled by the law
to do so this week. Morgan had been a
frequent patient at the hospital, and was
last committed several months ago. Monday he got up and tore a bed sheet into
strips, made a rope of it and hanged himself.

A mission is being conducted by the
Jesuit fathers at the church of St Mary's

The newspaper report from the *Cambridge Chronicle,* October, 17 1903, announcing
Michael J. Mongan's (misspelled Morgan) death at Worcester Insane Hospital.
(Courtesy Boston Public Library)

to announce Michael's sad passing. The news arrived at 16 Dublin Street in
Longford ten days later. The trauma sent shock waves reverberating through the
family – and then a deafening silence. The grief, shame and guilt were too much
to bear. Mutual blame festered in their beleaguered minds.

The news was also picked up by the local *Cambridge Chronicle* newspaper on
17 October 1903. Under a by-line headed 'Cambridgeport – In and About
Central Square', they filed the following report:

> Michael J. Morgan [again the name misspelled] aged 36, whose home was in
> this city, committed suicide by hanging from an iron window grating at the
> Worcester Insane Hospital on Monday, Oct. 5. The Hospital authorities did
> not report it until compelled by law to do so this week. Morgan had been a
> frequent patient at the hospital and was last committed several months ago.
> Monday he got up and tore a bed sheet into strips, made a rope of it and
> hanged himself.[3]

By a typographic error, the Mongan family in Boston were somewhat
shielded from the humiliation of Michael's death being made public. Yet it could
not shield them from the feelings of shame, guilt and resentment at their loss.[4]

During my research, I consulted a probing work *The Enduring Asylum*, on the history of the institution, by Dr Joseph Morrissey among others. He had worked at
Worcester State Hospital in the mid-1960s and 1970s. He recalled:

> Your report brought me back a number of years to my days at Worcester
> State Hospital... Being of Irish ancestry myself (both my parents were emi-

grants), I have a lot of empathy with the story of your grand-uncle and the many Irishmen and women who lived and died at the Hospital over the past 150 years, Suicide, regrettably, is often associated with serious mental illness both today and at the turn of the century period at Worcester State Hospital… Suicide rates can be an indicator of poor care, but specific incidences are often difficult to anticipate and it does occur even in the best facilities. The diagnosis you mention, 'constitutional inferiority' does sound archaic by today's standards. I, too, am unsure of its exact meaning.[5]

Dr Morrissey was instrumental in helping me access an important document from the archives. He was able to locate a copy of the 1902 Worcester Insane Hospital annual report which threw revealing light on the running and organisation of the institution at that time. Dr Morrissey had some revealing insights into the report's findings:

> The list of trustees is interesting as in includes members of the local Yankee aristocracy and class of industrialists – Lincoln, Moen, Ely, Hoar, Whitin – all are names I associate from my youth with local factories in the Worcester area. Of particular note is Samuel B. Woodward, who must have been the son or grandson of the founding superintendent at WSH in the 1830s.

Discussing the meaning of the use of the term 'constitutional inferiority', Dr Morrissey noted that the first time it was mentioned in the transcripts of Michael's questioning, it had a political interpretation which is misconstrued because the reference is something about the status of the individual in the Supreme Court had changed that decision.

> I think it is much more – at the time – a kind of clinical sort of statement, as part of the their notions as to what insanity – [or] the cause of insanity – was. Something about [being] unfit or biologically inferior, because one thing that was going on during this time was the heavy influence of a kind of social Darwinism and eugenics, and the purifying of the races, etc.[6]
>
> I think there was a prevailing notion at the time about moral weakness I mean that, the Irish in particular, might have been seen as particularly susceptible to alcoholism, and I have a feeling that the term is capturing some of that. I think that was the understading. You know what happened over the latter half of the 19th century – was that most of the hospitals, with the waves of Irish immigration after the Great Famine. Some of the backdrop to the story you're telling [is about how] your grand-uncle ran into hard times. So what happened was that a lot of the state hospitals began to be filled with Irishmen, and so, being Irish and being insane almost became co-linked – so there was this kind of perception of the Irish as being a kind of underclass and inferior. So I have a feeling that the term [constitutional inferiority] is somehow or other related to that view, but I'll try to get a better understanding

for you. And yet it could be one of those terms that [psychiatrists used as] part of their jargon at the time, , and you wouldn't necessarily find it in a medical dictionary.[7]

A contemporary 1907 group photo of streetcar conductors and drivers survived in the archives. It showed a group of Boston Elevated Railway Company staff posing in front of a street at North Point Car House, located at P and East Second Street in South Boston.[8] These men had been Michael's peers and contemporaries; probably men with whom he had worked with for years since he joined the West End company in 1888.

The men stood proudly in front of – or perched on – an electric tram, with those in front hunkered down for the photo. They all wore their dark uniforms, eight-button double-breasted jaclets, white shirts and ties; some even sported smart bowties, while other had pipes stuck at rakish angles between their teeth; others had fob watches on a chain in their waistcoats. They looked a contented, professional bunch, proud of their status as members of a major Boston transportation company, with steady and guaranteed employment. All these men lived in the City Point neighbourhood and resided within walking distance of the North Point Car House. Michael, living at 21 M Street until 1898, would also have been only minutes away on foot. Their streetcars travelled from City Point heading along Faragut, East Fourth Street, to L Street, Broadway, on to Boston and finally Harvard Square in Cambridge.

The group exudes a sense of shared camaraderie and they look like a reasonable, relaxed, friendly men. Yet sectarian strife was rampant amongst streetcar staff around that time. Were these the men who had gone on a wildcat strike at the Car House back in 1897? Had they resented Michael, a non-union member, for not taking part in their strike? Was one of the group a man called Tom Frankley, Michael's 'friend' and colleague, with whom he had differences over religious beliefs? Had Frankley spitefully denounced Michael to the police and set his life on a disastrous downward spiral? Were these the men who had mocked and laughed at Michael after he had been 'living with the loonies' at Worcester Insane Asylum? Was one of these men Michael's harbinger of doom?

I struggled to understand what motivation might have led Michael into deciding to take his own life – a devastating act that tore apart a close-knit family on both side of the Atlantic and lead to a deafening one hundred-year silence, only finally broken by my inner young boy's instinctive need to discover the truth.

13

Transatlantic cousins. Charlie and Reg

In 1983, I felt I had hit a dead-end. Essential information on Michael and the exact details of his incarceration at Worcester lay blocked in his vital medical records – tantilisingly out of reach in the archives. Little did I realise that it would be some fourteen years – until 29 July 1999 – before I would finally get access to them.

As I was waited and wondered about what information lay in the archive at Worcester, I decided to try and learn more about how Michael's two children, Charles and Mary coped with the terrible trauma and get on with their lives. How do you deal with a suicide?

Charles and his Irish cousin Reginald, had been contemporaries on opposite sides of the Atlantic. Yet, they would have no contact throughout their lives, the stigma of Michael's death precluding any transatlantic reunions. However, my research revealed some interesting parallels in their respective careers – both were railway company employees and both served in the military. I eventually discovered that Charles had a naval career from archives at the US Military Personnel Records Center in St Louis, Missouri, which provided details of his service.

Charles Joseph Mongan was a true 'Southie'. He was born on 12 May 1895 at 21 M Street. In those days, most births actually took place in the family home, assisted by a neighbourhood midwife, and Charles' was no different. Though, right next door, at 15 M Street, Michael's sister Mary Anne and her husband James Keough were on hand to give support during the birth. Charles was baptised at the old Gate of Heaven church on East Fourth St, on 23 May 1895, with his aunt Annie Hurd as sponsor.[1] Two years later on the far side of the Atlantic at 16 Dublin Street, Longford, Charles' cousin Michael Reginald, was born on 29 April 1897. Now both brothers Michael and James were proud fathers, exchanging transatlantic best wishes by letter. Michael had sent James a studio portrait of his daughter Mary Elizabeth, born in May 1896. Charles and Mary spent their early childhood in Southie, taken in their double-pram for walks from M Street to the beaches at City Point. Their parents strolled around Castle Island, watched the elegant yachts sailing in the harbour and enjoyed the cool sea breeze. They held picnics near L Street Beach, often joined at the weekend by Michael's sisters; Elizabeth, Catherine, Delia and Maria-Theresa. The couple moved to 32 Bay Street in Cambridge in 1898 and, two years later, Charles, aged five, started at a local pre-school.

Throughout his father Michael's dramatic incarceration, Charles attended Houghton School, a neighbourhood elementary grammar school, on River Street (now the Martin Luther King Jr School), off Putnam Avenue. He graduated grade school in 1910, aged fourteen, and, through some friends of his late father, found employment as an apprentice railway guard with the Boston Elevated Railroad. As he progressed he was earning $135 dollars per month as a fully fledged railroad guard. Then on 28 August 1912, seventeen-year-old Charles enlisted with the American navy, though whether from patriotic fervour or peer pressure, we don't know.[2] He was sent to the Naval Training Camp located, ironically, on Deer Island in Boston Harbour, where he received basic training from 1 April to 10 May 1912. Charles was posted on active duty to serve as Able Seaman 1st Class on board US naval dreadnought battleship USS *Louisiana*. He had followed his late father's footsteps into military service. At that period, American presidents William Taft and, later, Woodrow Wilson had sent US warships into the Gulf of Mexico to protect American interests in Mexico during a period of turmoil in the country.

In 1912, the US navy was a relatively small force of just over 3,000 officers and 47,515 men. Stern naval traditions of wooden ships and iron men still prevailed; discipline was rigid and punishment swift. Yet the navy guaranteed three

The battleship USS *Louisiana* (BB-19) photographed in 1906, was in service with the US Navy from 1906 to 1923. Charles Joseph Mongan, first cousin of Reginald Michael Mongan, served as Able Seaman on board from 1912-16 and saw action during the US Naval landing at Veracruz, during the Mexican Campaign in 1914. He later served in the US Navy Reserve as Coxwain (Petty Officer) during the First World War from 1914-18. (*Courtesy US Naval Institute Photo archives*)

meals a day, foreign travel, adventure, camaraderie and a vague, if alluring, possibility of romance.[3]

With a displacement of 16,000 tons, the USS *Louisiana* BB-19, was a 456-foot long battleship of the Connecticut class, and had been commissioned on 2 June 1906, with Captain Albert R. Couden in command of an 827-man crew.[4]

Having been part of President Roosevelt's 1907 'Great White Fleet' designed to impress other nations and deter any hostile action, the USS *Louisiana* sailed, on 19 November 1910, as part of the Second Division of the Atlantic fleet, which visited English and French ports before returning to the United States in the spring of 1911. The warship returned to Europe during summer of 1911, making formal visits to Denmark, Sweden, Finland and Germany, where the Danish and Swedish monarchs, the Kaiser and the Tzar were honoured guests on board.

Between 6 July and September 1915, with Able Seaman 1st Class Charles Joseph Mongan serving on board, the USS *Lousiana* made three voyages into Mexican waters. On the first trip (6 July–29 December 1913), she stood by to protect American lives and property and enforce the Munroe Doctrine and arms embargo established to discourage further revolutionary turmoil in Mexico. The second voyage (14 April–8 August 1914) came at a time when tensions between Mexico and the United States had reached crisis point, with the shelling and occupation of Veracruz. The battleship was to sail a third time for Mexican waters from 17 August to 24 September 1915 with Charles on board.[5]

The landing at Veracruz, on the Mexican Gulf coast, began on the morning of 21 April 1914 when a force of 787 officers and men, 502 of whom were Marines, landed in the city. Led by three rifle companies from the Florida, they had orders to seize the Customs House, the focal point of the operation. Initially, the men were met by desultory sniper fire and several were wounded as the shooting intensified. As further battalions came ashore from the *Utah*, the Customs House was captured and occupied. By 24 April, American forces had taken control of Veracruz. A Third Seaman Regiment had been formed from the newly arrived battleships *Louisiana* and *North Dakota*, together with men from the *Michigan* and *Minnesota*. By then the Naval Division at Veracruz had grown to 5,800 men (with 3,300 blue jackets and 2,500 Marines) and twenty US naval vessls lay of Veracruz and nineteen off Tampico.[6]

There were some skirmishes at Veracruz, as part of the Third Provisional Regiment, Advanced Base Brigade. The USS *Louisiana* Marines of Company E, with 119 men under the command of Captain Arthur T. Matrix, became involved in some of the action on land. By then, however, most of the fighting was over. The USS *Louisiana* held off Veracruz from 22 April to 29 May when it sailed for Norfolk Naval Base. On 27 April, the American flag was raised over Veracruz, as the band played the *Star Spangled Banner* while the battleship *Minnesota*, fired a twenty-one-gun salute.[7]

After his honourable discharge at Norfolk on 11 May 1916, Able Seaman 1st Class Charles Joseph Mongan was awarded the Mexican Campaign Medal for his services. He returned to his civilian employment as railroad guard with the Boston Elevated. However, barely a year later, on 2 June 1917, he re-enlisted as America became involved in the First World War.[8]

Charles, at twenty-two, with his military service number No 143 4049, re-enlisted with the US Naval Reserve Force as coxwain on board USS *George Washington*, berthed at Commonwealth Pier in South Boston. As coxwain, Charles, with the rank of petty officer, was the senior NCO of the ship's boat and wsa charged with maintaining discipline among the the seven-man crew of the captain's launch. He also shouted out steering instructions to the helmsman. Some coxwains were also called on to pipe the ship's officers on board.

The USS *George Washington* was a former German-built Lloyd Line passenger liner, which had sought refuge in New York, as a neutral port, in 1914. Commandeered by the Americans, she was transformed into a troop transport ship and sailed with her first load of 'Doughboys' on 4 December 1917, and over the next two years, she made eighteen round trips to Europe.

The USS *George Washington* carried President Wilson and the American delegation to the Paris Peace Conference on 4 December 1918. (She also carried assistant secretary of the navy Franklin Roosevelt, and the Chinese and Mexican peace commissions to France in January 1919.) President Wilson was on board again when he sailed to France, arriving on 13 March 1919. He returned to America at the conclusion of the historic conference on 8 July. Charles' veteran's file reveals further details of his concerns for his mother's welfare at the time. On active duty from 8 August 1917 until 11 October 1919, Charles had taken out a $10,000 insurance policy in his mother's name while at Bumpkin's Island naval base in 1918.

Throughout his naval service, Charles continued to send a $90 monthly remittance to his mother who was living with his sister Mary, then employed as an $800 per annum telephone operator, at their new apartment at 112 Kinnaird Street – just a few doors away from his childhood home on 32 Bay Street. Charles received an honourable discharge on 1 June 1921 at Higham, Mass Naval Base. He was awarded the First World War Victory Medal for his services. He applied for a disability benefit due to 'loss of voice', affecting his lungs and throat, incurred by excessive 'hollering' and exposure while on duty as coxwain at Commonwealth Pier. His application was witnessed by his two Cambridge neighbours, Ralph Robart and Ralph W. Hamilton. On discharge, Charles moved back in with his mother and sister.[9]

After Michael J. Mongan's tragic demise in October 1903, his widow Maria and their two children, Charles and Mary, moved up to a new apartment building, dating to 1892, at 112 Kinnaird Street in Cambridge, where they lived along with Maria's brother John Hurd, then employed at Bennett Street Carhouse, until Charles married in 1925. The house, is a typical wooden-frame triple-decker building popular with emigrant families.

Charles' life changed when he met a girl from Baltimore. Mae Eisel was working as a waitress in Cambridge when Charles proposed. On 14 June 1925, they were married at St Paul's Catholic church, 34 Holyoke, at Mount Auburn, near Harvard Square, with Rev. W. Gunn officiating, and his sister Mary and friend John Coghlin as sponsors.[10] The Hurd family and friends turned out on a radiant summer's day; his mother so happy for her only son; his aunt Annie and uncle John 'Jack' Hurd, joyfully showering the couple with confetti. Mae's parents Harry and Annie Eisel, up from Baltimore, and her brother, Earl, were all glad to take part in the happy event. Sadly, none of his estranged Mongan aunts were invited to the ceremony. Michael's death still cast its long shadow over family contacts. By 1931, the newlywed couple were living at 1034 Masachusetts Avenue, in downtown Boston. Charles had returned to his conductor post with the 'El' and remained there until he retired on a railroad pension around 1940 after twenty-eight years service.

Close parallels can be drawn between the destinies of Charles in Boston and his cousin Reginald back in Ireland. As children, Charles, aged five, and Reg, aged three, had played together in the garden at 32 Bay Street in Cambridge during the family trip to America in August 1900.

They had returned to Ireland, as the 1901 census (taken in March) lists James as 'House Carpenter', with his wife Mary and son Reginald, aged four, living at 11 Fee's (later Ward's) Terrace, just outside the town.[11] James had been working on the new housing projects developed at the time. The family celebrated the arrival of a daughter, Esther Mary (Dolly), born on 7 April 1901.[12] More celebrations followed when James was hired as head carpenter by the Midland Great Western Railway at Longford Station on 27 January 1902, probably on the recommendation of friends of his later father, Patrick.[13]

Reginald had started as a pupil at St Michael's National School on 12

November 1904 and stayed there until he left Third Class in July 1906, aged nine, to attend another local school.[14] The 1911 census shows James, his wife Mary, and Reginald and Esther Mary, living at 11 Ward's (formerly Fee's) Terrace in Longford.[15] That year, Reginald, aged fourteen, sat the Board of Agriculture (Technical Dept) Scholarship Examination at his school and was awarded second place.

In 1912, Reg, had just turned fifteen, when he graduated from school and found employment as the assistant secretary with St Mel's C. D. Insurance Society, a local parish mutual company.[16] The following year, his father was promoted to foreman carpenter with the MGWR Railway at Longford Station on a weekly salary of £1.12s.0d. Then, on 14 January 1916, James was appointed leading carpenter at MGWR main Broadstone terminal in Dublin at £2 per week.[17]

Three months later, on Easter Monday, Ireland was shaken by the outbreak of the 1916 Rising centred on the General Post Office on O'Connell Street in Dublin. A small band of insurgents, led by Padraig Pearse and James Connolly, read out the Proclamation of the Irish Republic from the steps of the GPO headquarters, and then held out for a week against the overwhelming British firepower before surrendering. The centre of the city was devastated, and fifteen of the insurgent leaders were executed by a British army firing squad at Kilmainham Gaol. Following growing public outrage, other executions were halted.[18] James Mongan and his son were among the crowds of Dubliners who walked down O'Connell Street to view the shattered buildings.

James' career prospered when on 21 September 1916, he had received another payrise to £2.3s.0d. Through his father's connections, Reg was taken on as an assistant electrician with the MGWR Railway at Broadstone on 18 shillings per week.[19]

Whilst the rest of Europe was recovering from the First World War, the War of Independence raged in Ireland, when guerrilla warfare broke out between the Irish Republican Army and the crown forces. Among the IRA leaders was Seán Lemass, son of a hat-shop owner from Capel Street. In 1919, James Mongan had left Longford permanently to move his family to Dublin. They took up residence at 52 Fontenoy Street in Phibsboro, an impoverished north inner-city area, though only a ten-minute walk from Broadstone MGWR terminal.[20] On 3 March, James was made foreman of No. 1 Maintenance Service team.[21] However, Reg's budding career received a setback on 25 October when – still on a learning curve – he was demoted to apprentice electrician at 12 shillings; his wages were later increased to 14 shillings and he was again promoted to improver electrician on November 1919.[22]

Against a backdrop of increasing tension – as Ireland tottered on the brink of civil war – after Michael Collins signed the Anglo-Irish Treaty that brought into force the partition of Ireland, Reg Mongan resigned his position with the MGWR on 25 February 1922. With a colleague he established, as junior partner, a small electrical engineering company Murphy & Mongan at Brunswick Chambers, 200 Great Brunswick (now Pearse) Street, behind Trinity College in the city centre.[23]

'Irregulars', who didn't want to accept the Anglo-Irish agreement, took over the Four Courts and, on 27 June 1922, Collins' forces opened fire on the building – the Civil War had begun. As the fighting intensified, Collins was killed in an ambush on 22 August in County Cork. On 6 December 1922, the twenty-six counties of southern Ireland were proclaimed the Irish Free State and were granted Home Rule within the British Empire. Six northern counties, with their Protestant majority, retained their links with the crown, and partition came into existence. As the Civil War raged in Ireland with reprisal following reprisal, the Irregulars' chief of staff, Liam Lynch, was killed in action in April 1923.[24]

Reginald, patriotically inspired by Collins' oratory and the family's military tradition, became increasingly concerned by the worsening national situation. On 24 March 1923, he enlisted with the Irish Free State Army and was made Second Lieutenant with the Salvage Corps (Army Corps of Engineers) at Tallaght, under the command of Commdt Michael McCormack.[25] A negotiated truce between the warring factions led to a ceasefire on 24 May 1923. The Salvage Corps was put in charge of dismantling British army barracks and storing the recuperated material at the military dump in Tallaght, west of Dublin.[26]

In the aftermath of hostilities, military requirements were reduced and, on 20 December, after nine months service, Reginald Mongan, received an honorable discharge from the army. He had been a firm but popular officer with the men under his command and the NCOs and men of the unit presented him with an illuminated commendation on the disbandment of their unit. The commendation said the men wished to express their appreciation of:

> the interest he had shown in them and wished him rapid progress in his future career and that he would continue to shew humour and sympathy to those placed under his command.[27]

In June 1924, Reginald sat the Civil Service Clerical Officers Examination. He was amongst the 100 successful candidates and was appointed as clerical officer to the Ministry of Labour.[28] With new-found relative financial security, he was soon well-known around Dublin for his sartorial elegance, a snappy dresser in his well-tailored suits. With his dark hair and fair complexion, he had the look of a Spanish hidalgo. Reg's style and charm soon attracted the ladies. He spent his weekends at Shankill Tennis Club, looking dapper in his white tennis flannels. On 17 August 1927, he took a short break in England from his civil service work and, on impulse, aged thirty, took the plunge and married his twenty-four-year-old Dublin girlfriend, Mary Taggart, daughter of a King's Dragoon Guards sergeant major, at the Church of the English Martyrs, Withington, south Manchester.

However, the couple quickly found that they were incompatible and the marriage was never consummated. Reg was to spend over seven years seeking an annulment of his Manchester marriage.[29]

Portrait of Second Lieutenant Reginald Michael Mongan, who served with the Free State Army, 1923, with the Salvage Engineer Corps. Oil painting, based on contemporary 1923 photo, by Paris-based Canadian artist Murray Stuart Smith (1925-1998) in 1985. (*Courtesy Reginald Mongan archives*)

US Naval Veteran Charles Joseph Mongan and his wife Mae lived at 118 Hancock St in Cambridge, MA, just off Massachusetts Avenue [left]. They were regular patrons during the 1940s and 1950s at the nearby Elite Spa Bar [right], now the landmark The Plough & Stars pub established in 1970 in the same premises) located at the end of Hancock Street, at 912 Massachusetts Avenue.

In Boston, Charles retired around 1940 after twenty-eight years employment as a railway guard with the Boston Elevated Railroad. He had followed his father's example by moving from his military service back into the mass transport industry. However, his working career was far from over. As a forty-four-year-old navy veteran of the First World War, he found congenial employment as staff chauffeur with the Cambridge Public Library. With his wife, Mae, he moved into a small apartment at 118 Hancock Street, off Massachusetts Avenue, in Cambridge.[30] Sadly, as the couple were never able to have children, they only needed a two-room home. This part of Cambridge was only ten minutes from where he had passed his childhood on Kinnaird Street. At the end of Hancock Street, on the corner with Massachusetts Avenue, was The Elite Spa, his local hostelry where, during the 1940 and 1950s, he would drop in for a beer with Mae, friends and colleagues, after his day at Cambridge Public Library.

During the 1946 congressional elections, The Elite Spa was much visited by campaigning candidates vying for votes, one of whom was twenty-nine-year-old John F. Kennedy.

In political terms, Cambridge was part of the eleventh congressional district and it reflected Charles' own political leanings. The seat had been held by veteran politician and one time Boston mayor, James Michael Curley, with 30 per cent of the registered votes. With his father Joe's financial backing, John F. Kennedy had been persuaded to run for the seat, something that was made possible because Curley had been convinced to step aside and run again as Boston's mayor. Joe Kennedy also agreed to discretely pay off Curley's substantial debts and finance his mayoral campaign.

Jack Kennedy had no real connection with the district and faced strong local opposition. The other candidates were former Cambridge mayor and state legislator Mike Neville, who was well-ensconced locally, and Dan O'Brien, a Cambridge undertaker whose funeral parlour was located on the corner of Hancock Street, just opposite The Elite Spa. Never a natural mingler with strangers, Jack nevertheless campaigned incessantly. In spite of some initial hesitation, he dropped in to local saloons, barber shops, restaurants and pool halls to talk with local residents.

As a war hero himself, Jack was instrumental in setting up the Joseph P. Kennedy Jr Veterans of Foreign Wars post in the eleventh district. He even took on the role of post commander, presided over a national VFW convention and became a member of the American Legion.

Joe Kennedy spent an estimated $250,000-300,000 on his son's campaign, blitzing the district with billboard, subway, newspaper and radio ads, and direct mailings – all proclaiming 'Kennedy for Congress'.[31]

Some 1,500 Irish ladies were invited to an elaborate soirée at the plush Hotel Commander in Cambridge to shake hands with the new, formally attired Boston brahmins. The hard-nosed Kennedy campaigning guaranteed a decisive primary victory: Kennedy won 22,183 votes to Mike Neville's 11,341, John Cotter's 6,671 and Joe Russo's 5,661 – 40.5 per cent of the overall ballot, though with a turnout of only 30 per cent, this represented 12 per cent of the district's democratic vote. However, on 5 November, in spite of a Republican overall victory, Jack Kennedy defeated his Republican opponent, Lester Bowen, by 69,093 votes to 26,007. The votes of Charles and Mae Mongan probably helped to launch JFK on his way to the White House.

Former Cambridge Head Reference Librarian, Marguerite Lechiaro, writing in 1997, had clear memories of a fifty-year-old Charlie Mongan at Cambridge Public Library:

> I write to you as one who worked with Charles Mongan at the Cambridge Public Library for many years. 'Charlie', as he was affectionately called, was the library chauffeur. He drove the library delivery van and his work consisted of delivering books and supplies from the main library to the six branch

libraries, daily visits to City Hall with communications, payables, etc., and servicing the sick, elderly and disabled with reading material.

I came to work at the library in 1945 and Charlie was already an indispensable fixture and I soon joined the ranks of the other employees who had come to depend on him for a ride to a city meeting or a supply needed in a hurry. It was always 'Charlie, could you do this errand for me?' He was a dedicated employee who never refused a request no matter how busy his schedule. If things got too much for him, he would mumble to himself and we knew we had asked too much of him. He was proud of his service and was keenly interested in veterans' affairs as well as City politics. He lived at Hancock Street in Cambridge near Harvard Square with his wife.[32]

Physically, Charles was about 5 feet 8 inches in height and weighed 170 pounds with a salt and pepper hair crewcut, and he always had a curved briar pipe in his mouth. Marguerite recalled his facial features – straight eyebrows, a short nose, even teeth, clean-shaven with a ruddy complexion. He usually dressed in a shirt and tie, slacks, black shoes, and wore a navy ski cap. A mild-mannered, relaxed, easy-going soft-spoken man, he often talked about his wife Mae, as they were a close couple. Marguerite remarked on his appearance:

I was thinking of it today. He had very nice skin, like as if he never shaved, shiny and smooth. I do remember that, and he was always clean-looking. He wore different hats, a ski cap, you know, when it was cold and he'd be out in bad weather. I would say [he was] a kind of character. Everyone at City Hall would say, 'Charlie? Ah, Charlie, Charlie'll do anything.'

In a further interview at The Charles Hotel on Harvard Square in October 2002, she remembered Charlie Mongan's time at the library in more detail:

[Charlie] lived at 118 Hancock Street in what in those days, I think was 'light housekeeping' [minimal household maintenance]. I'm not sure of that, but in 'light housekeeping', it meant just one, maybe two [rooms] at the most, with a hot plate for your cooking, and a sink, and probably share a bathroom. I am not really positive of that, the area where they lived was pretty much 'light housekeeping'.

And then nearby was the pub [The Elite Spa] we would call it a bar room, and Charlie and his wife I know frequented that. It was in the same block of stores because it faces Hancock Street. They shopped at the Manhattan Meat Market, which was a market on Central Square; got good bargains. He would report the bargains to us. He shopped for his clothes in a flea market, though nowadays we call them rummage sales, and he would have to tell you about this great bargain. I talked with him more than someone else because he'd go by my desk and he'd always have something to say and I would answer him.

The main entrance of Cambridge Public Library, Massachusetts Avenue, where Charles Joseph Mongan spent his later career as library chauffeur from 1940 to 1960.

Yes, he was sort of always around, I don't know, he was around all the time and we'd send him off on all kinds of errands. As much as you'd think he couldn't find a place, he would find it, you know, it was probably an Irish trait, he'd persevere and find it. And you'd say, 'Ah, Charlie will never find this', but he'd find it and bring you whatever you were looking for.

He always had a pipe in his mouth, never took it out. So you had some of the girls who were probably not as interested, who would say I can't understand one word he says, so don't bother me, you know, that kind of thing but I kind of knew what he was saying if I listened and paid attention.

Charlie had what you'd call a 'van' today. The van was really much too large for his work so we convinced him that he should get a station wagon. The city would only purchase a wagon every three or four years but Charlie was attached to the van, and kind of baulked at the time. But in the end, there was a photo I know of him standing with the new wagon, and he was proud of it. We always thought of him, in our feeble minds, that he didn't want the station wagon because he couldn't hide his wife in the station wagon. But in the end it worked out, and then Charlie retired. He enjoyed his weekly routine on payday of picking up his wife in the van and both would go to the bank to cash his paycheck. She would hide in the van because in those days non-employees were not allowed in City vehicles. It was perhaps his only indiscretion and we simply looked the other way. Otherwise Charlie kept pretty much to himself. I think he was happy to be part of City life.

We would go to cash our check. He'd get his wife first and go to Manhattan Market to do their shopping and then back home. He'd leave her and come back to work. It would be his lunch hour so I'm sure it was OK. It was just that no one was supposed to be in the truck and he laughed because we'd say nothing. We had one woman who was very friendly with Charlie. Her name was Florence Lyons, she died many years ago. She had a back office, she did the billing. And he would go down there and kind of drop in on her, you know. So she'd say, 'Charlie's gone for his wife, today's payday!' It certainly was a steady job. He would have had a good pension; it would have been 80 per cent of whatever he made.

Many of us were Democrats. There weren't many Republicans in Cambridge, I would guess. I think my tie to him [Charlie] was I always had a feeling that he was very fond of my father. My father was a sort of handsome man, a positively big, handsome man, with a handsome face. Not because he was my father! And very outgoing, liked every one, you know. Never disliked anyone. And I think that Charlie would feel he knew him. That sort of rubs off on someone like me, because Charlie would like to think I was probably OK because he liked my father or something, you know?

He was a steady, dependable worker, very proud of his position at Library Chauffeur. My father [Francis L. Sennott (1893-52)] was an early Mayor of Cambridge [1941-2, 1945, City Councillor c.1935-52, and publisher of the *Cambridge Recorder*] and because he had served in the First World War, and belonged to the American Legion, Charlie felt a special affinity to him and perhaps to me. He would often mention his service and the American Legion in conversation.

When the City would purchase a new truck for him, he would be elated. We never saw his wife only at a distance when he would smuggle her into the truck on payday to cash his check and do some grocery shopping. He pretty much kept to himself, once in a while he would bring back from his daily rounds to City Hall a bit of gossip. My mind is a blank when it comes to his retirement and death. I find this hard to believe because we were very good at remembering retirees and deceased employees.

Marguerite believed that Charlie had not requested any specific religious service at his funeral. However, it seems that his sister Mary and wife Mae ensured that he was waked at the local St Cecilia's Catholic church and a funeral mass was celebrated. Anxiously I quizzed Marguerite whether any photos of him had survived in the library archives:

I wish I knew more about him. I asked one of the boys at the library. I remember a couple of pictures. I can't say I remember [any] when I retired so they may have gone by then. But there was one in front of a new wagon, and one in a group picture. The boy [at the library] was really resourceful but he never came back to me. I told him to call me if he found anything. They know of Charlie, they would know the name, so I sent one of them to see what he could find, but he didn't find a thing. I'm sure the photo is long gone. He was our link to the City Hall, for bits of gossip and when he died, he was sorely missed. He was affectionately known throughout the city as 'Charlie from the library'. All of us at the library relied on him and he was in the truest sense a dedicated public servant.[33]

In 2000, Cambridge Public Librarian Susan Ciccone talked to other former staff members, who remembered Charlie as 'that little man with the pipe', whose job was to pick up and deliver books to the library branches and also drive staff members to various appointment or meetings. Another person remembered him as 'a very quiet man, who always wore a cap and smoked a curved pipe'.[34]

Charles had lost his mother Maria in 1936. His sister Mary had been living with Maria at 112 Kinnaird Street, when she died and they buried her at Cambridge City Cemetery. Charles remained in constant contact with Mary during his years at Cambridge Public Library. They met regularly after he retired from the library in 1960, aged sixty-five. I wondered if they ever spoke of their father's tragic destiny later when Mary visited Charles in a nursing home after he became ill. Charles finally died from broncho-pneumonia on 15 September 1963, aged sixty-eight, at the Veterans' Hospital in Boston. The D. F. O'Brien Funeral Home, near Hancock Street in Cambridge, handled the removal and he was laid to rest in the First World War Veterans' Plot at Cambridge City Cemetery. The entire cost, including $30 for a Mass and $5 for the priest, came to $1,485. Mae's shaky signature, evidence of her growing frailty, was affixed to the Veterans' Burial Allowance application form.[35]

My research revealed that, shortly afterwards Charles' widow Mae moved into the Pine Manor Nursing Home, at 6 Prentiss Street, a mile north in Cambridge, where she was visited by his sister-in-law Mary Mongan every week during her last years. She passed away on 12 March 1979, aged seventy-nine, at Cambridge Hospital. The attorney handling her affairs had established that from November 1968, five years after Charles' death, Mae was no longer able to care for her own property and possessions. He advised the court that her personal property amounted to $10,000. She had worked for the City of Cambridge and had been receiving a small monthly pension from them.

By January 1968, Mae had almost $19,000 in her savings account, though this was offset by nursing home costs and miscellaneous items purchased for her: fruit, a TV set, probably by her faithful sister-in-law Mary.[36]

Mae was survived by her unmarried brother, Earl, a retired textile worker, then living at 29 Chesnut Hill Avenue, in Brighton, near Boston College, in the west of the city. He died, aged seventy-nine, at St Elizabeth's Hospital in Brighton, on 26 May 1980, three months after Mary had died at Massachusetts General Hospital.[37] He was the direct last connection with the immediate family in America. Over a two-year period, the last members of that generation had all passed away.

It was the passing of a generation and, sadly, a few months too late for their Irish cousin (once removed) to make contact.

Charles had served with the US navy, worked with the Boston Elevated Railroad, and eventually became a Cambridge Library chauffeur. In Ireland, after working briefly with the MGWR, his cousin Reginald served with the Free State Army, then had a career with the civil service from 1924 until 1962.

In 1929, Reginald had met nineteen-year-old Agnes Staveley, daughter of a large Dublin merchant family, of North Great George's Street and Danesfort, Clontarf, Dublin. The family ran Staveley's Stores, hardware and china merchants, at 137 Parnell Street in Dublin. Soon the couple were dating regularly and Reg had begun the long negotiations to have his first marriage annulled. In 1930, he travelled on holiday to Rome to begin efforts to seek annulment of his Manchester marriage by the Rota Court in the Vatican. The complex, bureaucratic process was to continue for seven years.

About this time, Reg's father James, by then a maintenance service foreman, retired from the railways at Broadstone in July 1930, when he was granted an £30 annual pension.[38] In 1933, Reg returned to the Rota Court in Rome to continue the lengthy annulment process; in the Italian capital, he witnessed the growing rise of Facism under Mussolini. Finally, in 1935, he received the long-sought annulment from the Vatican. Just as he was celebrating the outcome of this long, frustrating period of matrimonial limbo, destiny struck again.

In 1935, further tragedy blighted the family when his only sister Esther (Dolly), died, aged thirty-four, during a routine appendicitis operation at Whitworth Hospital in Dublin, leaving her parents, James and Mary, and her brother Reg distraught. Dolly had been musically talented, and had taken part in Longford Operatic Society productions between 1914 and 1919. Later in Dublin, as an enthusiastic ballroom dancer, she had won several awards at dancing competitions in the city's ballrooms. She had been engaged to a man named Jack, a wealthy Irish-American, when she died. During the 1920s, she had studied at a shorthand typing course, where she befriended a a fellow-student, Claire Lemass, the sister of Seán, the future Taoiseach.

In 1936, Reginald, aged thirty-nine, finally married Agnes, twenty-six, at St John of God's Church, in Clontarf on Dublin's northside and gave the family something to celebrate. The couple spent their honeymoon in Jersey in the Channel Islands.

That year, Reg's entrepreneurial spirit took off. He founded Dublin's first bicycle delivery service, Messenger Services Ltd, with uniformed messengers wearing pillbox hats, based in Rutland Place, near O'Connell Street. James Moir and other Dublin businessmen were directors of the company. The company later developed into a van delivery and publicity leaflet distribution service run by Agnes, until it closed down in 1976.

Reginald Michael Mongan and his fiancée Ms Agnes Staveley at races in 1934.
(Courtesy Reginald Mongan archives)

James Mongan and his wife Mary (left), along with their new in-laws Arthur and Mary
Staveley of Danesfort, Clontarf, on the occasion of their son Reginald's wedding to their
daughter Agnes, at St John's Church, Clontarf, in 1936. *(Courtesy Reginald Mongan archives)*

Reg also bought a house near Rathfarnham at the foot of the Dublin mountains on the southside of the city. In the early days of his marriage, he travelled to Mullingar to introduce his new wife to his grand-aunt's daughter, Mary Josephine Duignam, who was living at 40 Mount Street. Mary Josephine presented him with a unique photo of her mother taken at Belvedere House in 1913, when she had been housekeeper.

In 1938, Reginald's wife Agnes gave birth to their first child, Norman Charles Michael, on 11 December, at a private nursing home at 12 Lower Leeson Street. The choice of his son's names was to prove significant. The following year as the Second Word War broke out, and Reginald was appointed District Leader of the LSF (Local Security Force) for South Dublin. (As Ireland is a neutral country, the period was known as the 'Emergency'.) As district leader, Reginald had a motorbike patrol squad of 100 men under his command for the duration of the Emergency. Their mission was to locate any downed German airmen or spies who attempted to parachute into Irish territory.

In 1942, Agnes presented Reg with another son, Denis Justin James, on 14 April, followed by a daughter, Carol Mary Bernadette, on 10 February 1944. In 1947, outside his civil service work, Reginald, now fifty, also established Mercantile Services Ltd, an import–export business, at Nassau Chambers, Nassau Street, Dublin. He was inducted as a Fellow of the Economics Society, and played with the Civil Service Cricket in the Phoenix Park, Dublin.

At this time, Reg delivered a talk to the Dublin Rotary Club, called 'Modern Mercuries', highlighting his vision for fast efficient, and inexpensive, Dublin messenger and delivery service.

In June 1947, he travelled to Spain on business, and stayed at the prestigious Palace Hotel in Madrid. He attended a bullfight there, and was in Spain when Manolete, Spain's greatest matador, was fatally gored by a Miura bull in Linares. He visited the Prado Museum and the famed Retiro Gardens.

In 1952, aged fifty-five, Reginald was working alongside fellow-Longford man, department chief John Leyden at the Department of Industry an Commerce in Kildare Street, Dublin, when he was promoted to Higher Executive Officer level. At the time, the Minister for Industry and Commerce was the visionary and former War of Independence volunteer Seán Lemass, who held the post continuously from 1932 until 1948. Lemass was again Minister from 1951–54 and 1957–59, when he was elected Taoiseach by the Dáil on 23 June 1959.

In 1954, as a life-long chain smoker, Reginald suffered an angina heart attack and was bedridden for several months after a serious heart condition was diagnosed. In 1962, Reginald, aged sixty-five, retired after thirty-eight years with the civil service and was looking forward to his golden years. On 17 March, I myself, his eldest son, had left home for Paris. However, just over two months later, I flew back again for my father's funera; my father had suffered a fatal heart attack at our home on 2 June. Reg, survived by his wife Agnes, two sons and a daughter, was buried as Cruagh Cemetery, in the Dublin Mountains, with its panoramic view of the city spread below.

My father took many unanswered questions with him to his grave. I sensed that he must have learned of his uncle Michael's tragic destiny in America, but wasn't certain. Was he aware that, in 1962, he still had two Mongan cousins living in Boston? As a child, he had played with them back in 1900 when he visited America with his parents. There had to be a reason why he never contacted them again.

I found the uncanny parallels between Reginald and Charles intriguing. Charles, born in 1895, had outlived Reginald by a year, dying in September 1963, aged sixty-eight. Both men had military careers in their youth – Charles with the US navy; Reg with the Free State Army. Both found steady, pensionable employment with large organisations – Charles with the Boston Elevated Railroad and Cambridge Public Library; Reg, after a brief period with the MGWR railway with the fledging Irish civil service.

I know Charles and Reginald had met once as very young children, aged five and three, in 1900 in the garden at 86 Kinnaird Street in Cambridge, but it had become a secret – maybe a hazy memory in later years. Because of Michael's tragic destiny, they were never to meet again, never to share happy times together, never to correspond with each other. The rift was complete. They could even have gradually forgotten about each other. The stigma and shame of Michael's suicide in 1903 had split asunder the transatlantic bonds between the two branches of the family. They were bound to silence. After James learned of his brother Michael's final act at Worcester, he must have decided to 'pull down the shutters' on all connections with the family in America. The grief, hurt and sorrow were just too much to bear.

I felt Reg must have been aware of the tragedy that had befallen his Uncle Michael in America, or that three of his six aunts had married there. Several possible clues suggested that he knew of his uncle Michael's sad demise. Reg had been baptised 'Michael Reginald' at St Mel's Cathedral on 29 April 1897. However, throughout his life, in all later official documents, his parents chose to use Reginald rather than the name of his ill-fated uncle, Michael? Pure chance or conscious decision?

Another clue lay in the fact that he named his eldest son Norman Charles Michael. Had he deliberately chosen the names of his doomed uncle and his American cousin? Had he learned of Michael's fate from his own father, James, but chosen only to refer obliquely to it through recurring family first names?

At the time of Reginald's death in 1962, Charles and Mary were still living in Cambridge, along with Charles' wife Mae. Did Charles and Mary remember they had living relatives back in Ireland, but chose never to contact them? The stigma and shame, even after so many years, was still too much to face if they ever met with their Irish cousins? Reg's death had left his eldest son with an enigma to resolve, sending him on a mission to seek out the long-hidden truth of the family's destiny in America. Fate ordained that his eldest son whose name connected him with the lost family was chosen to seek out the truth behind the cover up, the whitewash of the sad story in Boston.

The final resting place of Michael's son Charles Joseph Mongan, (1895-1963), Cox USNRF, in the First World War Veterans' Plot at Cambridge City Cemetery, Cambridge, MA

14

Mary's story. A spiritual journey

In October 2000, I stood – amazed – in the bright autumn sunlight, staring at the green, three-storey, wooden clapper-board house at 21 M Street, opposite M Street Park, in South Boston. I was stunned that the house was still standing a century after my relations had lived there. I had thought that old buildings didn't last that long in ever-changing America. Somehow, it had survived. It was typical of the Irish immigrant home from the turn of the 20th century – the three-decker, as its name implies, was a three-storey wooden house, with one apartment of six or seven rooms on each floor, opening off common front and rear stairwells.

Somewhat disbelievingly, I walked up the six steps to the entrance and stared at the brass numerals '21'. No mistake about it. This was the place all right. Michael J. Mongan had stood on these very same steps a century before with his baby daughter Mary Elizabeth in his arms. He had put his hand on the handle to open the door many times as he walked up the stairs to the family apartment above. Here they had spent happy times. The building was well-kept, painted a pale green, with a dark green door. I looked at the names on the letter boxes – Flaherty, McGrath, the Irish connection continued, though now these properties were much sought-after by upwardly mobile Boston yuppies.

Mary Elizabeth Mongan, daughter of Michael J. Mongan and Maria Hurd, had been born at 21 M Street, in South Boston on 29 May 1896.[1] Michael was especially overjoyed at the birth of a daughter; the pain of the loss of his first girl Annie from cholera in 1894 still haunted him. Mary was genuine Southie-born, having spent her first two years in South Boston until her family moved to Cambridge in 1898.

In Cambridge, little Mary was been surrounded by her dysfunctional Irish-American family; her Irish-born grandparents Elisha and Hannah Hurd, her aunt, Annie, and motor-mechanic uncle John, as well as her own parents in the 32 Bay Street apartment. Her early years were marred by increased family tensions; as her father's Michael's health went on a downward spiral. She probably had vague memories of her parents' arguments, shouts, tears and threats, which had led to her father menacing to 'shoot' her mother if she did not rear the children better. Did her father kick her, as her mother's friends had said at the time? All that strife must have sent worrying signals to impressionable young children. How well Mary even remembered her father, who died when she was only seven, is debateable. Mary and Charles had been frightened, traumatised and left crying at these outbursts.

Those harrowing childhood experiences marked Mary for life. Had she any recollection of playing with her Irish cousin Reg in the garden at 86 Kinnaird Street, when her uncle James had visited Boston in 1900? Her first seven years had been scarred by her father's declining health, his periods of unemployment and depression, disputes with her mother, and arguments with her grandparents living upstairs.

During my search, I consulted the Cambridge City directories, which showed the Mongan family continued to live at 32 Bay Street from 1898 until Michael died in 1903.[2] Michael was listed as 'motorman', while Elisha Hurd was a watchman at River Street stables. Elisha died on 16 February 1905, aged sixty, the Irish-born son of Edward Hurd, and was buried at Holy Cross Cemetery, in Malden just north of the city. Hannah, his widow, faithful wife and housekeeper – and contested guardian of her son-in-law's precious savings – survived until 2 April 1908, and at the age of sixty-two, was laid to rest beside her late husband. All this loss caused further sadness for Maria, who within the space of five years had lost her husband and her parents. Her life had also been marked by tragedy.

I discovered that Elisha Hurd's grave plot had been purchased on 17 September 1872 to receive the heartbreaking mortal remains of Edward Hurd, aged five months, buried on that day, then Hannah's brother, John McCarthy on 30 November 1883; followed by baby Sarah Hurd, aged eleven months, on 30 July 1883, finally Michael and Maria's first born, Annie Elizabeth, was buried there on 30 July 1894. The Hurd plot at Malden was purchased by the estate of Hannah Hurd on 8 October 1908. Both Annie, a spinster, who died aged fifty-six around 1932, and her brother, John, who died aged sixty around 1937, were interred there too. Two more witnesses to the dramatic events at 86 Kinnaird Street at the beginning of the 20th century had passed on.[3]

The evidence suggests that the Hurds had arrived in in the late 1860s, fleeing the traumatic aftermath of the Famine in Ireland. At just thirty-two, Maria had already suffered the loss of her two young siblings, Edward and Sarah, and her own firstborn, Annie.

Mary grew up in this troubled Cambridge household and attended the nearby Houghton School (now the Martin Luther King Jr School) on River Street with her brother Charles.

Mary Elizabeth Mongan (1896-1980), daughter of Michael J. Mongan, never married and lived with her mother Maria, who died in 1936. Mary became well-known as a psychic healer and medium in the wider Boston area, holding regular readings at several spiritualist centres. She was fondly remembered by people she had helped from the 1950s to 1970s, even being consulted by Boston Police Dept during the infamous Boston Strangler serial-killer murders in 1962-64.

The Hurds continued to live at 86 Kinnaird St. Her uncle, John, was employed as a a pitman at Murray Street stables until 1918, while her aunt, Annie, had found work as a manager. In 1919, Maria moved up a few doors up the street to 112 Kinnaird Street, where she resided, along with her son Charles, a conductor with the Boston 'El' and Mary, who was working as a clerk.[4] John and Annie Hurd were still living at 86 Kinnaird Street in 1926, by which time John was a car mechanic and Annie, an employment agent.

Charles had married Mae in July 1925, and the couple went to live at 1034 Massachusetts Avenue. Then, in 1931, as America entered the Great Depression following the Wall Street crash of 1929, Maria and Mary (still fortunate to be working as a clerk) moved to 26 Guyette Road in Cambridge.[5]

Mary, was living at home, unmarried, caring for her mother at 37 Yorktown Street, in north Cambridge, when Maria passed away in 1936. Coincidentally, Yorktown Street was only a few minutes away from St Paul's Cemetery in Arlington, where her father, Michael, lay in an unmarked grave.

Mary laid her mother to rest at Cambridge City Cemetery. By then Mary was employed as a seamstress and living at 1137 Massachusetts Avenue, close to Charles and Mae. With Mae's brother, Earl, they were now sole immediate family members in Boston.

Mary had already begun to lose contact with her Keough cousins, Josephine, James Jr and Helene, around this time. The shadow of Michael's death still hung like a pall over family relationships. Her aunt, Mary Anne, had died in 1929 and her retired husband Jimmy in 1932. She may have attended the Keough funerals, but Michael's demise had torn asunder close family bonds even with Mary Anne's family. Mary's cousin, Eliza Edgerly, daughter of her Aunt Elizabeth, had been working as a nursing assistant at the Peter Brigham Hospital in Boston when her mother died in 1925. Brave and resourceful, it was Elizabeth, who had stepped in to handle Michael's funeral arrangements in 1903, but had become estranged from the Hurd family, reproaching Maria for having her brother committed to Worcester. Mary gradually lost all contact with Elsie and her brother Charles Edgerly.

Among the few papers of Mary's that I recovered after her death in 1980, was an intriguing correspondence between her and Dr J. B. Rhine, of the Para-Psychology Laboratory at Duke University in Durham North Carolina.

Dr Joseph Bank Rhine (1895-1980) was considered to be the father of modern parapsychology and, along with his wife Dr Louisa E. Rhine, studied the phenomenon. He had coined the term 'extrasensory perception' (ESP) to describe the apparent ability of some people to acquire information without the use of the known (five) senses.

He adopted the term 'parapsychology' to distinguish his interests from mainstream psychology. Dr Rhine had moved to Duke University in 1927, where he joined Prof. William McDougall to explore the field of investigation into the unexplained powers of the mind, and was largely devoted to the study of mediums and the questions of survival of death. He undertook experiments on telepathy, clairvoyance and precognition were undertaken using specially designed cards called Zener cards. About the size of normal playing cards, and collected in decks of twenty-five, each card had one of five symbols on one side – a cross, star, wavy line, circle or a square.[6]

Carl Jung, the famous pioneering Swiss psychologist, was an admirer of Rhine's work and corresponded with him concerning the case of 'a young woman with marked mediumistic tendencies', and another case concerning strange 'explosions' involving a bread-knife with three unexplained breaks in the blade.[7] He acknowledged that J. B. Rhine's experiments in telepathy, clairvoyance and precognition had validated what Jung called the 'synchronistic principle'. 'Events must possess an a priori aspect of unity'.[8] Jung believed that Rhine had demonstrated that 'space and time, and hence causality, are the factors that can be eliminated, with the result that acausal phenomena, otherwise called "miracles", appear possible'.[9]

For almost fifty years, J.B. Rhine was the undisputed leader in the field of parapsychology and helped to develop it into a now recognised branch of science. The Rhine Research Center in Durham still continues the work he pioneered.

The Rhine letters I found revealed a previously unsuspected facet of Mary's personality and they were a revelation. Writing from her address at 675 Boylston Street in the residential Back Bay area of Boston near Copley Squre on 18 November 1957, Mary spoke of the psychic powers she had developed over time:

When you were in Boston, I spoke to you about being tested at your laboratory at Duke University. I spoke about my being a subject for E.S.P. cards, and told you I don't believe I could get two cards right out of fifty. But as you are interested in psychic research, I could tell you many proofs I have had of spirit contact. This may, or may not be of interest to you in your research of proof of spirit contact. You told me to write to you. Sincerely, Mary Mongan. [10]

She finished the letter with her flowing signature. Dr Louisa E. Rhine replied to Mary on 9 December:

This is in reply to your letter to J. B. Rhine. It's true we are interested in personal experiences that seem to involve elements that fall in the field of parapsychology. I don't know just what the nature of these of yours, which you call spirit contact, but if you would be willing to send me a short account of one or two perhaps I could tell you whether they are the kind we consider data for scientific research. With appreciation, Sincerely yours, Louisa E. Rhine.[11]

675 Boylston Street
Boston, Massachusetts
November 18, 1957

Dr. J. B. Rhine
The Para Psychology Laboratory
Duke University
Durham, North Carolina

Dear Dr. Rhine:

When you were in Boston, I spoke to you about being tested at your laboratory at Duke University.

I spoke about my being a subject for E.S.P. Cards, and told you I don't believe I could get two cards right out of fifty.

But as you are interested in psychic research, I could tell you many proofs I have had of spirit contact.

This may, or may not be of any interest to you in your research of proof of spirit contact.

You told me to write to you.

Sincerely,

Mary Mongan
Mary Mongan

Mary Mongan's letter to Dr J. B. Rhine, eminent parapsychologist at Duke University, from her address at 675 Boyleston St, in 1957. (*Courtesy Mary Mongan archives*)

Mary responded apologetically on 8 January 1958:

I was a little late in replying to your letter of December 9th on account of the Christmas rush where I work. I believe Dr Rhine and his associates at Duke University are earnestly trying to get proof of what I call Spirit Contacts, but they are interested in P.K. and E.S.P. tests of which I know nothing about, having had no contact or experience with either tests.

What I call spirit contact, proof of some person or persons who are the so-called Spirit, helping people on this earth, even though they are not seen. It is so much easier to talk to a person than to write about these contacts but you are in North Carolina and I am in Boston, but I will do the best I can. Personal experience of seeing a grandfather of mine [Patrick Mongan?], a girl friend [and] two so-called ghosts I didn't know, is something no one can ever take away from me. These personal contacts I cannot prove to you. Sixteen times I have tried, with the help of the Spirit, to bring relief to people in sorrow and confusion.

One case was a child in Quincy, Massachusetts, who disappeared, the parents, the newspapers were asking for help from anyone who would help them. I talked to Captain Farrazie of the Quincy police and he and two others, interested in the finding of the boy, took me in a police car to the quarry and I pointed out to them where I believed they would find Danny Matson's body. Many months passed by, the search never stopped, they did not find his body in the quarry, and they believed that he might have been kidnapped and taken to some distant place.

One night I went over to Mrs Matson's home and talked with her and I tried to explain the work I was doing as mediator between the two worlds and I told her I firmly believed her little son was with his own, and her husband's loved ones, who had gone to a higher life and that they should keep up the search of the quarry as that is where her little son's remains were. I left a little medal with her and told her to keep faith and courage, for if I was right at least she would know where the boy was. They started another search of the quarry and after many months they found the body.

A lady up in Fitzwilliam, New Hampshire was missing and in the papers it showed a picture of a searching party dragging a pond, but they couldn't find her body. I asked Spirit could I help them out and I was impressed to write to Governor Gregg who was interested in the search and I told him I believed they would find that woman's body in the woods about one mile from her own house. A short time later he sent me back a note of thanks and said the case was closed. I never read papers that they had found her or her body and often wondered what happened. Then one day, much time later, there was a small piece in the paper on the finding of the body of the lady one mile from her home in the woods.

These are two of what I call help of Spirit. I cannot show you a spirit person nor prove to you I was in contact with persons from a higher life. By that kind of proof. All I know is the help I have given to others comes through help of an unseen spirit helper.

I do not know what, if anything, this means to you, but I do know this – there are many people interested in psychic research, much proof had been given by mediums that loved ones do live and know what is going on around their own and try to encourage them and quiet them. One request I have always made to the people I helped was to keep my name out of the paper. Sincerely, Mary Mongan.[12]

Dr Louisa E. Rhine replied on 23 January 1958:

Thanks for telling me the successful results of some of your attempts involving what you call spirit contact. I can see that the differences between your experiences and ESP test of which you say you know nothing is not very great. You are using out in real life the same ability we are studying in the laboratory. With appreciation, Sincerely yours, Louisa E. Rhine.[13]

Around 1962 to 1964, Mary's psychic powers were called upon by the Boston Police Department during the infamous 'Boston Strangler' serial-killer murders, that traumatised the city at that time.

Between 14 June 1962 and 4 January 1964, thirteen single women in the Boston area were victims of either a single serial killer or possibly several killers. At least eleven of these murders were popularly known as victims of the Boston Strangler. Mary was part of a team of international psychics consulted by Massachusetts Attorney General Edward Brooke, a handsome, intelligent and polished professional. He was also the only Afro-American attorney general in the country – and, even more remarkably, was a staunch Republican in a solidly Democratic state. He set up a Crime Research and Detection task force under his close friend Assistant Attorney General John S. Bottomly. This choice was controversial as Bottomly was a man of non-traditional methods (Edmund McNamara, Boston Police Commissioner reportly described him as a 'nutcake'). Among Bottomly's team of crack Boston detectives was Dr Donald Kenefick who headed up a medical-psychiatric advisory committee with several experts in forensic medicine.

At Bottomly's suggestion, Brooke eventually consented to a risky move and agreed to the involvement of Peter Hurkos, a well-known Dutch psychic. Hurkos did identify a suspect, a shoe salesman with a history of mental illness. However, no evidence was found to link that man to the murders. Most people believed that Albert De Salvo, who confessed in detail to eleven of the killings, was the murderer. He was later found in his cell, stabbed through the heart in 1973.[14] In spite of Mary Mongan's express wishes, Ed Hines recalled seeing her name as a psychic in the newspapers between 1962 and 1964.

Further confirmation of Mary Mongan's psychic powers came from people she had helped at Spiritual Church meetings in Methuen, Massachusetts. Several people answered letters I had sent to local newpapers in the Boston area requesting information from Mary's friends and acquaintances. On 10 August 1981, I received a letter from friends in the Methuen area, north of Boston:

Good Morning Editor,
Mary Mongan did indeed have several friends in Methuen. She stayed overnight at my home several times while she was in town. We had many pleasant hours together. Sincerely, Pricilla Hughes.[15]

Boston resident Joseph Viglione remembered her well:

Mary Mongan was a very good living person. She was a spiritualist medium and practised for years with the spiritualists at such centers as the White Rose Center, the Psychic Center, and at the Copley Square Hotel on Sunday once in a great while. Mary O'Shea at 80 Mason St, Boston, was a great friend of hers. The last time I saw Mary Mongan was at the Lutheran Church lunch site. Mary lived in the Marble House, Section 8, subsidized housing building on Mass Ave in Boston. [opposite the Christian Scientist Church on Copley Square] She was found peacefully deceased in her room where she passed away. I hope this helped you. Sincerely yours, Joseph Viglione.[16]

Another lady, Arlene Fitzpatrick, wrote on 7 August 1981, from Medford, a suburb north of Boston with a vivid pen portrait of Mary's personality:

Mary Mongan was quite a 'girl'; really spunky, independent and a determined lady. I met her when I went to a spiritualist church, 'The Ladies Aid' in the old Copley Hotel. They moved since to Quincy, Mass. She was the guest medium. She was the first in my life. She was not a spiritualist, but a willing medium. Her Catholicism prevented her from joining, but usually went and was active.

In Methuen, there was a small spiritualist church and every Wednesday, she went. The ladies running this were her friends, and she was often used. I do not know if they exist now! She was born with this psychic gift and used no tools, just the sound of your voice. She had visual imagery and 'trust the Blessed Mother' was always the answer to your questions; to how or what's the answer – if there wasn't a ready psychic answer for your question in her reading. She was farsighted in her gift, reading two to eight years ahead – and often into years to come.

At one point, she had a small third floor apartment (no elevator) around the corner on St Botolph Street. There, crossing the street, she received a broken knee? – a car accident as she crossed the street. Peter Bent Hospital eventually treated it. She used a cane on occasion. She also was robbed once on Massachusetts Avenue. The last time I spoke to her she said she never went out after 5 p.m. It was no longer safe, in a known, mugged, neighbourhood.

Her apartment was sparsely furnished. It was the way she wanted, as housework and cooking wasn't her forte. I tried to fill in her tools (dishes, etc.) in the kitchen shortly after she moved. She did not want more than service for one or two, and I was told so in a very positive way. She kept one or two cans, in case she didn't feel like going across the street to a restaurant.

She took advantage of free education at Northeastern CE courses for the elderly. I bet she never yielded a point of issue with her Northeastern University professors. I don't know what [courses] she took, but she was very quick. Her brother [Charles] was in a nursing home in Brighton or Newton, and she visited her sister-in-law [Mae] often.

Since I work, I didn't see her but called her approximately once or twice a year. I was never sure whether she wished to hear from her admirers. I yearly sent her a note for Christmas. My neighbour Ann Feragamo, spoke to her every so often. I showed her the newspaper piece in the *Herald*. I'm sure you'll hear.

For St Patrick's Day one year I had bought her two figurines that were appropriate for the time of the year. In 1973 I bought her a Celtic cross on a chain from Ireland. She always wore the rhinestone one that was meaningful to her. I doubt she ever wore the one brought from Ireland.

I wonder where she was buried!! I had called and was told her phone was disconnected. I believe Mary knew you were doing this genealogical research and could have reached you if she wished, providing she was still clear at her death. She was fast, precise and all knowing – and independent as they come. Great, smart, quick.

Mrs Crane [George-Gussie] in Medford ran the Lady's Aid Church until her husband became ill and she retired. Gussie Crane is as old as Mary M was – or older. If I can help you more, please advise. Mary was my first introduction to a medium and quite a 'girl'. I admired her. Sincerely (Mrs John J.) Arlene G. Fitzpatrick.

P.S. She rarely read outside of the Spiritualist Church she serviced, but would occasionally help out a troubled soul.[17]

In another letter in September 1981, Arlene Fitzpatrick had written to people who had known Mary as a psychic medium:

Mary was a speaker at the Ladies Aid Church when it was on Longwood Avenue often. She also went to Methuen Spiritualist Church, however, she never joined the Spiritualist Church but was their medium.

Anne's neighbour Ann Feragamo did, indeed, add her recollections of Mary:

Mrs Fitzpatrick is my next-door neighbour. She introduced me to Mary

Mongan almost nine years ago [1972]. She helped me physically and spiritually during a very trying time in my personal life. She was a wonderful warm and loving person. I once gave her a holy picture that she kept displayed in her rooms. We had lunch on two occasions and enjoyed each other's company. I know she went to see her sister-in-law [Mae] almost every other week. I hoped that this note will help you complete your study.

It's a shame that we didn't meet when you were here in Boston.

I know you'll get lots of information from the Spiritual Church both here in Boston and in Methuen. Your aunt [first cousin once removed] was a very religious person and helped many with her wisdom and understanding. She'd never abuse her psychic ability to my knowledge. I didn't know of her death until Arlene showed me the article. I had sent my yearly Christmas card and calls got no reply.

If I hadn't been confined to the house taking care of my father-in-law and husband I would have gotten over to see her. Please accept our sympathy and prayers for her. Any way we might help, please advise. Sincerely yours, Mrs Ann Feragamo. [18]

I was very touched and moved by the words of Mary's friends in Methuen and Medford. She had left a legacy of love, wisdom and understanding behind her. The evidence also confirmed that her apartment was located at Marble House, 221 Massachusetts Avenue, across the street from the First Church of Christ Scientist in downtown Boston. Ed Hines had traced her will on file at the Probate Court in Boston. It revealed that Mary, in her typical thorough manner, had pre-paid all her own funeral arrangements with J.S. Waterman & Sons, directing her remains to be buried in Cambridge City Cemetery (Range 234, Grave 106) next to her mother and sister-in-law.

Mary passed away on 21 February 1980, at eighty-three, alone and independent to the last, at her Church House apartment, and was removed to University Hospital, Boston. Her attorney stated that she had furnished him with an information sheet confirming her father's name as Michael Mongan, of 'Dublin, Ireland' and the maiden name of her mother as Maria Hurd of Cambridge, Massachusetts. Her last employment had been as a news stand operator. She gave the names of her aunt Mary Anne's daughters, Josephine and Helene Keough 'of Los Angeles' as her closest relatives. [19]

A funeral service was held two blocks from her home at St Cecilia's Church, 31 Belvedere Place, with Monsignor Mackey officiating.

Interestingly, St Cecilia's, a red-brick building dedicated in 1894, was located on the fringe of the Yankee Brahmin Back Bay residential area. The church had been constructed by the faith and hard-earned wages of Irish domestics working in the mansions lining Beacon Street and Commonwealth Avenue. With its predominantly unmarried female congregation, few baptisms took place and, during the summer months, church attendance dwindled when servants accompanied their Bramhin employers and families to the Berkshires and the ocean. Mary's aunt Delia had worked with a family on nearby Clarendon Street back in 1900.[20]

Mary was waked for only one afternoon and there were no family members or friends at her funeral. Her friends in Methuen had not been informed of her passing. Her Keough nieces, Josephine and Helene, had pre-deceased her in 1970 and 1976 respectively; her sister-in-law Mae had died a year before and her brother-in-law was confined in a Brighton nursing home. All her estranged Mongan aunts had long passed on.

Mary's will revealed that she had left any remaining monies in her bank account to the 'Home for Little Wanderers' in Boston, a private non-profit child welfare agency. She had a personal estate of her bank account with a Social Security Death benefit of $255, leaving a total of $2,601.70. When all expenses incurred by the estate had been deducted, the home received $1,237 and her long-serving attorney about $800 dollars.[21] She had passed away as she had lived, fiercely independent, aware, wise, generous to others and loved by many. Little did she realise that her cousin Helene's husband, Bob, his sight failing, was still living only 16 miles away on the South Shore.

Mary had lost her father as a seven-year-old child. I like to think that she had inherited some of Michael's best qualities. I wondered if I had come to the end of the search for the truth. Yet my inner boy was still not totally satisfied. Was there was still more information to be discovered? What had happened to the Keough girls in later years? Had they married and had families? Might there be relatives out there still somewhere? The search had to continue.

15

Helene and Bob. A South Shore romance

I decided to concentrate the next stage of my research on the Keough family. By 1916, Mary Anne and her husband, James Keough, had spent forty-two years living in South Boston since their arrival in America in 1874. James had quickly found work as a brass melter in the local iron foundries, while Mary Anne had worked as a domestic servant. They were finally able to marry around 1886 and their four children – Josephine, James, Hubert and Helene – were born in Southie between 1887 and 1898. They changed addresses in the area several times: from 7 P Street when Josephine was born in 1887, to Second Street at James' birth in 1889, (Michael and his new bride Maria lived at 112 Second Street in 1893), to 8 Kemble Place, when Hubert arrived in 1892 and 21 M Street, when Helene came into the world in 1898. All the children were baptised at the old Gate of Heaven Church on Fourth Street.[1] During Michael's internment at Worcester between 1900 and 1903 the Keoughs had been living at 15 M Street.

As his death certificate showed, James Keough had retired in 1912 after twenty-eight years as a foundry brass melter.[2] Finally, around late 1916, as the First World War intensified in Europe, the family finally decided to make an exodus to South Shore. Many inner-city Irish immigrant families had begun to move out around that time.

The decision to move was probably influenced by their growing children needing more space, and the fact that Mary Anne's sister Catherine was living on the South Shore with her husband David Aherne in nearby Abington. The Keoughs found a house in Holbrook, Massachusetts, a small town just 16 miles south of Boston. Holbrook and Abington were adjacent; just 2 miles apart and linked by trolley cars. The towns lay in Plymouth County, which covered all the area south of Boston; and included the towns of Quincy, Weymouth, Braintree, Scituate, Randolph, Stoughton, Rockland, Brocton, Hanover and Marshfield, extending all the way down to Plymouth and Cape Cod.

In late 1916, Mary Anne and James, along with their three adult children, Josephine, aged twenty-nine, James, twenty-seven, and Helene, aged eighteen, set up home at 62 Pleasant Street in Holbrook. I never learned what happened to Hubert. No reference to him emerged from the archives – had he died as a child? The town's origins went right back to the earliest colonial period. It lay on the

Cochiato river, in the former lands of the Wampanoag native people. 'Cochiato' was an Indian name meaning 'swift flowing', and the river flowed from Lake Holbrook to Braintree. Tradition said that the first white settlers had found just one family of Indians on arrival.[3]

The first recorded house to be erected in the Holbrook township was built in 1712 by John French, and stood on the site later occupied by 240 Center Street. He was shortly followed by some old colonial families: Capt. Elihu Adams (1741-75), brother of President John Adams around 1765; Capt. Nathaniel Belcher (1732-86) built a house in 1754, which survived at 326 Franklin Street, while his brother Joseph (1743-1818) came from Quincy around 1770, as a revolutionary soldier and first shoemaker in the town. Colonel Barnabas Clark (1749-1862) a militia officer for forty years, built another house in the 1790s which survived at 185 Center Street. The Thayers − from Benjamin Thayer, to Simeon, Joseph, Napthali and Deacon Peter Thayer (1708-98) − were a distinguished family of revolutionary soldiers.[4]

Peter Thayer, who had been a captain of a military company in the French and Indian wars, had come from Braintree before 1750. He built a house at 176 Center Street, on an old woods track known in earlier times as Peter Thayer Road. In 1742, a road was built that became Center Street. While these men were mostly farmers, they began to develop small business enterprises; Peter Thayer and Barnabas Clark set up a gristmill and sawmill on the Cochiato River parishes. A new industry had already been developing in the early 1700s. War veterans like Belcher and Benjamin Paine (1759-1823) had established shoemaking as their trade. In 1810, Capt. Thomas White (1779-1862) began manufacturing boots and shoes on a large scale at a shop on South Street. Capt. John Wales (1774-1865) began a boot making business on South Street. He was the first one to crimp boots using a method he developed in 1818 by Micah Faxon (1783-1873), who had moved to North Bridgewater (now Brocton) and began the wholesale shoe-making trade there. By 1849, Holbrook had twenty-two individual boot and shoe makers in the town.[5]

As the population grew, it began to split into separate new parishes. Although opposed by Randolph and Braintree, in 1818, the parish of East Randolph came into existence, and eventually became know as Holbrook on 9 December 1872. It took its name from Elisha Niles Holbrook who had pledged to donate $50,000 to build a town house, library and pay of the town debt.[6]

The first recorded Irish resident in Holbrook was John Jones who resided on Weymouth Street around 1836. By the 1850s and 1860s, increased numbers of Irish and French Canadians began to arrive. In 1865, there were twenty-three adult males of Irish origin, while the French Canadian counted twelve men. The Civil War led to a growing demand for boots, and four local factories received government contracts as the business expanded. Holbrook's 'Golden Age' or period of greatest industrial activity, came between 1875 and 1885. By 1875, there were thirty-three manufacturing and associated businesses, producing boots and shoes with an annual turnover of $937,318, while the town population had grown to 1,726 souls. Ten years later, the turnover of manufactured good had risen to $1,548,038, employing 814 persons.

In 1883, Holbrook saw the town's greatest production record ever. In the week ending 15 September, exactly 1,986 cases of boots and shoes were shipped with the annual total amounting to a staggering 75,826 cases.

To cope with these huge production figures, the town population had begun to expand. From 1872 to 1882, Holbrook's initial decade, the number of houses increased from 283 to 441. By 1876, Snell Street, part of Pleasant Street had been built. Five years later, the entire length of Pleasant Street had been completed.[7]

Captain Peter Thayer, known as Deacon Thayer, had originally built a house and settled on the site at 176 Center Street before 1735. When it was burned down, it

The Burns family home at 176 Centre Street, Holbrook, MA. An original house, was built by Capt. Peter 'Deacon' Thayer on the site before 1735. Destroyed by fire, it was replaced by this two-storey wooden frame building between 1839 and 1854. It was sold to Irish-born Garrett Burns by Mary Thayer in 1870: his brother James, a Westmeath carpenter, bought the ground-floor shortly afterwards. This 1905 image shows his wife Elizabeth (Hamilton) Burns standing at the front door. Robert Burns, their youngest son, married Helen (Mongan) Keough in 1925. The house was demolished after Robert Burns death in 1986. (*Courtesy Dr Owen Kiernan archives*)

James Keough and his family moved to his wooden frame house at 62 Pleasant Street, Holbrook, MA, from 21 M Street, South Boston in 1917. He lived there with his wife Mary Anne (Mongan) Keough, his son James Henry, and daughters Josephine and Helene until his wife's death in 1929. James Keough, a retired brass melter, died in Hyde Park, Boston, in 1932.

was replaced by a 2½ storey clapper-board building between 1839 and 1854, where his great-granddaughter Harriet Thayer lived in the late 1860s. A Greek-Revival style dwelling on 4 acres, with wooden window sashes, it was built on granite foundations, with clapboard walls and a roof asphalt shingle, and the main block façade had five windows and a central doorway. Inside there were two interior brick chimneys and two separate floors. The house was sold, in 1870, by Mary Thayer to Irish immigrant Garrett Burns,[8] who lived there with his wife, Alice and their children and shortly afterwards his brother James, a carpenter, bought part of the house and moved into the ground floor.

James Burns (1841-1924) was the son of Francis Burns and Catherine Reilly, who had emigrated from County Westmeath. He had married Elizabeth Hamilton (1851-1936) and had eight children: Francis F. (1869-71), James S. (1871-1901), Elizabeth (1874-1922), Samuel J. (b.1875), Thomas F. (b.1889), Catherine (b.1886), Anne, Eileen and Robert (b.1891). James had an uncle Patrick, who had a large family in Randolph, Massachusetts (which was near Holbrook). He had worked in the woollen mills in the Blackstone Valley and throughout Massachusetts, Rhode Island and Connecticut.[9]

All the Irish families in Holbrook were connected through marriage, and the majority lived on South Franklin Street. They used to graze cows on Adams Lane. While the Burns family had a Westmeath background, other families like the Barrys and the Fitzgibbons came from Kerry, the Cronins from Cork, the O'Neills from Limerick and the McGaugheys from Antrim.

James' fifth son, Robert Hamilton Burns, born in 1891, grew up in Holbrook and attended the Roberts School. On graduation, like most of the town's population, he started out working in the burgeoning shoe factories, but later trained as a car mechanic.

A portrait of Helene Keough, youngest daughter of Mary Anne (Mongan) Keough, born at 21 M Street, South Boston, on 4 July 1898. Married to Robert Burns in 1925 she died in Holbrook, MA, in 1976 and is buried in St Mary's cemetery, Randolph, MA. (*Courtesy Robert Burns archives*)

Initially on settling in Holbrook, the Keough family had acquired a small property at 148 Center Street, 100 yards from the Burns homestead at No. 176. The properties overlooked a small pond called Silver Lake. The Keoughs later moved to 62 Pleasant Street where they were living in the late 1920s.

The 1920 US census showed retired Irish-born carpenter James Burns, aged seventy-nine, residing at 176 Center Street in Holbrook, along with his wife Elizabeth, sixty-nine (nee Hamiliton from Westmeath) and their children, Katherine, thirty-four, Thomas, thirty-one, and Robert, twenty-seven. All were employed in the local shoemaking factories where Katherine was a stitcher, Thomas, a heeler and Robert, a welter.[10]

I discovered that around 1924-25 Helene Keough began working as chief telephone operator at the well-known Filene's Department Store in downtown Boston. Both she and her sister Josephine, a sales lady, travelled by trolley into the city every day to their work at the store. An attractive, stylishly dressed young woman, with blue eyes and rose-bud lips, Helene had started dating local car mechanic and sports-mad football coach Robert 'Bob' Burns in the early 1920s. They apparently had a long engagement, as they only finally tied the knot on 17 January 1925, when Bob was thirty-four and Helene twenty-seven, at a service at St Francis Xavier's Church in neighbouring South Weymouth.[11]

I imagined among the guests at the wedding were Helene's elderly parents, Jimmy and Mary Anne, her sister Josephine, and her First World War veteran brother James, with her aunts Catherine, now widowed, and Delia visiting from Abington for the occasion. On the Burns side, there was a modest turnout: Bob's brother Thomas, his sisters Kate and Anne, along with her French-Canadian

During their courting days around 1920-25, Bob Burns drove his fiancée Helene Keough in an elegant Stearns-Knight coupé out to Nantasket Beach, near Higham, MA, where they were photographed in Roaring 20s beachwear. (*Courtesy Dr Owen Kiernan archives*)

husband Napoleon Pechette. Sadly, their estranged Mongan relatives in Cambridge were not invited.

Bob and Helene had been an oddly contrasted couple – he was outgoing, loquacious and congenial, while she was a quiet-spoken, reserved, demure and stylish, with no interest whatsoever in sporting activities. Clearly, it seems to have been a case of opposites attracting. The guests struggled through the snow to the wedding celebrations, while Bob, deliriously happy, could not resist throwing a snowball at his brother Thomas. It was a memorable occasion. Helene carried her mother's Mongan blood in her veins. Toasts were made and songs were sung. Bob and Helene could look forward to a bright and promising future. Helene's mother Mary Anne was enchanted to have her two sisters Catherine and Delia, present at such a marvellous historic family occasion. Even the shadow of their brother Michael's traumatic end was forgotten for that special day. Yet no word of the celebrations filtered back from Mary Anne to her brother James in Ireland.

In the days leading up to the marriage, James and Mary Anne bought a home for their daughter on 12 January 1925, from Fanny Trenouth at 20 Oakdale Street in South Weymouth. A typical detached two-storey clapper-board house, it stood on 12,492 square feet of land, in a tranquil rural setting in a wooded area. *The Weymouth Town Directory* (1926-27) listed James J. Keough, his wife Mary Anne and his eldest daughter, a saleslady, living there at that point. However, after less than two years ownership, and probably financially overstretched, they released the mortgage back to Fanny Trenouth on 27 October 1926.[12]

On 6 January 1929, Helene gave birth to a baby girl, christened Mary Eileen. Congratulations poured in from all sides, and the little girl's health was drunk. Helene's aunts Catherine and Delia came over from Abington with presents of baby clothes for the tiny new addition to the family. Helene's parents James and Mary Anne were ecstatic with their new granddaughter. Helene, however, was soon back working at Filene's Store in Boston, leaving her newborn infant in Mary Anne's care at 62 Pleasant Street. All was well as the child blossomed.

Then disaster struck again. Baby Mary Eileen began coughing uncontrollably. The doctor diagnosed severe bronchitis. Two months and nineteen days later, she died; carried off on 25 March 1929 by acute bronchitis allied to broncho-pneumonia.[13] Helene was shattered, weeping floods of tears, heartbroken, and Bob mute with inconsolable sorrow, as the family reeled in total shock.

Mary Anne was horrified by the news. Was there a jinx on the family? First the death of her brother Michael and subsequent detachment from her brother James back in Ireland, now her hope for the family's future had been dealt a cruel blow. The family gloom deepened even further when Mary Anne, traumatised and heartbroken at the loss of her first granddaughter, suffered a heart attack and passed away on 13 July 1929. She had survived her granddaughter by just three months. Three days later, Mary Anne was buried alongside her beloved Mary Eileen at St Mary's cemetery in adjoining Randolph.[14]

The sad bereavements shattered Bob and Helene's relationship. America entered a bleak economic period, with the Wall Street Crash and the subsequent Great Depression. Helene and Bob's marriage was torn apart by the bereavements. Her father James, the retired brass melter, went to live at 940 Hyde Park, nearer to Boston, where his son James Henry was employed in a local foundry. There James' chronic cardiac problems worsened and he passed away on 27 August 1932.[15] Neither he nor his wife Mary Anne had ever taken out naturalisation papers, and were still classed as 'aliens' in the 1920 US census. James was laid to rest at St Mary's cemetery in the same plot as his wife and their granddaughter.

Helene and Bob, guilt-ridden and emotionally drained, decided to separate for a while. Helene left Holbrook and took an apartment in Boston with her sister Josephine, who was still working as a saleslady in a dry goods store. A former neighbour, Mary (Smith) McAvoy, writing in 2001, had crystal clear recollections of them at the time:

> My cousin Mal Harpins, has mentioned to me a couple of times that someone was seeking information on the Keough family who were neighbours of mine, probably in the late twenties. They lived two houses down from my family [Frank Smith] at 48 Pleasant Street, where we lived. It was the corner house at Sprague Avenue where there is a newer house now on that property.
>
> I remember two young women who worked in Boston and took the train. Their names were Helene and Josephine. Being plain little Mary Smith then I was always impressed with what I thought were glamorous names. Their mother took care of a little baby which was an attraction, as well as a player piano they allowed me and my brother Joe to insert rolls and pull the keyboard prongs to operate it.
>
> I have a vague recollection of that baby becoming very ill and dying. I'm certain of the location of the house and those two names. Sincerely, Mary McAvoy.[16]

After receiving Mary McAvoy's letter, I had a phone conversation with her in April 2001 at her Norwood home. A former teacher, her memory was crystal clear, sharp and accurate. She distinctly remembered the death of Helen and Bob's baby girl:

> I remember the mother, and when we'd go into the kitchen, she'd be taking care of that baby. They were very nice, cause how many people would have let little kids come in and out of the house, but we were always welcome there. I can remember going into that living room where there was a child laid out. I'm eighty-one now, so I'm talking about a long time ago. I remember them well.
>
> The Burns…were down on Center Street. Bob, he became quite disabled and I had a brother Joe, he was in the service, but when he came back Bob Burns couldn't really walk and Joey used to go down and visit him and bring him little treats, but Bob became quite disabled.[17]

She had clear recollections of the Keough family's mechanical player-piano and the local Irish community:

Yes [it was] one of those rollers. You put in the rolls and there were little prongs in front of the keyboard, and you just pressed them together. You could play one tune after another. Player pianos at that time were a popular thing. I do remember them living there. It was a nice home. My mother came from Cork. She was Mary McCarthy before she became Mary Smith, when she married Frank Smith, and his father built a house two up the street from where the Keough's lived... That street, Pleasant Street, that runs parallel to South Franklin Street, that's where most of the Irish people with Irish roots, came to [either] direct from Ireland or second-generation Irish. There was an Irish community down in there. Holbrook itself was an old Protestant town to start with. My father came from Avon, a nearby town, to Holbrook, when he was about twelve or thirteen [c.1910] and about that time it was all Protestant. And even when we were going to school, we were what you might call a minority. Times change. Its very different from now from when I grew up, because so many people came out from Boston.[18]

I had first discovered the existence of Bob Burns from a Californian researcher Dorothy Dingfelder in 1982, while following a false lead for Helene and Josephine Keough out in Los Angeles on the West Coast. She had found him in the 1920 US census. I then contacted the Holbrook Police Department where I spoke with Police Officer Jack Reddy who was able to confirm that Bob Burns was still living at 176 Center Street in Holbrook. Amazingly, I was right on target and I had located him at the exact same address. From my home in Paris, I phoned Robert Burns, then ninety years old and with failing eyesight. It was an exciting and emotional conversation, as my mind raced with a thousand questions. Not wanting to exhaust him with a barrage of family data, I hung on to his every word. He mentioned that his late wife Helene, had a brother James, who had owned a garage in Spring Valley in upstate New York in the late 1930s. He remembered that James' wife had been killed in a car accident around that time. He also remembered that his wife Helene had an aunt Theresa (Maria-Theresa) in Abington and her mother's maiden name was Mongan. Bulls eye! Although the information was fragmentary and muddled, I now had confirmation of the family connection with the Burns family in Holbrook. Now I had more digging to do to tease out the full story.

In October 1982, I wrote to Bob Burns in Holbrook with a list of questions about his late wife Helene's family background. His cousin Mary Ellen McLaughlin had been taking care of him at that time and she wrote back on his behalf:

We received your letter the other day. We were waiting for your reply before we sent the enclosed photos so that we would be sure we had addressed our letter to you correctly. I'm afraid Bob can't give you any information on the Keoughs and he has no pictures or papers of any kind except for these I am sending.

Bob had been quite sick for the last week and is very weak due to his not eating. He seems to have lost his appetite. He ate very little but I'm worried about his condition. He will be ninety-one next Friday, November 5th, so I suppose we must accept a slowing down. I am enclosing several photos. I don't know how old the one of Helena alone and Ms Keough and Josephine are. The ones in 1971 and 1980 are dated at the back. Sorry we can't be of more help but hope the photos will be of interest. Yours, Mary E. McLaughlin and Bob Burns.[19]

The photos she sent were a revelation. There was a formal sepia-coloured studio portrait, probably taken in Boston around 1910-12, with an enigmatic nautical backdrop, with what looked like a battleship's deck rail immediately behind the seated two ladies. Here at last was an image of Mary Anne Keough, Michael's closest sister, who had stood by him during his darkest days at Worcester. In 1910-12, Mary Anne had been about fifty-five years old. In the photo, she was seated on a wooden chair, her broad, open face expressing a mixture of compassion and determination, her light-blonde hair cut in a bob-style below her ears. Her face, broad, peaceful, with a benign expression, yet touched by a hint of melancholy. Her arched eyebrows curled over hooded eyes, hinting at a steely determination, with a potential for sternness when necessary. She had a strongly marked chin, with a delicate, well-formed short, aquiline nose and a slightly sad smile flickering on her thin lips.

Esther Mary Dolly Mongan, (right) Irish neice of Michael J. Mongan, shared similar broadfaced features as her aunt Mary Anne Keough (left) in Holbrook, MA. (*Courtesy Reginald Mongan archives*)

She wore a long, bodiced dress, pulled tight at the waist, around a matronly figure, that draped down to her ankles. A loose bow was tied down the front of the bodice, with a light-coloured sailor-style lace collar draped down her back. A string of possibly amber beads hung around her neck.

The overall impression was of a gentle yet resolute woman, who had experienced deep sadness, yet had not become embittered. It was then only seven years since her brother Michael's death. Although the trauma of his suicide had left the family with a sense of grief, guilt, shame and recrimination, nevertheless, she had battled on for her own family's sake.

She appeared to be a wise, good-hearted, gentle soul, who undaunted, and with new-found serenity, had moved her family into the growing ranks of the 'lace-curtain Irish', with a parlour and player piano, in Holbrook on the South Shore. She had stood by with compassion as Michael's health had taken a downward spiral in Worcester. Straightaway I noticed that her broad-faced expression bore a close resemblance to her brother James' daughter Esther Mary (Dolly) back in Ireland.

Mary Anne's daughter Josephine sat, probably somewhat awkwardly, on the right armrest of the chair, leaning towards her mother. The pose suggested a warm, loving, understanding relationship between mother and daughter.

Josephine had a long, narrow face with a soft rounded chin, probably reflecting her father James Keough's genes. Her hair, darker then her mother's, spilled down over her forehead, parted in the middle, over her well-drawn eyebrows. Her eyes were large, open and wide, with a quizzical expression and a mischievous glint, her hair held up in a demure bun.

Her short straight nose and high cheekbones, were highlighted by a hint of a smile on her lips. She would have been about eighteen and wore a long, light-coloured dress, draped down over her knees to the floor; with a scalloped-edge lace collar, and a small string of pearls. She gave the impression of being a well-brought up young girl, part of the first American-born generation. Had her mother told her about her uncle Michael's tragic destiny? Did she realise she had two Mongan cousins, Charles and Mary, still living in Cambridge? Or her cousin Eliza, daughter of her late aunt Elizabeth? Had Mary Anne preferred to cover up the whole tragic episode?

I also found the backdrop used for the photo very intriguing in itself. It showed them sitting on the wooden deck of a battleship with a protective rail running behind them. Beyond the rail on the left was the outline of a naval battleship advancing through the waves, its great twin turret pointing to the right. Further right was another ship with smoke billowing around it. A direct hit from the battleship's guns? I found the image quite enigmatic. Had it anything to do with Mary Anne's nephew Charles, who had begun his naval service with the

USS *Louisiana* in 1912? Whatever the reason, the pose of mother and daughter in front of a battleship appeared both incongruous and anachronistic.

A second image was a tinted colour portrait of Helene c. 1920-25, her medium-length dark-auburn hair curled on her forehead, with well-shaped eyebrows, wide grey-blue eyes, and a timid smile hovering on her rose-bud lips. She had a soft, appealing, pensive sad look. She wore a pale-blue dress with a white lace collar, a pearl necklace completing the picture of a demure young Irish-American colleen. At that time, she would have been working as Chief Phone Operator at Filene's Department Store on Washington Street, near where her uncle Michael had met his nemesis in 1903.

Deep down inside, I felt my inner young boy was glad to have found an actual image of his Irish-born grand-aunt and her Irish-American daughters. It had proved him right to have persisted with the search. It now made her existence in America a reality. He had unearthed his long-lost American cousins and had re-established the severed links with Ireland, with Mullingar. His instinct had been right on track and he had followed it without hesitation, knowing it would lead to the truth. His vague instinctive hunch had been vindicated.

Mary Anne, along with her five brave sisters had set off – naïve and eager – into the unknown, full of aspirations and hope for a better life in a harsh, competitive and challenging new world. Now the healing of the psychological wound suffered by the family could begin.

During my trip to Boston in October 2000, I travelled down to visit to explore the town where Mary Anne and her family had settled around 1917. I stopped in front of 62 Pleasant Street, a classic two-storey, wooden-frame house, bathed in the New England sunlight. Miraculously, it had survived almost unchanged. I dropped over to Holbrook Town Hall where the staff of the town clerk Shirley Austin were most welcoming and helpful. They made a phone call to Rick McGaughey, who ran the newsagent's shop in town. Rick remembered Bob with great affection, as he had been coached by him during his football days. He had often visited him during the 1970s after Helene had returned to Holbrook and was living at 176 Center Street with Bob and his sisters Kate and Annie. I asked him about Helene. He remembered her clearly saying she was 'quiet as a mouse, spoke very softly'. He also put me in touch with Elaine Bowers of the Holbrook Historical Society, who later provided me with a unique tape recording of Bob Burns.

In 1980, Bob was eighty-nine, had been interviewed by two Holbrook schoolgirls as part of a school project to record the memories of the town's senior citizens. Bob's memory was clear and sharp, and he could vividly recall his earliest days as a child at 176 Center Street. It gave me a fascinating insight into the man who had married Helene. His warm, engaging personality shone out from the tape, revealing a true small-town hero with a life-long passion for sport. As an enthusiastic coach, he had had a positive influence on generations of Holbrook youth. Interviewed at his home, in his broad South Shore twang, he spoke of his childhood:

Well, my mother and father got this, bought this house from the Thayers, and there were three brothers, my father [James], my uncles John and Gary [Garret]. They decided they wanted to buy this place…so my Uncle Gary lived upstairs, and my mother and father lived downstairs for quite a few years.

He talked about his High School education:

In order to get a diploma you had to write an essay and you had to memorise it. You didn't read it. You had to get up on that stage before 600 people, and speak, and remember every word. I picked out a good subject at the time, the Panama Canal. They were cuttin' that across and I knew all about it. I guess… the people in Holbrook found I was the Head Engineer when I got through my speech!

He also studied algebra, geometry and in third year studied languages:

I took German for two years. I'll tell you I went from Fifth grade in Roberts School, to Sixth grade, and I went to Sixth, Seventh and Eight downstairs in the summer school.

Ever passionate about sports, his loyalties were torn between Holbrook and Randolph High School:

I played football at [Randolph] High for their school. I wasn't allowed to play but I played. My father was annoyed, buys me a hockey stick and says, 'here's something to play hockey with', and I always found that rougher then football…So I always went to St Mary's and to…Sunday School, and I was christened in Holbrook and I received my First Communion. I was confirmed in Randolph and I hung out with Randolph High School boys all the time.

We had good teachers, and we had nice people, very nice people…we were like one family, the whole class. I didn't like school when I went to Roberts School. My sister used to have to write excuses. I went when I was four years old [1895] – stayed out when I was four years old – stayed [out] when I was five and went back when I was six. So anyway I went at six and I didn't like school… but when I got to Sixth grade I liked school, and when I graduated I didn't like to leave. You know, you feel like cryin'. Honest, you have all your friends and it's the last time you are all together, and you don't see each other any more.

Bob graduated on 25 June 1905 and immediately had to start working at the local shoe factory:

> I went to Rice and Hutchince…and was workin' there from the June 26th that I got out. You didn't hang around top say I think I'll go to college or anything – you were OUT! – and you started packing straight away. They didn't have any Social Security – they didn't have anything in them days at all. If you were ten minutes late in the factory they took it out of your pay.

He talked about the importance of the shoe industry:

> Well, mostly everything was shoe factories. A lot of people left because [while it] wasn't a bad place to work. You know – you could make money and everything, the families wasn't rich, any of them. You know in them days… there wasn't too much work but they didn't pay too much money. And anyway we were glad to get out, get doing something, everybody wanted to work… Rice & Hutchince was a good stable factory. I worked there until they went on strike like… and I coulda' had a good job if I stayed, but I wouldn't stay there. They wanted me to go on salary, wanted me to stay. I wouldn't stay. I said my work is better that what you were paying me. You can't buy me.
>
> There was new Superintendent that came in from Wynn – his name was John Bolger, and I never knew it until afterwards, but he was Ray Bolger's father, the one who was a dancer, you know, he was in the *Wizard of Oz*… He had charge the whole factory, you see, 'How would you like to work for me?' I say I got a chance to learn breast up with my brother-in-law. Well, if you work for me you got a chance to learn anything in this factory. I says all right, I'll work for you. He says… we made a store room like down the North end. Anyway John Bolger, he say I'm goin' to put a desk in there and I want you to keep track of all the welt and needles and supplies. But they needed it the room, so he made a good job there – and I learned a lot there – and it was considered one of the best jobs in the factory at that time, you see.

Bob spoke of his great enthusiasm for sport and for coaching:

> Well, I coached the St Joseph's. I played a game of ball up there when I was sixty-seven years old, up at the back of the school. I took over the ball team when I was sixty-three years old – the Holbrook St Joseph's CYO team – and I was in the Holy Name Bowling League for thirteen years… anyway, why… I had all the ball players. I got about four or five ball players on the Police Force, and I got some in the Fire Department.
>
> I had that All-Star game down in Milton and Brockton team, and I was manager of that, and coach, and I had thirty-two players on the bench, and they came from Franklin, Foxbury, Medway, Millis, Mansfield, Walpole. There was [some] from Needham, and Norwood, Quincy, Higham, Weymouth,

Holbrook and Randolph. All of these places had thirty-two players, and I had seven-player practises before we played and in the first year we got beaten five to nothing by them. They were a bunch from Park Lee in Boston. But this time we had a practise game down in Kincaid Park in Quincy – and the next game we had up here in Town Park in Holbrook. The next practise was in Randolph, and the next two was [at] Milton Town field, that was our home field, and we had 4,000 at the game, that was a lot of people at a ball game.

Bob reflected on the other changes he had seen in Holbrook:

Well, one thing I'll tell you – when you went to St Joseph's Circuit Church, you thought you were a Sue Fark! At one time… they thought you were a foreigner, there was only a few Catholics in Holbrook, they had a hard time getting a Catholic Church in Holbrook… but us kids at school, we were all one, there were no differences no matter what you were, they were all alike, in fact we had a coloured [girl] at our school, and she was just the same as we were, she was a wonderful girl.

His life-long love of sport came back into the interview:

I tell you, we had a lot of fun… but we never broke windows.

We behaved ourselves, and we played ball all the time, we had a baseball, and we had a pair of skates, skatin' down here, playing hockey and baseball, our court in the back of the Sunday school. A couple of pine trees with a couple of hoops nailed to them, and then you had to buy the basketballs, by a penny a week. Holbrook didn't buy nothing.

My father, my brothers years ago, used to play football, we played on the first football team that Holbrook ever had. His picture was in the paper one time, he played full back. We had no gymnasium, nothing like that and the basketball where I went. I played ball with Randolph. I had a good lot of ball players from CYO Open in Holbrook High. I had a nice ball team and I think I won about three trophies, I got a St Joseph Trophy…a Quincy trophy. I got a Little League team, and I had them nine years. I used to have them practisin' four nights a week, so you see, they were so tired they couldn't do anything. [2]

By the 1920s, Bob had, apart from his passion for sports, built an enviable reputation as an outstanding car mechanic. He became a specialist in repairing and maintaining fabulous Stearns-Knight touring automobiles – vivid symbols of the Great Gatsby era. They were some of the biggest, most powerful and well-constructed cars of their day. Built for the well-to-do sporting motorist, they were favoured by kings, emperors, governments and wealthy industrialists.

The company had been founded in Cleveland, Ohio by Frank Balou Stearns in 1896. By 1902, it was producing a 20 horse-power model retailing at $3,000 dollars. Three years later a 40 horse-power model was selling for $4,000 dollars. In 1905, they introduced the striking white trim on the facade of the radiator shell, proclaiming their trademark slogan 'The White Line Radiator belongs to the Stearns'. The cars went on to capture numerous speed, hill climb and endurance trophies. In 1911, Stearns became the first US manufacturer to adopt the patented Knight sleeve-valve engine for the 1912 model. From that year on, the cars were known as Stearns-Knight. By 1917, over 3,000 cars were being produced annually including the powerful V-8 model.

Founder Frank Stearns had to retire due to ill-health in 1917, when the company was taken over by a new management. They took huge profits of the company while cutting back on investment in developing new models. Sales dwindled from almost 4,000 cars to 1920 to less than 700 in 1922. A new six-cylinder was introduced in 1923, and a smaller version in 1925, which only sold just 100 units in 1925. In spite of these diminishing sales, the Stearns-Knight of the late 1920s were considered amongst the highest quality cars of the day – King of the American Motor cars. The 1929 Stearns-Knight M America model was an exceptionally elegant, classic two-door sports machine with a six-cylinder sleeve valve engine, a folding soft roof and wire wheels. It literally epitomised the 'Roaring Twenties' era.[21]

Another poignant image later turned up amongst Robert Burns papers at 176 Center Street after his death in 1985, which I finally obtained from his nephew Owen Kiernan. The tinted colour image appeared to date from the early 1920s when Bob and Helene were dating. The photo, probably taken on one of their excursions to join the crowds at glorious Nantasket Beach on Higham Bay in one of Bob's borrowed Stearns-Knight open-top tourers, showed Helene wearing a typical short black, flapper-girl style outfit with dainty silver shoes on her feet. A red shawl was tied artistically around her shoulders, and a red bandana around her head. She stood close to Bob, his arm wrapped protectively around her waist.

Bob wore a black armless singlet and black shorts set off by a white belt; his hair worn in the 1920s fashion, parted in the centre, and cut tight above the ears. The relaxed, intimate pose, spoke volumes of their golden, halcyon days of the 1920s; redolent of beach parties and barbecues along the South Shore, girls in flapper skirts, young men in straw hats, the Charleston danced to the sounds of Dixieland Jazz bands. At twenty-two, Helene looked at though she had found Mr Right and the couple were looking forward to a happy life together. I felt that the image gave me a glimpse into their lives far from the estranged family back in Ireland. Another part of the jigsaw had fallen into place.

During my phone call to Bob back in 1982, he had mentioned that Helene's brother James had lived in upstate New York after serving in the First World War. I now wanted to learn what I could about his destiny and strove to recover glimpses of his life from archival obscurity. I discovered that James' life had also been marred by tragedy. His baptism certificate showed that James Henry Keough was born on 12 July 1889 at 7 P Street in South Boston and that he had been baptised at the old Gate of Heaven Church on Fourth Street, with his seventeen-year-old Irish-born aunt Delia and John Downing acting as sponsors. Like his siblings, James was also a true Southie, spending his formative years in the predominantly Irish enclave and attending school locally. He had grown up opposite M Street Park and probably remembered kicking a football with his little Irish cousin Reg, as an eleven year old. He was fourteen years old at the time of his uncle Michael's sad demise at Worcester. He would have witnessed his mother Mary Anne's grief and anguish on learning of the news of his uncle Michael in October 1903. He followed in his father's footsteps and had become a brass molder at Estabrook & Sons foundry nearby in South Boston.

When the Keough family left South Boston in late 1916, James Jnr moved out to Holbrook with them. By then, aged twenty-seven, he was living in a house at 25 Center Street when America declared war against Germany on 6 April 1917. This address was not far from where James Burns and his family were living at 176 Center Street and where his future brother-in-law Bob, had his first glimpse of an attractive young Keough sister, Helene, just eighteen, at that time.

Once war had been declared, the army attempted to mobilise troops very quickly. At that point, America had a standing army of 127,000 officers and soldiers. By the end of the war, 4 million men had served in the United States army, along with another 800,000 in other military branches. I was able to locate James' military file in the archives. It stated that James Henry Keough, of 25 Center Street, Holbrook, had enlisted in the US army in Rockland on 28 March 1918, when he was twenty-eight years old.[22] He gave his mother's name as 'Mary Keough'. Like his uncle Michael, and his long-forgotten cousin Reg back in Ireland, he had answered his Mongan clan ancestors traditional call to arms, in the service of America.

The American Expeditionary Force in the First World War was the first time in American history that the United States had sent soldiers abroad to defend foreign soil. In May 1917, after the declaration of war, General John Joseph 'Black Jack' Pershing had been designated the supreme commander of the American army in France. Pershing and his staff soon realised just how ill-prepared the United States was to transport vast numbers of soldiers, and their vital equipment to the front. In Europe, the battle-weary British and French troops, who had been in the frontline since August 1914, were in dire need of the relief the Americans were bringing to them. As there was a scarcity of ships to bring American troops to France, the army pressed into service any cruise ships they could find, seized German ships, and borrowed allied ships to transport the massive military contingent from New York, New Jersey and Virginia.[23] Among them was the USS *George Washington* with his cousin, coxswain Charles J. Mongan on board.

James initially served as private with the 151st Depot Brigade until 1 May 1918, when he was posted to the 58th Massachusetts Infantry Regiment. The regiment formed part of the Fourth (or Ivy) Division, under the command of Major Generals John L. Hine and M.L. Henry. On his shoulder was their famous insignia: a green four-leafed ivy in a circle, in a cross shape, superimposed on a square olive drab diamond. Now he was a Doughboy, a nickname American infantry men were proud of at the time. James Henry Keough, army serial No. 1. 686. 608, was now one of 500,000 US soldiers bound for France.[24]

Although the first American soldiers had set foot in Europe by June 1917, the force did not fully take part on the frontlines until October of that year. The First Division, one of the crack divisions of the American Expeditionary Force, then took up positions in the trenches at Nancy in France. Throughout 1917 and into 1918, American divisions were usually employed to augment French and British units in defending their lines and staging counter attacks on Germany positions. Early in May 1918, the United States troops had their first victory at Cantigny, as their AEF commanders gradually assumed sole control of American forces in combat. General Pershing continued to deploy US troops to help defend the Western Front during the Aisne offensive in May and at the Marne in June. US troops also took part in the allied attacks at Le Hamel and Canal du Nord. By July 1918, roles had been reversed as French forces were assigned to support their American allies in operations.[25]

The German-held St Mihiel salient was chosen for the US army's first offensive, when General Pershing assembled 500,000 troops at this sector in early September 1918. Alerted of the impending attack, the German High Command ordered a partial withdrawal of their troops. As the Germans began pulling out, the Americans pounced on 12 September. A parallel assault by 110,000 French troops took place three hours later, while over 1,400 aircraft supported the advancing US and French units. By 16 September, the entire St Mihiel salient was under allied control. During the Battle of St Mihiel, Pershing had been in command of the First American Army, comprising seven divisions and more than 500,000 men, in the largest offensive operation ever taken by US armed forces.

Col. George Mitchell had the monumental logistics task of bringing 400,000 troops from the successful St Mihiel Campaign to take part in the Meuse-Argonne offensive on 26 September 1918. The US army used more then 300 tanks and 500 aircraft from the United States Air Service to support the offensive. Two thirds of the advancing troops had arrived from St Mihiel and the exhausted soldiers only advanced 3 kilometres along the wide 64-kilometre front

An 1971 photo of (from left to right) Annie, Kate, Helene and Bob Burns, photographed outside the Burns homestead at 176 Center Street, Holbrook, MA, with grand-nephews Steven and Vincent Kiernan. (*Courtesy Robert Burns archives*)

on the first day. Progress slowed down, with the offensive coming to a halt on 30 September.

James was posted with the 58th Massachusetts Infantry Regiment with the Fourth Division, (part of the Third Corps) when they attacked on the first day of the Meuse-Argonne offensive on 26 September. In just twenty-four hours of the bloody fighting, they advanced 6.5 kilometres. They continued their offensive until 19 October, when the Fourth Division was relieved while holding the important Bois de la Core and Bois de Brieulles positions. The Meuse-Argonne offensive restarted on 4 October. The German army, many now suffering from a debilitating influenza epidemic, held out until 4 November, when they began to pull back.

Fresh US troops were moved to the front and had advanced 32 kilometres when the Armistice was declared on 11 November 1918. The Battle of Argonne had lasted from 27 September to 6 October 1918, during which time Pershing had commanded more then 1 million American and French troops and when allied forces had recovered more then 200 square miles of French territory from the German army.

In the immediate aftermath of the fierce fighting, James Keough, physically

The Keough family grave at St Mary's cemetery, Randolph, MA, where Irish-born James J. Keough, wife Mary Anne, two daughters, Josephine and Helene and Bob Burns lie buried.

and emotionally exhausted, was totally unaware of his Irish grand-aunt Mary Dignam's passing on 23 November, 1918 at Belvedere House, Mullingar.

By the time Germany signed the Armistice, the American Expeditionary Force had been transformed into a modern, battle-hardened army acknowledged as one of the best in the world. The United States had endured an estimated 360,000 casualties during the war, including 126,000 killed in action and 234,000 wounded. James Keough, with a little luck of the Irish, had come through physically unscathed, if emotionally marked for life, from the bloody two-year conflict.[26]

James returned to the United States where he received an honourable discharge at Camp Devens, Massachusetts, on 2 July 1919. His safe return was marked by an emotional reunion with his relieved mother Mary Anne, and retired father James, while his sisters Josephine and Helene hugged him joyfully. Helene's fiancé Bob, stuck a beer in his hand and welcomed him back to civilian life.

No doubt, James was among the happy guests at Helene and Bob's wedding on 17 July 1925. He must have rejoiced that his youngest sister finally, after such a prolonged engagement, was getting hitched to the man in her life. He had witnessed the family's joy when Helene announced she was pregnant in April 1928 and was delighted when the couple's first child was born on 6 January 1929. After the tragic death of infant Mary Eileen on 25 March 1929, James provided support and tender brotherly love as the devastated couple mourned their loss. He then endured further heartache with the death of his beloved mother Mary Anne.

James H. Keough's veteran's file showed that he went to live in New Jersey, at 608 Hudson Street, in Hoboken, just across the Hudson opposite Manhattan, where he was working as supervisor in a laundry business in the early 1930s. By then he was married himself, to a widow called Stashia Mae, who provided him with a little step-daughter, Beatriz. His veteran's file contained a number of letters in his own spiky handwriting. He had applied for a $1,000 dollar United States Government Life Insurance in August 1930, and during his medical check-up the examiner noted that he was 5 feet 9 inches tall and weighed 173 pounds. By 1934, James had moved the business to 311 Washington Street in Hoboken and then moved across the Hudson to New York in February 1935.[27]

His wife, Anastasia 'Stashia' Mae Cable, hailed from upstate New York. She was a native of Spring Valley, a small village near Ramapo, at the foot of the picturesque Ramapo Mountains, south of Lake Sabago. A country girl, she had been employed as a laundress in private homes. On their rare weekends off, she brought James up by train to meet her father Charles, from nearby Arden village, and her mother Harriet, a native of Hewitt, N.J. near Wanaque Reservoir.

As the Great Depression began to loosen it stranglehold on the American economy, their laundry business picked up. James, Stashia and Beatriz moved into a fashionable apartment at 1125 Grand Concourse in the Bronx around 1937.[28] Between 1900 and 1930, the resident population of the Bronx shot up from 200,000 to 1.2 million inhabitants, almost 50 per cent of whom were Jews, who commuted to work in Manhattan. The new Grand Concourse development, inspired by Paris' great Champs Elysées boulevard, had been completed in 1914. By the 1920s, the Fordham-Grand Concourse intersection had become a thriving commercial hub; a centre of tree-lined avenues, with luxurious homes, and apartments designed in the latest art deco and modernist styles. The new housing development on Bronx Main Street had featured, for the first time, the most up-to-date facilities – private bathrooms, central heating, hot water and air conditioning. For James, it was a stark contrast to his childhood memories of growing up at 21 M Street in South Boston. Nearby, stood such landmarks as Fordham University, the famed Yankee Stadium, home to the New York Yankees, and Lowe's 4,000-seater theatre, built for $4 million in 1929.[29]

James and Stashia Mae were living at the Grand Concourse complex in the

Bronx in early 1938, when they decided to take a trip out to western Massachusetts.

I wondered whether or not they might have been on a trip out to visit his enigmatic seventy-eight-year-old aunt Bridget, who may have been living at Holyoke, near Springfield, at the time. His cousin James Mongan had visited Springfield with his son Reg back in 1900, possibly to visit the same aunt. The 1920 US census had shown a Bridget Monaghan (another misspelling?) running a boarding house in Holyoke at that time. On Sunday, 13 February 1938, they were heading westwards past Worcester, scene of Michael's death, when, in the growing dusk, with heavy sleet impeding visibility, when the hand of destiny intervened into their lives.

The Southbridge Evening News on Monday, 14 February 1938, reported the horrific details of the accident:

FIVE PERSONS HURT IN CHARLTON CRASH.
New York and Springfield cars collide Head-on near Tiberii's Stand.
Five persons were injured, four of them seriously in a head-on collision late yesterday afternoon near Tiberii's roadside stand not far from Charlton City. All were brought to Harrington hospital and today, one had been discharged, one was on the danger list and the other three remained in serious condition. Mr and Mrs Howard Hilliker of Springfield, aged 34 and 31, respectively, were riding in one auto and Mr and Mrs James Keough, both 44, of New York City were riding in the second machine. Also riding in the Hilliker vehicle was David Labeau, 18, of Aldenville, who had been given a ride by the couple about ten minutes before the crash. He was given emergency treatment for injuries to his right arm and left knee.

Mrs Keough is the most seriously injured. She is on the danger list at the hospital and is suffering with fractures of both legs, a fractured left wrist, lacerations over her right eye, and possible internal injuries. Mr Keough fractured both knees and has lacerations of the face.

Mrs Hilliker has a fractured jawbone, possible fractured right wrist, injured right leg, and lacerations to the face. Mr Hilliker suffered face and leg lacerations and possible internal injuries. State patrolman Edward Eidt of the Brookfield police barracks is investigating the crash. Mr Hilliker, police said, was driving on the car heading east and Mr Keough was operating the machine headed in the opposite direction. Mr and Mrs Keough were taken to hospital in the Town ambulance and Mr and Mrs Hilliker and the Labeau youth were brought to the institution by passersby.[30]

On Tuesday, 15 February, a further report was published in the newspaper:

WOMAN INJURED IN ACCIDENT DEAD
Mrs Stashia Keough, 48, of New York died today at Harrington Memorial

Hospital of injuries received in an auto accident in Charlton near Toberii's roadside stand.

She sustained fractures of both legs, a fractured left wrist, lacerations over her right eye, and possible internal injuries. Her name was placed on the danger list when she was taken to hospital. The car in which she was riding with her husband, James Keough, collided with a car driven by Howard Hilliker of Springfield. Mr Keough is also a patient at the hospital where he is being treated for fractured knees and lacerations to the face. His condition was reported improved today.[31]

Shocked by the horrific news, Helene and Josephine rushed out by train from Boston to be at their brother's bedside in the Harrington Memorial Hospital. In the aftermath of his wife's death, James, agonisingly immobile with both knees fractured, was unable to attend her funeral. Helene and Josephine were there to pay their last respects, along with Stashia's daughter Beatriz Cable. Stashia's body was brought back to her home village of Spring Valley, near Ramapo, and laid to rest at Brick Church Cemetery. An obituary was inserted in the *New York Times* to inform friends and neighbours of the sad news.[32]

James spent two and a half months recovering in hospital until released on 1 May 1938. He had to face into a long painful and arduous rehabilitation process to learn to walk again. His step-daughter, Beatriz, wrote to the Veteran's Administration in Washington DC on 21 February 1938, to inform them of the situation:

Dear Sir, I am writing to you about Mr James Keough of 1125 Grand Concourse, New York, New York. Mr and Mrs James Keough met with an accident Sunday, February 13, 1938. Mrs Keough died from her injuries February 15. Mr Keough was also injured and is confined in the Harrington Memorial Hospital, Southbridge, Mass. and expects to be there for some time. Mr Keough has asked me to take care of his insurance until he can come home from hospital. I am Mr Keough's step-daughter.

I am sorry I cannot get his signature as you request on your change of address slip. If there is any doubt of sending the receipts to me, write Mr Keough at the Harrington Hospital, Southridge, Mass. But he is going to make his home in Spring Valley, N.Y. Yours truly, Mrs Claude Curtis.[33]

James had to spend a long convalescence at Harrington before recovering from his injuries. His morale would have hit rock bottom on hearing of his beloved wife Stashia's death.

He needed his closest family around him to give solace in his pain, loss and self-recrimination. At that time his sister Helene was living in Quincy, south of Boston, and she immediately stepped in to help. On being discharged from hospital, James went to live at Helene's home. From 65 Greenleaf Street, he wrote, in his idiosyncratic spiky hand, to his insurance company:

> Dear Sir, I was in an automobile accident in February, and I have not been able to take care of my business till now. If there is anything due on my insurance I would like this opportunity to pay it up immediately. My wife was killed in the accident and I would like the beneficiary changed to my sister Ms Helene Burns, 65 Grassleaf St, Quincy, Mass. Very truly yours, James H. Keough.[34]

By 23 August 1938, with Helene's nurturing and encouragement, his health had improved, and James relocated to his deceased wife's town in upstate New York, and was living with his step-daughter Beatriz, at 15 Johnson Street in Spring Valley, N.Y.

As part of Ramapo, Spring Valley village was located 27 miles north of New York City, at exit 14 off the New York State highway. Lying at the foot of a rugged mountainous region, the area had been developed by Scottish settlers who originally called it 'Scotland'. In 1823, the district had one store and a public house, and had become the centre of activities for a large area. The Scotland Post Office was established on 29 December 1827 and, by 1870 Spring Valley had 1,500 inhabitants. Spring Valley was finally incorporated on 9 July 1902. Dairy farmers later successfully petitioned the Erie Railroad for a freight stop so they could speed their milk into New York. As its waters were highly reputed for their purity, Spring Valley was to gain fame as a popular health resort area, as its elevation at 500 feet was thought to be both invigorating and beneficial. The extensive Memorial Park an ideal retreat for swimming, basketball and other sports activities, while some fifty hotels sprang up to cater for the needs of visiting New Yorkers.[35]

Initially, James moved into 15 Johnson Street with his step-daughter and her husband Claude Curtis in 1938 and then, from September 1939, had his own two-storey wooden-frame home at 9 Johnson Street, off Maple Avenue.

From then on, aged forty-five, he spent the next twenty active years working as a 'vulcaniser' retreading car tyres with the Henry Kulle Tyre Co. on Main Street. His sisters Helene and Josephine came up on summer weekends to escape torrid New York heat and humidity over the years. With picnics and barbeques, they soon became close friends of his step-daughter Beatriz and her husband Claude.

When James was sixty-seven, he suffered a fatal stroke on 21 May 1957, and was buried next to his wife at Brick Church Cemetery. His veteran's file showed that his sister Josephine had made a successful application to have an United States flag draped on his coffin of her brother, a veteran of the First World War. They watched through their tears as his last remains were lowered into the earth.

Once again, Helene stepped into the breach to handle the funeral arrangements. By then she was living in New York at 315 West 74th Street on the trendy

Upper West Side with her sister Josephine. She settled the $1,092 funeral expenses and then had to write to claim the costs against her brother's insurance policy:

> Dear Sir, In regards to my brother's (James H. Keough) insurance, I have the policy which is dated to May 1931, and made out to his wife, it reads as follows: Beneficiary: Stashia Mae Keough, his wife, one sum. His wife died in 1938 and then he made me the beneficiary. He intended this for his funeral expenses I am sure. He was buried from the Allen B. Sniffen Funeral Home, Spring Valley, N.Y. I paid Mr Sniffen in full the sum of $1,070 on May 22nd the day before the funeral. You may verify this either by writing to Mr Sniffen or I could send you both the policy and the receipts bill here with. Please return them to me. Thank you. Yours very truly, Helene Burns.[36]

I also tried to follow up the leads on James' step-daughter Beatriz. I learned that she survived him until 1989, and was buried next to her husband Claude, who had passed away in 1969, in Brick Church Cemetery. The trail had come to a dead end – or so I thought.

In May 2001, I received a small padded envelope in the post from a newly found Kiernan relative on Cape Cod. It contained the last poignant personal effects of James Henry Keough, recovered among the documents found at 176 Center Street in Holbrook before it was demolished in 1999. A copy of his birth certificate confirmed that he had been born at 806 East Third Street in South Boston (on the corner of 7 P Street); a $200 dollar invoice from Dr Ralph S. Perkins MD for professional services to Mr and Mrs James Keough on 13 February 1938 had survived; and a $57.56 dollar Harrington Memorial Hospital x-ray bill. All these items had been preserved as a poignant memory, by his sister Helene and her husband Bob in Holbrook.

Two metal dog-tags with 'James H. Keough' stamped on the surface along with his army serial number – 1686608 – told the story of his military service. The rainbow-coloured ribbon of his First World War Victory Medal with battle clasps brought into sharp focus his time on the battlefield in the Aisne-Marne Somme Defensive Sector and the St Mihiel-Meuse-Argonne action.

On the reverse side raised lettering spelled out the words: 'The Great War for Civilisation'. All these items had been preserved as a family souvenirs by Helene and Bob in Holbrook. They honoured the life of Mary Anne Keough's son and nephew of his ill-fated uncle Lance-Corporal Michael J. Mongan. James had served his new country with valour and distinction – for me another part of the quest had been completed.

16

Helene Burns. A West Side story

At the time of her brother James' death in May 1957, Helene and her sister Josephine were living at 315 West 74th Street, on the trendy Upper West Side in New York.[1] To my utter surprise, I learned that, from around 1950, Helene had been employed with the United Nations based in the tall, slim skyscraper at United Nations Plaza, at First Avenue and 46th Street on the East Side.[2]

She had initially worked with the UN Special Fund, later amalgamated in 1965 to form part of the United Nations Development Fund which administered funds for resource exploration, combating desertification, technological developments and volunteers, and collaborating with other UN-associated agencies.

As a major global organisation, there was a constant stream of visiting foreign dignitaries to the UNDP headquarters for conferences, meetings and other official business. Helene's work as a social secretary at the UNDP, meant she organised travel and social arrangements for visiting delegates, scheduling their meetings with various department heads, spending much time on the phones every day, resolving planning details, co-ordinating diary appointments, booking flights, restaurants, limousines and getting the right people to right official receptions at the right time. Her experience as a chief phone operator at Filene's Store back in the late 1920s must have served her well, along with her soft-spoken, demure, unflappable, well-mannered 'lace-curtain Irish' persuasive diplomatic skills. Her days must have been hectic when a major international conference was being held at the UNDP, with hundreds of dignitaries arriving en masse.

In the evenings, she would walk back to the West 74th Street apartment in the faded glory of an elegant 1880s brownstone mansion near the Hudson river.

The Upper West Side stretched from 59th Street to 125th Street and was bounded by Central Park on the east, and the Hudson river on the west. The area was home to such venerable New York landmarks as the American Museum of Natural History, Colombia University, the Cathedral of St John the Divine, the Dakota Apartments and the Lincoln Center (in 1959).[3]

The district had been gentrified from the 1870s onwards as high-rise brownstone buildings shot up on the West End, and real estate investors backed major projects like the Dakota and San Remo buildings. Colombia University had relocated from the East Side to Morningside Heights in the 1890s, moving into the former grounds of the Bloomingdale Lunatic Asylum. As part of this burdgeoning intellectual and artistic trend, Colombia enhanced an already stimulating cultural life in the area. By the early 1900s, artists and academics were sharing the neighbourhood with a diverse ethnic population.

The Upper West Side was home to a wide array of exotic ethnic restaurants, delicatessens, markets, shops, cafes, bars and markets, catering to a Bohemian melting pot of New Yorkers. Although once perceived as a largely Jewish neighbourhood, an influx of African-Americans from the Southern States, Puerto Ricans, Dominicans and Haitians, along with Russians and Ukranians in the 1940s and 1950s – and another wave of Cubans, Puerto Ricans and Dominicans in the 1960s, kept the demographic melting pot on the boil.

Due to this wide diversity, the area developed a liberal and relaxed attitude to life. It had maintained a sense of community, where artists, writers, musicians and young families, could find relatively low-rent housing, and a neighbourhood spirit. Clearance of the sprawling slum area was at the centre of a furious debate as major urban renewal, pioneered by Robert Moses, which began in the mid-1950s, making way for the Lincoln Center in 1959.[4]

Helene and Josephine lived in the exotic and colourful Upper West Side for some two decades from the early 1950s. Over the years, Helene's ever-faithful husband Bob made periodic trips up from Holbrook to visit, but he was a small-town hero and living in New York was not an option.

On Saturday mornings, the sisters strolled over to Central Park, sat on a bench and fed the ducks. They talked about their long-deceased parents Mary Anne and James and their Southie childhood now so distant.

They were aware that their cousins Charles and Mary, Southie-

Helene Burns and her sister Josephine resided in this 1880s brownstone apartment building at 315 W 74th Street on Manhattan's trendy Upper West Side in the 1950s and 1960s. After Josephine's death in 1971 she returned to Holbrook, MA, where she lived with her husband Bob Burns and his two sisters Kate and Annie until her death in 1976. (*Photo Padraig O'Curry*) born like themselves, were still living in Cambridge, but they still didn't maintain any contact with them because of the circumstances of their uncle Michael's death.

They talked about visiting Ireland and touring around the Lakes of Killarney to admire the verdant landscapes of their ancestors. A nostalgic trip to their roots, quaffing a pint of Guinness, savouring an Irish stew or kissing the Blarney Stone, it all seemed so romantic. Their mother Mary Anne had told them stories of growing up with her sisters and brothers at Railway Terrace in Mullingar but any thought of visiting their mother's hometown, and maybe finding relatives, quickly caused any plans they did have to evaporate quickly. All those ideas were forbidden territory now. They had fast-fading memories of their little Irish cousin Reg who had played with them in M Street Park when he came to America in 1900. So far away now. They had no idea that Reg was still alive and well and living in Dublin at that point.

I had made my first trip to America from Paris in 1967, landing in a sweltering New York on 1 August. I found a room at a small centrally located budget hotel (which meant no air-conditioning) – The *Pickwick Arms* at 50th and Lexington Avenue. In the muggy, humid heat, I explored the city's famous tourist sights: the Empire State building, the Guggenheim, Museum of Modern Art, Soho, Greenwich Village artist's quarter, Washington Square and hip local jazz clubs. Many steamy nights were spent at the ultimate in-spot, Max's Kansas City, the trendy watering hole for emerging artists, writers, musicians, the New York underground where Andy Wharhol and Lou Reed reigned over their court of creative wild men. Located at 213 Park Avenue, between 17th and 18th streets, off Union Square, it lay, electric and eclectic, at the centre of the universe where 'the rules were being rewritten, molds being broken, trends being set, a cultural exchange centre overflowing with big names and aspiring nobodies'. Nobody cared that the food was so-so and the wine cheap and cheerful. Mickey Ruskin (1933–83) had created a unique setting where artists, writers and musicians ruled, attracting a motley crew of future superstars such as Robert Rauchenberg, David Bowie, Jimi Hendrix, Dennis Hopper, Truman Capote, James Baldwin, Barnett Newman, Brian Epstein, William Burroughs, John Lennon, Janis Joplin, Jim Morrison, Peter O'Toole, Jane Fonda, Bobby Kennedy, Sargent Shriver, Michaelangelo Antonioni, Verouska, Allan Ginsberg, William Burroughs, Loulou de la Falaise… a boundless inventory of creative genius; fuelled by drugs, sex and the wildest artistic possibilities.[5]

At that point in my life, aged twenty-nine, I had still had little interest in my Irish background, having come to the United States to view it from a French or, more exactly, Parisian perspective. I had travelled to New York with Paris advertising friends and Irish family connections were nowhere in my mind. I was far more interested in living for the moment, in the arts world, in jazz, and the effervescent non-stop New York club scene. Never for a moment did it cross my mind that I actually had close American family relatives actually living in the city. They were only a few blocks away at 315 West 74th Street. I might have passed them on the street without having the slightest idea who they were. In a city of 8 million souls, they would have just been another two anonymous faces in the crowd. As far as family connections were concerned, I was on another planet – it was a case of missed opportunities, my mind not attuned to those possibilities.

I also spent some time doing the rounds of the major advertising agencies; Young and Rubicam, J. Walter Thompson, Doyle Dane Bernbach, Lord Geller & Frederico, with my portfolio of work, just testing the waters as to whether I was good enough to find work there. However, I had already had been hooked by the attractions of the Parisian lifestyle, the architecture, the food, the wine, the cafés and Les Parisiennes. To my romantic mind, it had much more to offer than pressurised, frantic, dirty New York, all geared to doing deals, business-based and money-driven. I found it exciting and stimulating yet, compared to Paris or San Francisco, too crowded, unyielding and impersonal, where everybody was in a hurry. That constant striving, relentless pressures, allied to the climatic extremes, soon decided me against seriously seeking work there. The overpowering heat and 100 per cent humidity made it feel like I was living in a steam bath during the meltdown highs of the summer months. It left you gasping for breath and needing a shower every hour. I soon realised that any sensible New Yorker who could, fled to the Hamptons for refreshing sea breezes or stayed put inside their air-conditioned, refrigerated sky-scrapers.

I showed my portfolio to several agencies and even got two jobs offers – one with the ABC TV channel another with a leading pharmaceutical advertising agency – though I was reassured that my work was of a sufficiently high professional standard to find my place in the world's advertising capital, but after a month, I'd had enough. My beautiful Paris beckoned. So not only did I reject the seductive sirens of the city that never sleeps, but I had also missed the opportunity of possibly encountering my grand-aunt Mary Anne's two surviving daughters living on the Upper West Side. I did, eventually, return to work in New York in 1970 where I collaborated as a designer with James Fenton & Associates on Fifth Avenue, not far from Central Station. At that point, I still ignored that my grand-aunt Mary Anne's daughter Helene was still living only a few blocks away, and working with the UNDP at United Nations Plaza. Frustratingly close, but I was in a Parisian frame of mind. Any searching for lost American cousins had not even entered my mind. Destiny was working against me.

Helene's UNDP career came to an end with her retirement around 1963 when she turned sixty-five years old. The sisters continued to live at their 315 West 74th Street address during the 1960s. Then, in 1971, Josephine, aged eighty-four, passed away with her young sister at her side. She was returned to Holbrook and interred with her parents at St Mary's cemetery, in Randolph, attended by Bob and his two sisters. Now Helene, at sixty-nine, was alone; like a homing pigeon, she decided to return to her husband Bob in Holbrook. She took up residence with him and his two sisters, Annie and Kate, at the old Burns homestead at 176 Center Street. Rick McGaughey, Bob's friend and football pupil from his coaching days, recalled how, 'Helene just turned up at 176 Center Street one day unannounced and moved back in with Bob and his two sisters. She was as quiet as a mouse.'[6]

Bob Burns' nephew, Dr Owen Kiernan, was a regular visitor to 176 Center Street around that time:

> When Helene arrived back permanently – it was many years after I left Randolph – she had gained weight and had naturally taken on a more elderly appearance. At the time Annie served as chief cook and bottle-washer, with no help from the others. She started her day at 5:00 a.m. and retired after the others at 10:00 p.m. In winter, her last chore was to douse the kitchen fire (they were all fearful of fires). After years of trying the Kiernan brothers finally put in a hot water heater. They had been concerned that the pilot light flame would start a fire while they were sleeping. In all my visits over those years, I never saw Helene do any housework or chores, and yet Annie was happy doing everything – she was an excellent cook.
>
> In spite of her quiet personality, she handled her communication job very well. Helene would have been the last person in the world to enjoy the rough, cacophonous environment of the Boston Garden Bruins games or the stadium used by the New York Giants football games. Yet, she always went along with Bob. I mentioned their late summer visits (in the 1920s) to the Giants training camp at Bear Mountain, NY, on the Hudson river.[7]

Owen sent me a photo of Bob, Helene and his two sisters when they celebrated Bob's eightieth birthday in 1971, showing them sitting on the sunlit porch at the side of the house. Helene had her hand placed affectionately on Bob's knee. Helene regularly played whist with her sister-in-law Kate, while Annie busied herself in her role of housekeeper and cook. Cousins and nephews visited regularly; Owen Kiernan, with his sons, dropped over to liven up their existence. I recovered a more recent photo showed a grey-haired seventy-three year old Helene, together with husband Bob in his baseball hat, Annie and Kate, along with Kiernan grand-nephews Steven and Vincent, standing in front of 176 Center Street in 1971.

Vincent Kiernan, Dr Owen's nephew, later recalled visits to the old Burns homestead after Helene had returned to live there:

That must have been when I came out of boot camp, after I joined the navy. I came out of the service in 1974, so I'm sure I did go back [there]. Yeah, she was a quiet lady. We just remembered stories of her. Bob and Helene used to go out to Nantasket Beach, that was Lovers Lane. I recall she was a very successful woman and had left [Holbrook]. She went off to New York, and then came back fifty years later. I do remember that she showed back up and Bob was quite in love again, which [I thought] was a little odd. I don't remember Bob ever leaving Holbrook, actually, he wasn't much of a traveller. But my father, he's been dead for many years, he would have known. Bob was an automobile mechanic, and was big into sports. My father used to say, when the cars came in they never left!.[8]

Helene spent her last years in Holbrook where she and Bob were together again at 176 Center Street. I wondered if their conversation occasionally had turned to the sad memories of their lost baby girl Eileen, and how different things might have been if she had lived. Helene's health finally began to decline and she entered Franvale Nursing Home in nearby Braintree, where she died, at seventy-eight, on 7 December 1976, and was buried next to her Irish-born parents at St Mary's cemetery in Randolph. Then, in 1981, Annie suddenly died, followed by her sister Kate two days later. In spite of these bereavements and ensuing solitude, Bob, now ninety, and with failing sight, preferred to continue living alone in the old Burns' homestead, with his cousin Mary Elen McLaughlin coming over regularly to take care of him.

His final years were spent there, his backyard still filled with rusting Buicks and Packards awaiting his mechanical talents to being them back to life. He became wary of prowlers on the property and threatened to shoot any intruders who strayed on to his property. Visiting friends had to identify themselves before he would put away his shotgun. Finally, in 1985, Bob, aged ninety-four, gave his last breath and passed away. He joined his wife Helene and her family in the grave at St Mary's cemetery, Randolph. Shortly afterwards, the 176 Center Street property was demolished for redevelopment. These were precious glimpses of the long-lost generations in America. Piece by piece the mosaic of the lost lives was taking shape.

By early 2000, I felt I had accumulated enough research to make a return pilgrimage to Boston. I wanted to see if I could locate any of the homes where Michael and his sisters had lived out their lives. After almost a century, it was time to try to reconnect with any living relatives in America. Filled with hopeful anticipation and some trepidation, I flew in to Logan airport in October 2000.

During the summer of 1999 in Dingle, I had spotted an American visitor wearing a T-shirt with 'South Boston' emblazoned on it. I immediately approached him and told him about my research for lost family members in his hometown. Jake Manning, a strapping, fair-haired, freckled, thirty-five-year-old Irish-American was a true Southie and generously offered to help. He passed me his card and e-mail address and said to contact him when I was coming over. So, true to his word, when I came through the baggage area Jake was there to welcome me. Now I had a friendly guide to the city.

Jake kindly drove me across a rain-swept, traffic congested city caught up in bottlenecks caused by the gigantic 'Big Dig' construction works to build a traffic tunnel right under Boston. We arrived in Cambridge where I had booked a room at Jean O'Hara's B&B on Leonard Avenue, close to Harvard. There I was received by a charming, warm New England hostess, who immediately made me feel at home – just like a visiting cousin from the 'Ould Sod'. She plied me with tea and we chatted away until the jetlag started to kick-in and I decided to call it a day.

Next morning, I checked my map and saw I was quite close to several addresses in Cambridge where Michael's woes had begun almost a century before. I hopped into a taxi and gave the driver the address at 86 Kinnaird Street.

I wondered if this was a wild goose chase. Had the building even survived over all those years? We drove down narrow leafy streets in the bright autumn sunshine and, as the taxi slowed, I saw the building. Amazing. Nothing had changed since Michael problems had started there in May 1900. It was uncanny; it felt like I was stepping on to an imaginary film set. Pure serendipity.

I hopped out and started to film and take photographs of the street. I went up close to film the number 86 plate on the wall. The house was a small wooden, two-storey building, painted in a blue-grey, with the window frames picked out in white, a garden and yard at the back. Had Reg played there with his cousins Charles and Mary back in 1900? Questions swirled around in my mind about what happened in this house on the corner of a pleasant, quiet, leafy street.

I was intrigued to see that all the surrounding buildings, mostly dating from the 1880s, had survived 'progress' and demolition. The house formed the corner block of Kinnaird and Bay streets. I walked around into Bay Street, where I found the separate entrance to No. 32, exactly on the opposite side of the building. I stared at the front door. This was where Michael, with Maria, Charles and Mary (Minnie) had lived, with Maria's parents next door on the first floor of the building. Almost a century later, nothing had changed whatsoever; the house, the street, the streetscape, all had survived destruction in an otherwise ever-changing American landscape. I later discovered the reason: the whole district was a protected heritage site, preserving these buildings against any future developments.

I was amazed. After nearly one hundred years, nothing had changed. I listened at the front door, but the house was silent. No one at home. I thought of knocking on the door to make enquiries, but hesitated. The present owners would probably know nothing.

I decided not to disturb any neighbours with enquiries about the Mongans or Hurds; too much time had lapsed since John Hurd had passed away in 1937. But I was greatly reassured that the building had survived. I took more photos, mentally absorbing the dimensions of the house, the peaceful, sun-filled, leafy street, to burn it on to my brain. This was where Michael's dramatic downward spiral had begun.

While the taxi waited, I walked farther up the street looking for 112 Kinnaird Street, where Michael's widow Maria had lived with Charles and Mary from the 1920s until her death in 1936. At first, I could not find No. 112. I walked up and down past No. 110 but could not see No. 112. Then I realised that, in fact, Nos 110 and 112 were in the same building, with two separate entrances side by side. I spied the second entrance door with the numerals '112' over the left hand doorway. It was a large three-storey, clapper-board wooden building, with its '1882' construction date marked on a front panel. Its light-blue paintwork, high-lighted by white window frames, gleamed in the bright sunlight. It was in very good condition, obviously well-maintained, and had endured the passage of time relatively unscathed – though I was just startled to discover it had survived at all. I had reconnected with the exact locations of Michael and Maria's family drama as though frozen in time. The physical surroundings of their dark days were still in place a century afterwards. I took more photos and filmed the silent building.

The street remained quiet in the bright autumn sunlight, the russet gold of the leaves contrasting with the pastel tone of the buildings. I was still stunned that the streetscape I was standing in had remained practically so intact Michael, in panic, had left 32 Bay Street at 4 o'clock in that fateful morning on 16 May 1900. History seemed to have stood still, as if waiting for me to come and discover the location of the drama for myself. I felt like a forensic historical detective, combing the street for evidence of the tragic event. As Michael's grand-nephew, it had taken three generations for someone to seek out the truth. I knew it had been preordained. Deep down my inner young boy was smiling. He had been right to lure me 3,000 miles across the Atlantic to resolve the enigma. I could hardly believe I was there – yet fate had preserved the evidence.

Next morning, Jake picked me up at the B&B and we drove south through the delightfully wooded South Shore region through Braintree and Weymouth to Holbrook. At the Town Hall on South Franklin Street, I went in to talk with the town clerk, Shirley Austin, with whom I had corresponded during my research. Unfortunately, she was out, but the staff took me around the building to meet some people who had known Bob Burns, notably the town surveyor Frank Smith, who greeted me like a lost friend. He suggested I talk with town historian Wes Coty farther up on Union Street.

Michael J. Mongan moved from 21 M Street, South Boston, to Cambridge, MA, in 1898, where he lived in this two-story, wooden-frame house, on the corner of 86 Kinnaird Street and 32 Bay Street (above), not far from Central Square. He lived there with his wife Maria, children Charles and Mary Elizabeth, on the ground floor, while his in-laws, Elisha and Hannah Hurd, lived on the first floor. The house, now a classified building, still stands on the site.

The separate entrance to 86 Kinnaird Street, Cambridge, where Michael J. Mongan's Hurd in-laws lived during the period of family conflict from 1898 to 1903.

We drove over to the house where we were welcomed by Wes and his wife. Their home was a veritable treasure trove of militaria – old uniforms, plumed cavalry helmets, swords and flags covered the walls. His wife's fascinating doll collection took up any remaining available space. Wes was very knowledgeable, having research and written several books on the Holbrook's early history. He filled me in with details of the of the old Burns' property at 175 Center Street, confirming that it had been torn down just a year before in 1999. He even produced an intriguing photo of the house taken in 1905, showing Bob Burns' mother, Elizabeth Hamilton, from Westmeath, standing in the doorway. Now I began to have a much clearer vision of the man Helene had married. On leaving Wes, we drove around the town as I strove to capture all the charming small-town American athmosphere of the area; detached, well-kept wooden clapper-board houses, tidy gardens, surrounded by the russet shades of the New England woods. More elements of my quest were falling into place.

Back in Boston the next day, I met up with my long-time researcher Ed Hines. Although he was a busy professional civil engineer with a major Boston construction company, married to an estate agent called Betsy, with three grown daughters, Ed had a passionate interest in Irish-American historical research that filled any spare moments he could snatch from a tight schedule. We sped off in his 4x4 from my guesthouse on Leonard Street heading for St Paul's cemetery in Arlington, just north of Cambridge on a pilgrimage to the last resting place of Michael J. Mongan, his courageous and intrepid sister, Elizabeth, and her daughter Eliza (Elsie). For over eighty years, his grave had remained unmarked and perhaps deliberately forgotten. Back in 1987, four years after I had learned of Michael's tragic end at Worcester, I had organised to have a headstone erected over the grave. Now, I was eager to see it for the first time.

St Paul's Cemetery in Arlington was located off Alewife Brook Parkway, less than a mile from Fresh Water Pond, near where Michael had been picked up by a Cambridge police officer in May 1900. At first, Ed, who had helped with the erecting of the gravestone, could not recall exactly where the grave was located. He had a general idea of the area but we were unable to pinpoint it exactly. We tramped up and down intensely scrutinising the rows of headstones. No luck. I began to panic at the idea of not being able to find it after coming all the way across the wide Atlantic.

Worried we called at the guardian's office but no one was there. We even called the Boston Archdiocese office to no avail. We doggedly continued out

After Michael J. Mongan's death at Worcester State Hospital on 5 October 1903, his resourceful sister Elizabeth Edgerly immediately bought a grave plot at St Paul's Cemetery in Arlington, MA, not far from her home at 29 Reservoir Street, Cambridge. Michael, his sister Elizabeth, and her daughter Elsie all now lie buried at St Paul's.

search until, almost despairing, we finally stumbled on it. The grave was located away from the main burial sector, on the edge of the cemetery, next to the small Alewife Brook stream, towards the Turnpike side. I wondered if this had been unconsecrated ground at the time of Michael's burial. However, his sister and niece were buried there too. It lay at the foot of an elegant American oak, in a most appropriate setting. The stone had been perfectly executed following exactly the design I had sent.

At the top of the stone, they had carved the Mongan arms, which I had retrieved from Spain, borne by the last member of the Spanish branch – Don Vincente Mongan Losada, an officer who had served twenty years with the Spanish army in Cuba, until his death in La Corunna in May 1913. The arms had come full circle. They had been carried to Spain by Mongan trooper in Col. Nugent's Regiment of Horse around 1710, who had served with a handpicked detachement of forty-five officers and men who sailed with the Pretender, James Edward Stuart, to Scotland in December 1715 and again March 1719. Following the failed Jacobite rebellions, he returned to Spain where his descendants settled near Orense, in Galicia, and married into the aristocratic Losada family, Lords of Quiroga Valley, and Condes of Bornos. Finally regranted to the Irish branch in 1984, they now adorned Michael's last resting place in America.

Tres gavilanes de oro, three golden sparrow-hawks on a field of gules, red, with a border of fourteen elements, red and yellow, seven on each side. Like his Spanish kinsman, Michael also descended in direct line from Brian Mungan, the Titulado, probable last recognised clan chief in 1659. I crouched down to read the inscription, with the initial part in Gaelic lettering.

O Mongaín i Baile Uí Mongaín
MICHAEL J. MONGAN
The O Mongan of Monganstown
Chief of the Name
Mullingar, Ireland
(1863-1903)
ELIZABETH MONGAN EDGERLY
(1872-1925)
ELSIE E. EDGERLY
(1896-1956)

I had given Michael back the ancient Gaelic aristocratic designation 'Chief of the Name' of his O Mongan of Monganstown clan, attempting to heal the wound caused by his tragic last act. Here lay Michael, doomed head of the family in America, along with his brave sister Elizabeth and her daughter Elsie, their names etched in black in the grey granite. I hoped his tortured soul could now rest in peace. It was another milestone in my quest.

The next day was Colombus Day and a national holiday in America. The weather had turned cold, damp and grey to suit my somber mood. I took the train from South Station for Abington. After a thirty-minute journey through a thickly wooded area, I arrived at Abington station. Outside the station, I found a taxi and headed for 33 Charles Street. Here, again, I was foraying into the unknown, hoping that the house where Michael's sister had lived with her Irish-born husband David Aherne, had survived. I began filming as we drove along until I saw the road sign for Charles Street appear.

We turned into the street and, suddenly, there it was – No. 33. Amazing. I paid off the taxi and began taking photos of the building. After a few minutes, the owner stepped out and I explained why I was there. He had thought I was maybe interested in buying the house!

David Evans told me something of the history of the building, a typical wooden-frame two-storey structure, probably built in the 1890s, like most of the houses in the area. He couldn't recall ever hearing about the Aherne family, who had lived there until the late 1930s. As we talked, a neighbour opposite, John Minihane, stepped out to say hello. I told him of my research, little realising that his wife, Mary was, in fact, a secretary with an living Aherne relative.

Another part of the jigsaw had fallen into place with the discovery of the old David and Catherine Aherne home. Catherine had also been a distraught witness to her brother Michael's last despairing act in 1903. Again history had preserved a clue to resolving the family enigma in this small rural South Shore community. Waiting on the cold platform for the express back to Boston, I reflected on the progress I had made in a few short days on the ground. I felt that the ancestors were propelling me forward on my quest.

On the last day of my Boston expedition, I travelled out to Boston College on Chestnut Hill campus to meet the distinguished, erudite, Irish-American historian Dr Thomas O'Connor for lunch. He was a Southie, who had grown up on Emerson Street, and was the author of several major books on the history of the Boston Irish. An urbane, soft-spoken gentleman, he spoke of how the Irish immigrants had survived in the Irish-dominated enclave around the turn of the 20th century. He had some fascinating insights into the subtle differences between the residential City Point area, where Michael, Maria and their children had lived in the mid-1890s, and the blue-collar Lower End industrial zone around Dorchester Street. I outlined my own research project which he encouraged and offered to help with any queries I might need. My whirlwind seven-day visit came to an end as I headed for Logan airport the next day.

As we soared back over the Atlantic, I felt I had made progress and now had a much clearer comprehension of the exact circumstances surrounding of Michael's sad destiny in America. I knew I'd be back to Boston to search for living American relatives and it was a stimulating and exciting prospect.

17

Family reconnections. A happy ending

In October 2000, during my trip down to Holbrook, I had met Rick McGaughey, who, as a young baseball player, had been coached by Bob Burns. Several months later, he sent me a tape recording of an 1980 interview with Bob, in which Bob had mentioned that his nephew, Owen, had been Massachusetts State Commissioner for Education. I listened intently to Bob's South Shore twang where he pronounced his cousin Owen's family name as 'Kearney'. I immediately contacted the State Education Bureau in Boston where they could find no mention of that name in their records. Yet Boston phonebooks listed pages of Kearneys. I was, once again, left wondering if I had hit another dead end. Research ground to a halt. I was stuck. Then, in April 2001, I received a note from Rick who told me that the person I needed to talk to was Dr Owen Kiernan (not Kearney), living in retirement down on Cape Cod, and he included an address. Another lucky break! I was back on track.

I immediately sent Dr Owen Kiernan a file containing the proof of our family relationship to him through my grand-aunt Mary Anne (Mongan) Keough's daughter Helene and her marriage to his uncle Bob Burns in Holbrook. Shortly afterwards, I received a large file from Owen outlining his long career in American educational circles and confirming the family links. Eureka!

Finally, in September 2001, I made an historic transatlantic call to Cape Cod from where I heard the warm, burnished baritone of Dr Owen Kiernan waft loud and clear across 3,000 miles of ocean. After 100 years of silence, I had finally reconnected with a living relative in America. A twenty-year quest for the truth had at last found the proverbial needle in the vast United States haystack. The conversation just flowed, as more parts of the jigsaw started to fall into place.

At eighty-nine and naturally eloquent, with a very Irish 'gift of the Blarney', Owen sketched the outlines of his distinguished forty-year career in education; the holder of over 100 honorary doctorates and more than 200 distinguished service awards. He had been Massachusetts State Commissioner for Education during the period of racial tensions over school busing in Boston in the early 1960s. Now retired, he still actively served as an advisor to the Washington-based Horatio Alger Association of Distinguished Americans, that provided over $4 million per year in scholarships to deserving students. I listened in awe to his words. Owen's remarkable longevity – a Burns family trait – had provided me with a direct and vital link with past generations; he was the living proof of the family's struggles in their new homeland. His mother Elizabeth was Bob Burns' aunt. He had known Helene and remembered her well. Now I had a direct personal connection with someone who had known her in the 1920s.

I was elated and dancing with joy inside. I had been reading Owen's biographical material and I saw that he also had played piano in jazz bands in his early days in Randolph. With my own intense love of that art form, I immediately warmed to the man. Straightaway, I proposed to travel over to Boston to meet up with him down in Cape Cod so we could really delve in detail into the family history. I suggested that I might fly out to meet him in October. Just as I had booked my flight I was stopped in my tracks.

On the morning of 11 September, a friend phoned me frantically from London and told me to turn on the television. I watched horrified as the second plane exploded into the World Trade Center. At that instant the world changed and any plans for visiting newly found American relatives were put on hold as America and the world went into shock.

My research into other branches of the family had also continued during this time. Ever since I had discovered that my grand-aunt Catherine Mongan had married David Aherne in Abington, I had been hoping to find present-day descendants of one of David's three brothers – Cornelius, James and Patrick. Research at Abington Town Hall established that David and Catherine had no children themselves, but I felt that at least one of three brothers must have had a family and present-day descendants could be living in the Abington area.

I made countless phone calls to various Ahernes around Abington but was unable to discover anyone with a specific family connection. I had established that David G. Aherne, Catherine's husband, had died on 16 December 1921, aged sixty-six, having worked for the New Haven Railroad in his final years.[1]

In 1923, Catherine was rejoined by her sister Delia, who had finished her days at Groton School, and they lived together for almost a decade at 33 Charles Street until Delia's death at sixty-one from arterio-sclerosis at Massachusetts General Hospital in Boston on 4 May 1932.[2] In her last years, Delia had returned to working as a domestic with a private family at 275 Clarendon Street, off Boylston Street, in the Bramhin Back Bay residential neighbourhood of Boston. After Delia's death, Catherine, now alone, moved to 75 Central Street, nearby in Rockland, near St Patrick's cemetery, where, having qualified, she worked from home as a registered nurse. She probably kept in touch with her niece Helene and Aherne brothers-in-law who were then living on North Street and Birch Street in Abington. She spent her last days at the Lonergan Rest Home, 56 W. Water Street in Abington, where she passed away, aged seventy-two, on 20 July 1942, as America went to war. She was interred with her husband and two sisters in St Patrick's cemetery, Rockland. From there the trail went cold.

Frustrated by this apparent dead end, I nevertheless persisted with other leads. In March 2002, as a last-ditch effort to find the elusive Ahernes, I wrote to local Abington historian Kevin Donovan explaining my quest. Some weeks later he wrote back with positive news:

> I believe I have found your long-lost relatives. I happened to enquire of our Superintendent of Schools whose name is Dr John J. Aherne if his father's family had any relatives that you listed for me. Apparently, the Ahern's of Ireland added an 'e' at the end of the name after arriving in the United States. Dr Aherne spoke with his mother as his father recently passed away and his mother was in contact with her husband's only living sister who kept track of the family history and sure enough David Aherne would have been Dr Aherne's grandfather's brother [grand-uncle]. I am told the family is looking for possible pictures for you.
>
> In any event, Dr Aherne indicated that he would be most happy to speak to you. He can be reached at his office telephone number. As a matter of fact, Dr Aherne's secretary, Theresa Minnehan, lives on Charles Street and remembers you knocking on doors attempting to locate any relatives. I hope this has been of help and good luck in your search. Yours very truly, Kevin R. Donovan. [3]

After so many setbacks, delays, roadblocks, frustrations and dead ends, I had now located a second family of relatives in America. Years of dogged persistence, propelled on by my inner young boy's unwavering insistence, were beginning to pay off at last. It showed that even on my initial exploratory visit to Abington, by pure chance, through chatting with John Minihane of his doorstep, I had already come close to finding the Aherne connection.

I called Dr John 'Jack' Aherne at his Abington office and he confirmed the news. I was elated to hear his voice over the phone. He promised to contact his late father's one surviving sister Marguerite, retired down in Florida with her husband, who was the most knowledgeable on the family history.

Two weeks later, I received a letter containing remarkable photos of her grand-uncle Cornelius (b.1847) and his family, taken around 1910. David Aherne's elder brother and Catherine Mongan Aherne's brother-in-law. I had made the connection. It confirmed my hunch that some Ahernes had survived down to the present. I told Dr Jack Aherne that I was planning a return visit to Boston in October 2002, and hoped to come down to Abington to meet my newly discovered American relatives. I found it quite ironic – a topsy-turvy situation. Here was an Irishman seeking his ancestors in America, when it was usually the other way round; Irish Americans looking for their roots back in Ireland. An upside-down world.

I finally flew back to Boston in October 2002 to meet face to face my new-found American relatives. During my two-week stay, I planned to try to cover as much ground as possible. My South Boston contact, Jake, was on hand at Logan airport to welcome me and ferry me down to Braintree, where I had booked myself into a small motel on Boston's south side. It was ideally located to explore the adjacent South Shore localities of Holbrook, South Weymouth, Abington, Randolph. Rockland, Marshfield and farther south to Cape Cod. We planned to meet later on to give me a guided tour of his native South Boston.

I had been in contact with a South Weymouth historian David Smith who picked me up next morning and drove me over to 20 Oakdale Street, in South Weymouth where Mary Anne and Jimmy Keough had owned the property between 1925 to 1927. The area had retained its rural wooded character and the house, a large wooden-frame building, had survived the passing years. We also visited the South Weymouth Museum, where old 1890s photos showed fascinating images of hundreds of women seated at long tables in the shoe factories of the era. Another element of the search slotted into place. He then drove me down to St Mary's cemetery in Randolph were we eventually located the final resting place of the Keoughs: Mary Anne, James and Josephine, alongs with Helene and Bob Burns, and their lost child Mary Eileen; now tranquil in the shadow of the trees. I stood in silence reflecting on Mary Anne's heroic steadfast efforts to save her doomed brother Michael, and how she had her heart broken a second time by the death of her little grand-daughter. I filmed and photographed the gravestone and felt a pang of regret at never having known this part of my American family. I had another emotional moment outside their 62 Pleasant Street home.

I also spoke on the phone with another Burns relative living in retirement nearby in Braintree, who confirmed Helene had worked with the UNDP in New York and his cousin Bob Burns had visited her periodically over the years. Next morning, Dr Jack Aherne came over to take me down to meet the present generation of the long-lost Aherne relatives.

He had brought along his mother Mary, his sister Mary and her bank-director husband Clyde to meet their visiting Irish relative. We went to lunch at his country club where we exchanged notes on David Aherne's marriage to Catherine Mongan back in 1886. I felt excited and a little apprehensive and, with my sleeveless body-warmer, multi-pocket photo jacket, baseball cap and money-pouch, not at all dressed for the occasion. Fine food and a glass of wine soon relaxed me as I told them about my long quest to locate them in Abington. I showed them the exact family connections from David's brother Cornelius, down to their generation. How David's wife, Catherine, was a younger sister of ill-fated Michael, whose tragedy had cut off all contact with the American side of the family. Michael had probably met David and his brothers in his early days in America before he moved back to Boston to work as conductor with on the West End Street Railway.

These were descendants of David's brother Cornelius, whose son, Jack, had also worked as a motorman with the Brockton Street Railway around the turn of the 20th century. On retirement, he had run the service station in Abington. Soon our cameras were out capturing the historic occasion for posterity. Jack Aherne was the Abington Schools Supervisor, while his father Charles, and uncle Raymond, and his sisters and nieces, had all chosen careers in education. His father had lectured at Boston University. As third-generation Irish-Americans, they had benefited from the struggles and hardship of their grandparents, who settled on the South Shore and eventually had spawned a dynasty of educators.

After lunch, Jack and the Ahernes took me on a guided tour of Abington. We went by 33 Charles Street where David, and then Catherine, had lived from 1886 until the 1930s. Catherine's sisters, Maria-Theresa and Delia, had also lived there with her. Then they brought me down to see the old Aherne house on the corner of North and Birch streets, just off the main thoroughfare.

I was amazed to see that all these 1880s clapper-board houses were still standing, looking in pristine condition, and well-maintained by their present owners. In front of the building, a light breeze billowed the American flag in the bright autumn sunshine. The detached houses were surrounded by gardens and well-trimmed lawns, little changed from when they were built. Like Holbrook, Abington had retained its tranquil, rural, leafy 19th-century character intact. I reflected on how David Aherne and his wife Catherine had made a new life for themselves, putting down roots in this small town.

We paused while I took some photos at the old E.P. Reed's Lumberyard site, now converted into a modern road haulage hangar. From there we drove past St Bridget's church in Abington, where David and eighteen-year-old Catherine had married in 1886, then over to St Patrick's cemetery, in nearby Rockland. They led me to the impressive pink granite headstone at the Aherne family grave. It summed up the story of the Ahernes in America, and their gradual evolution into the professional classes. Education was the revenge of the downtrodden Irish immigrants in America. As Jack's mother filled me in with family stories across the generations. I reflected on how different things could have been for Michael J. Mongan's family.

At St Patrick's, we enquired about Aherne/Mongan grave location at the guardian's office, but Judy, the supervisor, explained that the grave plot maps had gone missing. She gave us some approximate indications about where David,

Catherine and her sisters might be buried, but we were still not sure of the exact site – though I knew that they were located closeby. I had to find them. Then Jack's mother decided to call her cousin's husband Eddie Franey, former graveyard caretaker, who arrived ten minutes later. Unerringly, he guided us to a plot some 30 feet from the Aherne monument and pointed to what he recalled was the David and Catherine Aherne plot.

For eighty-five years, the grave had remained unmarked; since exactly 1916 when the first of the Mongan sisters, Maria-Theresa, had been interred there. I immediately made a decision to have a memorial erected and had a small marker stone placed there in November 2004.

I felt I had finally closed the circle. Now I stood at the final resting place of three brave grand-aunts in a quiet rural South Shore cemetery. My pilgrimage was complete.

The following day I boarded the Brockton–Plymouth bus at South Station to head down to Cap Cod to spend the weekend with a man who had left his mark on the Massachusetts education. Dr Owen Kiernan was to be a vital link with Mary Anne and James Keough's family in Holbrook as his uncle Bob Burns had married their daughter Helene. I knew he would have many recollections of the contrasting couple. We sped down the highway to Hyannis, where Owen was waiting at the bus station.

I stepped off the bus to be welcomed by a fit, agile, smiling octogenarian, wearing a white baseball cap, who ran forward to greet me. I recognised him immediately from the photo he had sent me. I embraced him with a bear hug, overjoyed that I had reconnected with another living American family relative and straight away I felt at ease with him. We set off for lunch at a seafood restaurant, where Owen's remarkable 'gift of the gab' went into overdrive. I was amazed by his vitality, sharp mind and good humour.

He delivered a fascinating monologue on the Cape Cod, his family history, and his most impressive and distinguished long career. I told him of my twenty-year quest to find him and his family, my long-lost relatives in the United States.

He talked and talked and I listened and listened. Delighted to actually be there with him after so many years yearning and searching, I soaked up every syllable he uttered.

Here was the living proof that the young boy inside me had been right all along. All his kicking and screaming, cajoling, haranguing and nagging had led to this moment. Owen represented a living contact with my grand-aunt Mary Anne and her daughter Helene. As we savoured the home-made Cape Cod chowder, looking out over Nantucket Sound, we lifted our glasses of chilled Chablis to toast our transatlantic reconnection.

Dr Owen Kiernan (b.1914), son of Thomas F. Kiernan, employed at the Diamond Shoe Factory in Brockton, MA, lost his mother Elizabeth Burns, when only seven years old in 1921. He earned a master's degree at Boston University and a doctorate in law from Harvard. From 1957 to 1969, he served as Massachusetts State Commissioner for Education, and was advisor on education to seven Presidents. His aunt Helene Keough Burns found him his first student summer job at Filene's Department Store in Boston in 1930. (*Courtesy Dr Owen Kiernan archives*)

After lunch, Owen took me on a tour of Cape Cod, driving out to Hyannisport to show me the Kennedy family compound near the beach, where Jack Kennedy had wooed the beautiful Jaqueline Bouvier.

We drove up along the coast to Hyannisport Golf Club where, by coincidence, they had just held the Robert Kennedy Memorial Golf Championship. He told me that his son, John, had been golf caddy to President Kennedy back in 1961. We stopped at the impressive Kennedy Presidential Memorial in a park overlooking the windswept waters of Hyannisport Bay.

That evening back at his home, we were joined two of his six offspring: school assistant principal Joan came up from New York to cook a wonderful meal, joined by his son John, partner with his leading Boston law firm, and his lawyer wife Susan. The pot roast dinner, with plums and prunes, was a delicious New England feast; as the wine flowed, and the atmosphere warmed up. After dinner, Owen took to the piano, revealing his instinctive musical flair, taking us on a musical journey through the great American songbook. Songs by Hoagy Carmichael segued into Rogers and Hart, to Gershwin and others in his wide repertoire.

As he played I filmed him, wanting to capture the magic of the historic moment. We all took turns playing our favourite melodies. John picked out a few tunes encouraged by Owen. I was delighted to have finally met such charming, talented and successful people. I played a few jazz standards as my contribution to the evening's celebrations, trotting out the sentimental hoary old chestnut *Danny Boy* to honour the memory of all those millions of Irishmen and women who had emigrated to America over generations.

It forcefully brought home to me just how much the post-Famine third-generation Irish were now an assimilated part of mainstream American society as they had struggled up the social ladder. John Fitgerald Kennedy's presidency had given them the long-sought social status and respectability and, now, they were in the driving seats of power. President Bill Clinton, with his Cassidy mother's roots in Fermanagh, had shown his deep interest in helping to find peace in Northern Ireland. The descendants of the Irish immigrants were coming home to roost. With the jetlag catching up with me, I slept well that night, dreaming of past generations who had left the Emerald Isle to brave the challenges and uncertainties of the New World.

Next day when Joan, John, and Susan had left, I sat down to film an interview with Owen. He had been born in Randolph, Massachusetts on 9 March 1914, just two miles from Holbrook. He was the second son of Thomas Francis Kiernan and Elizabeth Agnes Burns. She was the daughter of Westmeath-born carpenter James J. Burns and elder sister of Bob. I listened as he spoke of his mother's Burns connection:

My mother, incidentally, was born at a time when Randolph had split into two communities [1874] – separated by the New Haven Railroad tracks. On one side was the new town of Holbrook, and on the other side the existing town of Randolph. It was a large family, they lived on a farm at 176 Center Street in Holbrook. It was a well-knit family too, as I came to know my grandfather and grandmother, and all of my mothers' sisters and brothers – each of them went their own way. We were pleased to note that they wanted us to have what I would call a gourmet meal. It was Sunday so sometimes we would walk the 3 miles from our home on 9 North Street in Randolph to the Holbrook farm. It was a beautiful area, cows, chickens and turkeys, don't know how many cats the Burns had, but it seemed liked several thousands. I'm exaggerating, of course.

Aunt Katie had the responsibility for housekeeping and cooking, the reason being that Aunt Annie worked in a shoe factory in Boston, though originally in Brockton… but her longest period of working in a shoe factory was in Boston.

I mention cooking idiosyncrasies, which I have today, was that as a youngster, most youngsters are not too happy looking at an oyster, to me I thought that was top of the line in terms of Epicurian delights, and they made a marvellous oyster stew. The only thing that puzzled me was that after the stew was ready to be served, the oysters were removed and given to the cats! So I ended up with the liquid which was delicious, and the oyster crackers that came with it, and I thought I was living on the hog!

Not every Sunday, but I guess I'd have to say every other Sunday, we were privileged to have dinner, a very fine dinner, with even dessert, which we seldom had, at 176 Center Street with the Burns family. It was a 3-mile walk which my little legs enjoyed... and first left in Holbrook was Center Street. And I'd say it was about a mile and a half in to the Burns home, and we went by a very small lake called Silver Lake where in winter we went skating and were instructed occasionally by Bob Burns, who loved to skate and play hockey, and also coached, and was probably the No. 1 supporter in cheering the efforts of the Boston Bruins [baseball] team.

On the way to the Burns', I would pass a house on the right where the Keough family lived, and as I recall even as a young man or boy, where a very beautiful lady called Helene – we called her Aunt Helene – [lived] within 100 yards down a slight incline... to the Burns homestead which was on the left-hand side, and there we frequently we'd have our dinner. And after the adults were playing whist, we listened as best we could to the old radios that had earphones. Because they were so small, and didn't have enough to go round, Vincent would take half of one and I would take the other, because now we were in the World Series, and... on that little radio we got WHDA in Pittsburg... many miles from Randolph. We were about 12 miles from Boston and there was a trolley car which got us into Mattapan Square and the we took the subway to downtown Boston. But most of the time we used to use our thumbs and we'd hitch a ride – it wasn't as dangerous in those days as it is today.

At only seven years old, Owen suffered a tragic loss in 1921:

You maybe wondering also, where my mother Elizabeth Burns Kiernan was all this time. Unfortunately, she had been called to her eternal reward when I was seven and my brother nine... With her exception, and that of a brother James, the other children were blessed with impressive longevity. There were three other sisters and three brothers in the family. Two of my aunts lived into their nineties, and I remember what they said following the Class of 1931 high school farewell address, 'Young man, you have the gift of the gab.' I am not sure [if] they were referring to idle chatter, but rather the ability to speak fluently, even when off-the-cuff.

The lack of a gentle and caring mother during those formative years quite obviously took its toll:

I always seemed to get the short straw and ended up as the family's full-time cook, while Vincent took over the duties of 'part-time' housekeeper. Our ice chest was placed in the back, unfinished section of the house and when I noticed water on the floor from the overflowing ice pan I knew his duties that day were conspicuous by their absence.

He remembered his father's own difficult start in life:

> My father, Thomas Francis Kiernan, born in New York City, left school when he was eleven to help the family by working in a Brockton shoe factory. He took the 6:15 a.m. streetcar to Brockton's Diamond Shoe Co., and returned at 5:30 p.m. six days a week. He worked his way up to the cutting room where he ran the skieving machine which slices off excess leather in preparation for stitching. He was paid in pennies for each piece and one of my monthly chores was to take what was left in his payroll envelope and present nine dollars to our landlord for our rent. Later, when the property was sold to accommodate a first floor Pontiac dealership, the new owner raised the rent to $14. We all agreed this was outrageous exploitation of prompt-paying tenants, but we knew we would have to accept the new rate.
>
> My father's income was stopped from time to time by strikes which turned violent. He was a member of the Boot and Shoe Workers Union and their jobs were turned over to strike-breakers. We watched each morning as these men passed through the square in a convoy of black Cadilliacs. The land paralleled to Route 28 in Avon and the Montello section of Brockton was higher, providing locals with a launching pad for rocks, bricks and even cobblestones. Considerable blood was spilled, and again when strike-breakers returned to Boston. During the payless days, the union provided canned goods in several storefronts. Some of our neighbours took advantage of the free food, but my father said that this type of welfare was for poor people only, and that we could get along without 'relying on charity'.

He remembered distinctly his Randolph neighbours on the Crawford Square area of North Street. He never considered his family to be poor, as the entire neighbourhood lived at the same income level:

> I suppose by today's standards we were all 'economically challenged'. The Crawford Square area of North Street had several two-storey tenements. We occupied the second floor of No. 9, overlooking the square and directly across from Howard House, Randolph's only hotel. We had a kitchen stove for cooking and heating, one water faucet, kerosene lamps and outdoor plumbing attached to the back of the second floor. We developed Olympic speed in getting to and from this frigid addition in winter. As one left the highlands of the Square and descended to valley where St Mary's cemetery was located, the mailboxes told the story of our background – Riley, Taylor, Dowd, Leary, Murphy, Hoey, Gavin, Daly, Hart, Donovan, Collins, et al.

Owen recalled how his Aunt Helene had found him his first job back in 1929:

> When I was fifteen, Aunt Helene was the chief [telephone] operator at Filene's Department Store in Boston, and I was delighted when I became the 'vice president' of the shoe repair and replacement [department] in Filene's Basement, the first discount basement in the world, and there was a time when they did a million dollars gross business per day. But she was influential, and not only was she beautiful and talented in many ways, but she had influence with the Filene's big-wigs and so I got my [summer] job, And I started at 20 cents an hour but then I moved up after a while, I had a promotion to 25 cents an hour!

He had clear memories of Bob and Helene dating at the time:

> During the summer, Bob and Helene would visit the New York Giants training camp along the Hudson where West Point [Military Academy] is located at Bear Mountain. Bob would check the new offensive sets, the defensive sets, and at least from what he told me, my Aunt Helene would go along with him, and enjoy seeing the professionals play. I had the feeling that Bob and Helene were engaged for years, for some unknown reason, and the [wedding] ceremony did not come until quite late in life.
>
> As I said, there were no luxuries in the Kiernan family. There were very few cars except for Bob Burns eight-cylinder Stearns-Knight, which I think he was the only mechanic in the United States who could get it started, with those cylinders, but he did and was an outstanding mechanic. I think it was interesting to note that, in turn, his reputation as a great mechanic spread way out of metropolitan Boston. Bob was more interested in doing a great job and finding a way to fix a car that was ready for the dump, and he did.
>
> But he was a little careless in sending bills, so there were a lot of people all the way from Boston Harbour on the Atlantic all the way out to the Bershires, who had their cars fixed for free – particularly the Stearns-Knights. He was a specialist so that [people] would come great distances to have him fix their car, which he did – an outstanding mechanic.

Owen also developed a lifelong love of music. Although he could never afford piano lessons there was a battered old upright piano in the Kiernan household. He soon found a way to get around the problem:

> I was about ten or eleven when I became interested in the piano. We didn't have one so we bought a kind of old upright. It wasn't too good but it helped out. I played a lot with one finger, but very close by was a five and ten cents store, Kressky's Store, and at the back of the store they had a raised platform with a piano, and a young lady selling sheet music, so you'd go and ask if she would play a certain number that you had picked off the counter. They ran from 25 to 40 cents. The ones that were popular were 40 cents, but

I didn't have any money so I asked if it would be all right if I could come occasionally and stand beside the piano, and watch what she was doing, and I'd go home and play it, you know, with one finger and get it and so on. Well, gradually, I discovered two fingers, and then ultimately ten, and playing in bands during high school and college, and then later in adult life. I was with the pros, the people from the big bands. I was the only one who didn't know music but they taught me chords and things like that.[4]

In spite of the demands of his hectic career responsibilities in education, Owen retained his love of music and always found time to play his chosen instrument. He went on to play with everything from trios to big bands, inspired by his favourite 1930s bandleader Vaughan Munroe. Later, he recruited retired big band members in the Cape Cod area and organised them into groups performing for many worthwhile charity events, county fairs, nursing homes and United Way fundraisers.

Owen earned a master's degree from Boston University and a doctorate from Harvard. His special interest in school law served him well during the twelve years from 1957 to 1969 when he served as Massachusetts State Commissioner for Education. He was appointed executive director of NASSP (the National Association of Secondary School Principals), which he headed from 1969 for ten years. He had been education advisor to seven presidents, and became a lifelong friend of vice president Hubert Humphrey. As a committed idealist, inspired by educational reformer Horace Mann, he resisted calls to run for Massachusetts State Governor, preferring education over politics.

After my weekend with Owen and his family, I already felt I belonged. They had welcomed me like a prodigal long-lost cousin. Owen, from very modest beginnings had risen to the dizzy heights of his chosen profession and remained true to his vocation. I felt honoured to have met him. Overjoyed, emotional and uplifted, I headed back on the bus to Boston brimming over with his inspirational energy. I felt so lucky to have encountered such an exceptional American relative. The years of hoping, yearning and searching had paid rich dividends indeed. Now I had another American family.

On the way north, I dropped off near Marshfield where I had arranged to meet my Boston researcher Ed Hines, whose brilliant detective work in the archives had brought Michael's sad destiny to light. He had invited me to stay overnight as I wanted to film an interview with him. As a successful civil engineer working on major projects with a leading Boston construction company, he had somehow found moments at lunchtimes or on weekends to dash into the Massachusetts State Archive and resurrect the truth of Michael's saga.

I wanted to present him with a gift I had brought over from Ireland. The polished piece of 5,000-year-old bog-oak, with a small gold clock inserted into the centre, had lain dormant, hidden in the depths of the peat for five millennia. Only through digging deep into the peat bog had it been revealed and, with care, had been polished to a fine ebony patina. With Ed's help and innate, instinctive sense of where to look, I had dug deep, back a hundred years, to reveal a long-hidden family secret that now had been resurrected and brought back into the light. I felt deeply indebted to him for having accompanied me on the quest for the truth, and the ancient bog-oak seemed to symbolise the journey we had accomplished together. That evening we sat with his wife Betsy, in a lovely seafood restaurant over looking the Scituate harbour, and talked about how the Irish had gradually escaped from the inner-city ghettos and moved to the South Shore.

Later that night at their magnificent home, with its stunning view right down through the woods to the ocean, I filmed an interview with Ed where he talked about his Tyrone grandfather who, like Michael, had come to Boston and worked as a motorman on the electric trolleys around 1910, until he lost his employment through 'drink'. Boston had been a harsh, competitive and cruel world where a job was vital to survival – and where Michael had not survived. The next morning, I thanked them for their hospitality and headed back to Boston where I had to face up to a more challenging encounter with the family past. I had a rendezvous with history at Worcester State Hospital, where Michael's days had come to an end.

18

Michael. A last goodbye to Worcester

My inner young boy listened to the hum of the 9:00 a.m. train out of South Station for Worcester as it sped through the golden New England landscape. Woods, lakes, clusters of wooden frame houses, seemed frozen in time. The train cast a shadow over nature as it raced past. He watched the play of the morning sunlight play on the russet autumnal leaves. He thought of Michael's final journey to Worcester a century earlier. Little had changed since then. His anguished gaze had seen these same rural scenes and pondered his fate. The train sped westwards past West Newton, Auburndale, Wellesley Hills to Natick, Framingham, through Southborough, Westborough and Grafton.

As the train glided into the station, my eye was immediately caught by the sign of the wall 'Worcester'. I felt a chill race down my spine. I was following in Michael's footsteps – walking through on his stations of the cross to his final destiny. I wondered around the deserted Union Station filming as I went. Thoughts of Michael flooded my mind. A century before, he had escaped from Worcester Insane Asylum and had come to the station where he desperately tried to catch a train back to Boston. With no money for a ticket, he was trapped. He was missing his wife, his children, his sisters, friends and his neighbourhood and wanted to get back to work. He had spent enough time in Hell.

With no taxis at the stand, I began walking up the hill towards the city centre. Finally, a taxi rolled into view and, a few minutes later, I was standing in the main square. Worcester Town Hall, a Gothic fantasy built in 1890, had been there when Michael had driven past in a horse-drawn trap. If only stones could talk. I walked around filming and taking photos to capture the atmosphere.

I jumped into another taxi and gave the address for the Worcester State Hospital. The driver glanced back at me through his sunglasses – not a popular destination. As we sped out through the town, I continued filming through the half-open window as low buildings flashed by. Barely five or six minutes later, we pulled into the grounds of the hospital. The new modern Bryant Building, built in 1957, now stood on the top of the hill dominating the landscape. Had the old building been pulled down? Some hospital patients sat on benches or shuffled around the garden. As the taxi pulled away, I got my bearings. Then suddenly there it was. A few hundred yards away to the right, I saw the formidable brooding

Gothic shape of the old mental asylum stark against the purple-blue sky. This was where Michael met his inexorable fate sucked into the vortex of custodial regime of the time. Even in the crystal-clear autumn sunlight, it still glowered balefully over the landscape. It was chilling reminder of a bygone age when mental hospitals truly were prisons. To be incarcerated was too often a life sentence.

As the taxi sped off, I reached into a pocket of my photo jacket to load another tape in the camera. As my fingers feverishly searched, I could not find one. I was sure I still had spare one somewhere. Nothing. I cursed – I'd come all this way and now I had run out of video tape at a most crucial point. OK. I knew I had to go back into town to get some.

No taxis around. I had planned to catch the 2:30 p.m. train back to Boston. Frustrated and annoyed with myself, I decided I'd have to hoof it back into Worcester to find a camera shop. Now, under time pressure, I headed off down the avenue at a fast pace and turned left for the city centre. I strode briskly along the main highway, feeling stressed, and begin to perspire in the warm sunlight. It dawned on me that I had unconsciously begun to trace Michael's route after he had escaped by jumping from the first floor T.1 ward window, leaving his shoes behind. By an uncanny coincidence, here was his grand-nephew – a hundred years later – also heading for town in a hurry. Twenty minutes later, after checking several photo stores on the way, and my feet aching, I finally located a shopping mall where I found a professional camera store. Saved. Just as I was walking out the door my cell-phone rang.

It was Dr Joe Morrissey returning my call from a conference in Philadelphia. I told him where I was and he laughed. I said I was under some time pressure and would get back him. Amazing coincidence. He had been so helpful with my research on Worcester. Now armed with three fresh tapes – not wanting to take any more chances – I hopped into another taxi and headed back to the hospital.

We drove down past the modern Bryant Building entrance to the gaunt, boarded-up old asylum building. I told the driver to wait. I decided it was wiser to hang on to the taxi this time. I filmed the neo-Gothic main entrance with its huge canopy still in place. Michael had walked through that exact doorway, stepping into Hell on earth. Sartre had been so right in saying *L'enfer, c'est les autres* ('Hell is others'). I filmed the large boarded-up windows and panned up the four storeys where so many immigrant inmates had spent years locked up, and where they had died. I scrutinised the first floor windows some six feet from the ground where Michael had made his last desperate bid for freedom. Quite a good drop in his bare feet.

Next we drove farther down towards the old wing of the original building. I got out and walked along the façade. Suddenly, I saw a window with its iron bars still in place. Another chill sent a shiver down my spine. It was at such a window that Michael had ended his days. I had come to the end of my quest. Face to face with the stark reality of his destiny. There was nothing else I could do other than trust that his soul was finally at peace. I had made a pilgrimage across the Atlantic to learn the exact circumstances of his final act and lay the tragedy to rest at last. It was a sobering moment. (A campaign had been launched to save the Worcester State Hospital bulding and preserve it as a memorial to all those unfortunate enough to have ended up there. On 22 July 1991, a devastating inferno engulfed the Kirkbride building, bringing down the roof and floors, except for the right wing and administration entrance tower. The fire-damaged sections were bull-dozed shortly afterwards. Sadly, in 2008 demolition of the wings of the Kirkbride building began, along with the two historic tours and employee residences. Plans are afoot to develop a new psychiatric facility on the site. Hopefully the main entrance clock tower may survive as a forlorn reminder of its sad history.)

I got back into the waiting taxi. Just twenty minutes to get back to the station. As we headed off I remembered that Michael had spent a night of his escape, alone and anxious, at the Bell Pond Lake. The driver knew where it was on the way back. He stopped for a few minutes while I raced across the road to film the small expanse of water scintillating in the sunlight. So peaceful now. It had been a night of anguish for Michael a century previously. We headed for the station where the 2:30 train was waiting to whisk me back to South Station. I had carried out the ancestral need to heal the wound caused by Michael's tragic

The main hall at Worcester Old Union Station, *c.*1900, where Michael J. Mongan attempted to return to Boston by train after jumping to freedom from a first-floor window at Worcester State Hospital on 10 June 1901. Having no money to purchase a train ticket, he spent the night at Bell Pond Lake before returning to the hospital. (*Courtesy Worcester Public Library*)

demise. A page had been turned. My inner young boy smiled wryly and murmured, 'Goodbye Michael.' At last, he could let go of the past.

Before I left Boston, I had more people and places to see. I met up with Denis Ahern, a retired IT technical writer and Ahern clan historian. A gregarious, droll, fast-talking Bostonian with a Kennedyesque twang, Denis had been researching in Dublin, where we met when he had given a talk about his impressive Ahern website to a research group.[1] As I had established my grand-aunt Catherine Mongan had married David Aherne in Abington in 1886, I discussed my research with him. I had told him of my plans to travel to Boston to research the destiny of another grand-aunt Elizabeth, who had married carpenter Charles E. Edgerly at Holy Cross Cathedral in July 1884. After their marriage, they lived initially at 31 Lowell Street, then 51 Mystic Street, in Arlington, north of Cambridge.

An Arlington native, Denis kindly proposed to take me on a tour of his childhood neighbourhood. I took the suburban train from North Station to Arlington, where he was waiting for me on the platform. We drove around the area on another bright autumn day as he gave me a rapid potted-history of West Cambridge, as Arlington was first known. We visited the Jason Russell farmhouse where the first shots of the 1776 Revolution had taken place. We drove along Mystic Street, near St Agnes' Catholic Church, along the Mystic river, where Elizabeth and her carpenter Charles had lived when their daughter Elsie was born on 27 November 1895. We stopped on the corner of Mystic Street and Mass Avenue, where Denis showed me the actual building where his grandfather Denis Ahern had run the local first-floor barber's shop, linked with a small pool hall, conveniently located in the customer's waiting room.

We surmised that by an amazing coincidence that my grand-aunt Elizabeth's husband Charles had probably come in for his weekly shave at Denis Ahern's barber shop – a small world indeed. Denis also mentioned that his grandfather had also been a volunteer fireman with the Arlington Fire Brigade. On more than one occasion, his grandfather suddenly heard the alarm bell ringing at the fire station just down Mass Avenue. Immediately, he downed his razor and dashed off to do his duty, leaving a startled, lathered, half-shaven customer abandoned in his chair.

By the time of their son Charles William's birth, on 22 June 1897, Charles and Elizabeth Edgerly had moved to 45 Arlington Street, in nearby Medford, even closer to Boston. By 1903, they were living at 29 Reservoir Street, Cambridge, an impressive wood-built three-bay mansion with a mansard roof where Elizabeth was a domestic servant to Professor Horatio S. White of Harvard University. It had a large annexe with two separate entrance doorways, one of which led to Charles and Elizabeth Edgerly's home, when she received news of Michael's tragic end at Worcester.

Michael's sister Elizabeth (Mongan) Edgerly was living with her husband Charles, and their two children, at 29 Reservoir St, Cambridge, MA in 1903 when she organised his burial arrangements. She was the resident housekeeper to Professor Horatio S. White of Harvard University. They lived in the large annexe with its own separate entrances. (*Photo Denis Ahern*)

Boston had long been nicknamed 'Bean Town' in honour of its long links with that popular vegetable, apart from the ubiquitous cod fish. Next evening, I had dinner with Denis at the landmark Durgin Park restaurant in the shadow Fanueil Hall, on North Marketplace. The popular venue featured classic New England seafood dishes – boiled scrod, clam chowder, lobster and crayfish. Seated at a long wooden table with a red-check tablecloth, and served by fast, efficient, wise-cracking waitresses, Denis tucked into a boiled lobster, while I purposely chose the original Irish immigrant Saturday-night culinary speciality; earthy, robust Boston baked beans, cleverly blended with onions, mustard and molasses, one of the inexpensive, hearty dishes that Michael and his sisters had relied on as they adopted New England culinary customs. I was beginning to run out of time.

During my final days in Boston, I spent two nights in the generous hospitality of the daughter of a childhood family friend. Kieran had studied at Oxford, and was lecturing in economics at nearby Harvard University. She gave me a sofa to sleep on in the front room at her leafy Dana Street in Cambridge (near Hancock Street) ground-floor apartment that she shared with two other young academics. She organised an enjoyable pasta dinner, washed down by a bottle of Valpolicella, as the stimulating conversation ranged from surviving in the academic world, to Kieran's passionate commitment to the pandemic Aids crisis in Africa. I had tried to succinctly explain my quest for long-lost grand-aunts and grand-uncle in Boston, over a century previously. Next morning, I emerged from my slumber to the sound of birds chirping in the front garden. As I lay there, a thought floated into my mind. I had been trying to sum up my quest. It had been a search for lost relatives cut off for over a hundred years. Michael's sad end had led to a century of silence.

I still felt a need to spend some time in South Boston. I met up with Jake, my Southie guide, who proposed to drive me around his home patch. He wanted to take me around to all the old addresses linked with Michael and his family. We headed down to Second Street, where Michael had first lived, then to 40 O Street, where the wooden frame building had survived; then past 8 Kimble Place, to M Street, where Michael had lived at No. 21, while his sister Mary and husband Jimmy Keough had lived at both No. 15 and No. 21.

Now, the houses stood as mute witnesses to so many forgotten human dramas.

I had met local M Street resident Tim Hayes while researching there, and he kindly invited me into his first floor apartment with its view over M Street Park. He showed me around the seven-room apartment as I got a feeling for the exact type of surroundings that Michael and Maria had lived in at the time of the births of Charles and Mary. I filmed the scene from his window overlooking M Street Park, imagining the balmy summer evenings in 1895 when Michael and Maria sat together with the crowds in the park watching the baseball games. Those had been golden moments for the couple when their future seemed bright and full of promise. In 1900, Michael's sister Mary Anne had watched from a window as her husband Jimmy took their children, Josephine, James and Helene, to play with their visiting Irish cousin Reg in the park, after Michael had been discharged from Worcester. These houses had seen Michael's drama unfold before them. As I filmed, children, shouting and laughing, excitedly played in the warm October sunset. It was time to turn the page of history. Time to move on.

I was still hoping that I might be able to locate a photo of Charles Mongan. As a veteran of the First World War, and his interest in veterans' affairs, I put in a phone call to the American Legion headquarters in Boston, and enquired if there might still be older members of Veterans Post 142 (Charles' veterans group) who might remember him. I finally heard back from veterans' historian Dan O'Leary who provided some extra information on Charles' military career but could not find anyone who knew him. The passing of a generation. I did take a taxi out to Cambridge City cemetery, where after some anxious searching, I found his grave in the veterans' plot near the main entrance gate. He was interred among his former comrades; his small leaf-strewn marker stone gave a tangible reality to his existence; a miniature American flag flew near the grave, added a heightened poignancy to his last resting place:

CHARLES J. MONGAN
MASSACHUSETTS
COX USNRF
WORLD WAR 1
MAY 9 1895 SEPT 15 1963

I then walked along another section on Range 235, looking for grave 106, where Maria Hurd, Michael's widow, Mae Eisel, Charles' widow, and Mary Mongan, Charles' sister, were all buried. Unable to pinpoint it, I realised that it had no headstone. I wondered whether, grief-stricken by Michael's sad demise, they had wanted to remain hidden and forgotten. I promised myself that I would have a simple stone placed over their final resting place.

I spent my last day with Jake, my Southie guide. We went out to City Point and walked around Marine Park. Michael and Maria had strolled there in happier times a century earlier. Far out on the horizon, I could see Deer Island, from where Michael's final commitment to Worcester had begun. Jake spoke of his experiences of growing up in South Boston, and how the enclave still had a strong Irish identity. We drove over to Fish Pier and had a clam chowder and seafood lunch. I sensed that I had got as close to the lost generations as I ever could. It was time to leave Boston.

19

Reflections. On finding a needle in the haystack

Flying back over the Atlantic, I had time to reflect on the progress the research had accomplished. Looking back at the destinies of my grand-aunts in America, it had became clear that they had somehow missed out on the American Dream; they had neither prospered nor multiplied. I had established that, out of the six Mongan sisters who had emigrated to America, only three had married – Elizabeth, Mary Anne and Catherine. Sadly, their offspring didn't produce descendants who survived to start a new generation.

The eldest, Elizabeth Edgerly had died on 25 July 1925 at the House of the Good Samaritan, an acute care hospital on McLean Street, near the Massachusetts General Hospital. Her husband, Charles, was also a patient there at the time, had probably died there shortly afterwards. Elizabeth's death certificate gave her address as 40 Lawrence Street,[1] off Colombus Avenue, Boston, close to Clarendon Street, where her sister Delia was employed as a domestic with a Brahmin family. According to the 1920 US census, Elizabeth shared that Lawrence Street address with her daughter Elsie, and her Edgerly relations, John and his daughter Grace.[2]

Elsie seems to have stayed at home caring for her parents. She was working as a domestic at the Peter Brigham Hospital until she, in turn, died, unmarried and unmourned, on 24 November 1956, aged sixty. She had been living at 22 Kempton Street in Roxbury, another old Irish enclave in Boston.[3]

Her doomed uncle Michael had worked in the neighbourhood as a coachman with the Peters family back in 1903. Eliza had become a welfare case, financially destitute, with no heirs. She seems to have been pre-deceased by her brother Charles William, who never came to light in the archives.

The estrangement from her Mongan cousins, Charles and Mary, in Cambridge had become absolute, as they were not mentioned as informants at her passing.

Mary Anne Keough and her husband Jimmy had four children of whom three survived, Josephine, James and Helene – Hubert's destiny remained an enigma. Did he also die as an infant? Only James and Helene married. James, the veteran of the First World War, had no children of his own with his wife Stashia Mae, only a step-daughter Beatriz, from his widowed wife's previous marriage. Helene, the youngest of the Keoughs, had married her sweetheart Bob Burns, but sadly their child Mary Eileen, had died from acute bronchitis as a small baby. That traumatic event appeared to have brought Helene's child-bearing days to an abrupt end.

Catherine Mongan had married David Aherne in 1886, but they never had any children to bless their lives at 33 Charles Street in Abington.

Michael's marriage to Maria Hurd had produced two girls and a boy. Little Annie had died from cholera in 1894, leaving the couple devastated. Their son Charles, the US Naval Reserve Coxwain or petty officer, had married Mae Eisel in 1925, but their union didn't produce any offspring. Mary Elizabeth, Michael's psychic daughter, had lived at home at 112 Kinnaird Street, caring for her mother until Maria died in 1936. By then aged forty, she had not found romantic love in her life. She had followed a spiritual path.

The other two sisters, Delia and Maria-Theresa, had, like so many Irish women in America, remained unmarried. As a domestic servant, Delia's live-in employment had never allowed her enough leisure time or social contacts to develop a romantic relationship. She died at Massachusetts General Hospital in 1932, after which her sister Catherine brought her remains back to St Patrick's Rockland, where she was buried.

Her younger sister, Maria Theresa, whose name Bob Burns had heard about from his wife Helene, had spent her days working alongside her sister Catherine in the Abington shoe factories until, her delicate constitution worn out, she died prematurely, aged only thirty-six, in 1916.

The sixth sister, Bridget, may have settled in Springfield, Massachusetts, where James and his young son Reg may have met her when they visited the town in 1900. A Bridget Monaghan (another misspelling?), aged fifty, did turn up in the archives, running a boarding house in nearby Holyoke at that time.[4] Had James Keough and his wife Stashia been travelling out to visit her when they had their fatal crash near Southbridge in 1938? Another question that could never be answered.

Nor did the family prosper greatly in economic terms. Only Mary Anne and her husband Jimmy Keough, eventually became part of the 'lace-curtain' Irish, after they moved to Holbrook on the suburban South Shore. The piano-roll player at their 62 Pleasant Street parlour showed they aspired to a more refined lifestyle only attained by their daughters Josephine and Helene in New York, they eventually lived on the trendy Upper West Side during Helene's days working a UNDP social secretary. I felt reassured that I had honoured their courageous, if anonymous, lives. I had at least been able to clear up some of the emotional and psychological wreckage caused by Michael's sad end.

I felt some frustration that, of all these relatives in America, I had only been able to locate images for four of them. I had recovered the studio portrait of Mary Anne, and her daughter Josephine, and her daughter Helene, from Bob Burns in

1982. An image of Michael's daughter Mary Elizabeth, who died before I could get to her in 1980, had emerged unsuspectingly, from its hiding place in an old family album in 1979, and had launched the whole quest.

No image of Michael ever turned up anywhere. I studied archival images of 1890s Boston streetcar conductors wondering if one of the men might be him. Nor had any images survived for his son Charles. His US navy service file contained no service image of him. Nor did any photos of his wedding to Mae Eisel in 1925 come to light. Photos of him with his new van were taken during the time as chauffeur with the Cambridge Public Library, but, in spite of searches, they never came to light.

Notwithstanding the meagre the results of twenty years research, I felt that I had been chosen by the ancestors to carry out the quest. I sensed, in fact, that I never had any real choice in the matter. It had become more important than having a family myself, which ironically, seemed to accentuate the importance of searching for the lost relatives in America. It had revealed the truth behind grandfather James' dismissive remark that he never wrote to them, 'Couldn't be bothered.' Now I knew that he had been hiding the shame and stigma of his brother Michael's suicide, protecting his son's family from the horrific truth.

However, there has been a happy ending to this long-drawn out saga.

I have now located Kiernan and Aherne relatives through Mary Anne and Catherine's marriages. The welcome they had shown me gave a tangible sense of reconnection to the lost generation of my grand-aunts, and their brother Michael. I trust they will look down and smile at my prolonged efforts to finally locate them in the vast American continent. In some way, they had made it easy. They had never moved far from where they originally landed in Boston between 1870 and 1890. Like so many Irish-Americans, they had stayed put in their local communities. While they had often stressful, demanding existences in a strange new land, cut off from the Mullingar streetscapes of their childhood, from family relatives and friends, they had made a major leap of faith into the unknown. They had escaped a repressed, stagnant and stifled society in 1880s Ireland. They had found better prospects, if modest destinies, in America.

These glimpses of their lives revealed the hard choices they had to make in their new surroundings. Survival came first and that meant finding work. Like so many young Irish women, domestic service had been their preferred choice. Although it meant living and working long hours, living at the beck and call of their employers, it had also provided them with good food and comfortable living conditions in good residential areas. It also enabled them to save their hard-earned wages and pay for tickets to bring out other siblings.

Michael, with his MGWR head freight clerk, and British army Commissariat and Transport Corps experience, had been well-equipped to find work with the expanding Boston street railways. Sadly, sectarian tensions had followed him across the Atlantic and led to his final downfall when he was being denounced by an embittered colleague. Although he had never been a heavy drinker, the peculiarly Irish vulnerability to alcoholic abuse had led in part to his last tragic act.

My only regret in this whole odyssey was in failing to meet with Michael's psychic daughter Mary. I have no doubt, with her psychic powers, that she had sensed I was coming to seek her out. Had that spurred her on to pass away sooner – unable or unwilling to deal with reliving the horror of her father's tragic end, even to her Irish family relative. Throughout her life she had borne her sorrow bravely, never wanting to burden others with the deep wound of her soul; the trauma, stigma, and feelings of shame, guilt, and pain, an inevitable legacy of those bereaved by suicide.

A sensitive seven-year-old in October 1903 when her father took his own life in Worcester, Mary had been old enough to read the horror, guilt and despair on her mother Maria's face. It must have scorched her soul indelibly. She must have discussed the sad episode with her brother Charles over the years in later life, trying to understand how their Irish-born father could have abandoned them – leaving them alone with their traumatised mother, and estranged from their Keough, Edgerly and Aherne relatives, and Mongan cousins back in Ireland.

Charles had only been eight when the drama had touched his young life. How could anyone live with such a tragedy? How could it be explained? Could he have ever come to terms with it or understand why? The trauma of their father's passing explained why they had never tried to contact their uncle James back in Ireland over the years. The sense of shame, of a stigma had been too over-powering, to difficult to admit – even to Michael's own brother – or to their Irish cousins. It was all too much. They only wanted to bury it away, and act as though the dreadful nightmare had never happened. To have contacted their relations back in Ireland would have only forced them to drag the whole horrific episode back into the open – to reopen the deep wound. Sadly, regretfully, the family rift had been copper-fastened for ever.

I could now better comprehend Michael's last tragic act as a desperate cry for help – in the midst of total despair at the idea of being condemned to a life sentence of incarceration at Worcester. Was it a vista too appalling to contemplate? What were his thoughts on that dark October dawn at Worcester? He had never actually assaulted his wife or children. Nor his Hurd in-laws. He had never attempted to kill anybody. He had sold his pistol. He had just taken a little too much drink with his friends on Washington Street, so he should have only spent a night at the police station and paid a fine for being drunk in public. He had been overcome by escaping gas in his boarding house bathroom. He had never admitted to being suicidal. No one had ever tried to cure his recurring headaches, dizziness or painful eyes.

Had a feeling of panic, despair, frustration, of injustice, a sense of being doomed, raced through his beleaguered mind? I wondered whether his old syphilis infection might have begun to affect his central nervous system, distorting, twisting his mental processes, confusing his thoughts, creating his delusions.

Had his doctor's remarks about him spending a lifetime custodial sentence unnerved him, crushing any hope for the future? He had enough to live for if he been released back into the care of his family. He had compassionate supportive sisters to help him recover. It's all speculation now. Nothing can ever be completely clear about his motivations. He had become another victim of the 19th-century American mental asylum system's crude, inhumane and barbaric custodial conditions. Had that been the final straw that had broken his spirit? Had that appalling vista pushed him over the edge of the abyss?

My entire quest had been a belated attempt to find out what had happened to him and to understand his last tragic act in the minutes, hours, days, weeks, months and years before his last irreparable decision was taken. Had it been a rational, reasoned decision, arrived at after he mulled things over for a long period? Or was it a panic reaction to his unnerving surroundings – cries, moans, screeches, from other inmates in the night, at being forced to 'live with the loonies', to hear the demented ravings, of his insane fellow inmates? I had wanted to accompany Michael in his last hours before he took that fateful decision. A decision that had brutally torn asunder close family bonds of both sides of the Atlantic; it had disintegrated close family ties. It had left his frightened, guilt-ridden wife and her two young children, without a husband or a father. And grieving sisters without their brother. Back in Ireland, two generations later, it would leave his grand-nephew pondering the destinies of his father's family, and needing to find out the truth.

I had resurrected and reconstituted the story of a devastated, long-lost family, if only in words. I felt that by bringing the dark family secret in America, Michael J. Mongan had been at last rehabilitated, and maybe some dignity restored. He was no longer an anonymous statistic buried in the Worcester State Hospital archives.

Finally, the young boy inside me could smile again. The mystery and enigma of his long-lost American cousins had been revealed. Now he had a whole new rediscovered family of American 'cousins'. He had resurrected glimpses of his six intrepid grand-aunts who had made a giant leap of faith in emigrating to America. He had been able to share in their lives; their trials and tribulations, their joys and sorrows, their triumphs and defeats. They had lived independent, if modest, lives. He had accompanied his doomed grand-uncle Michael through his good times and bad, on his slow agony into the hell of black depression at Worcester and his final death by strangulation.

He could now recall the joyous family moments. Michael's marriage to his lovely Irish-America sweetheart Maria and their hopes for their future. The birth of their first girl Annie, an innocent life swept by cholera; and their renewed belief with the birth of Charles and Mary, as hope sprang eternal. There had been the happy occasions of the weddings; strong-willed Elizabeth braving hostile opinion by marrying her New Hampshire Congregationalist divorcee Charles, a carpenter like her father Patrick and brother James. True love was not to be thwarted. And Mary Anne, who had stood by her doomed brother right through the downward spiral of his health problems. She had waited many years before she could marry her long-time fiancé, Irish immigrant foundry worker Jimmy Keough, a union blessed with four children. Delia, was one of the generation of Irish women who had sacrificed their lives as domestic servants in the stately mansions of the Boston Yankee Brahmins, her infectious optimism and Mullingar brogue had left indelible memories on young students at Groton School.

I have no doubt Charles, Mae and Mary Mongan and their Keough cousins, Josephine and Helene, must have applauded the election of the young, handsome, charismatic John Fitzgerald Kennedy as President of the United States in 1960. The election of a Boston-Irish Catholic to the highest office in the land, must have especially warmed the hearts of all those Irish-Americans who had struggled up the social ladder in America. They were the unsung heroes, who had made their modest contributions to the building of the American nation. In 1957, JFK's wedding to the beautiful Jacqueline Bouvier had set them on 'the road to Camelot', a young, attractive, intelligent couple who symbolised a new era in American politics. In Cambridge the Mongans must have cheered and applauded as Kennedy's narrow victory over Richard Nixon was announced nationwide on television in November 1960, raising their glasses in salute at The Elite Spa bar at the end of Hancock Street. At their apartment on 315 West 74th Street, on New York's Upper West Side, their surviving Keough cousins, Josephine and Helene, must had danced an Irish jig for joy as the electoral victory was announced. At last Irish-Americans had something to be truly proud of, a victory that they had finally found acceptance in the American society's mainstream.

During his official visit to Ireland in June 1963, President Kennedy visited the ancestral homestead at Dunganstown, near New Ross, where his great-grandfather Patrick Kennedy had departed from for Boston in 1848. There he met some Kennedy cousins and had a cup of tea. He travelled on to Galway on 29 June, where, in his memorable 'Remarks on Eyre Square' speech, he pointed out to a huge crowd how:

> If the day was clear enough, and if you went down to the bay, and you looked west, and your sight was good enough, you would see Boston, Massachusetts. And if you did, you would see down working on the docks there some Doughertys and Flahertys and Ryans and cousins of yours who have gone to Boston and made good.[5]

Out in Galway Bay a fleet of trawlers, each carried huge letters, which, together, spelled out KENNEDY. The president's final declaration before leaving Ireland was, 'I will return in springtime.' He never did.

He met his destiny five months later in Dallas, Texas, when shots rang out on Deeley Plaza. Some Irish-American families, like the Kennedys, have survived tragedy and heartbreak to continue a tradition of public service, while many others, like the Mongans and Keoughs, have faded from the American landscape.

My inner young boy now had a better understanding of his enigmatic grandfather James, and could relate to his suffering at Michael's tragic passing. No longer was James a Victorian stranger, he had lived through a turbulent period of Irish history, had been part of a dynasty of pioneer railwaymen at a time when such employment had considerable social status. The saga of his long-lost American relatives had emerged from the obscurity of history. Their lives had been acknowledged and their struggles for survival recorded for posterity. That was the seed that his grandfather had unwittingly planted in his young mind. It had taken roots and grown into an irresistible compulsion to seek out the truth, and he had allowed nothing to stand in the way. The call of the ancestors to heal the psychological wound in Boston had been answered. He felt a great burden lifting from his soul. It had been a vital if demanding endeavour to bring closure to a sad family disaster.

The quest was to the detriment of emotional relationships and it strained friendships; it diverted me from a professional career until it ultimately took over my existence. It got to the point where I began to neglect my business clients, spending huge amounts of time on personal research. I had become addicted to finding out what had happened. The discovery of Michael's suicide in 1983, followed by my mother's passing in 1986, led to a nervous breakdown in 1988, and the collapse of a serious relationship, as I sank into a deep depression. On top of that, I experienced a double bereavement, never having had time to mourn my father Reg when he died in 1962.

However, it seemed ordained that I should charged with clearing up the psychological and emotional wreckage in Boston. I had to deal with the debris of the past that had shattered lives in America and in Ireland. My inner young boy had been single-minded driven by the need to discover the truth; to reveal the dark family secret, to uncover the whitewashing of my grand-uncle's death. No doubt grandfather James had wanted to shield the family in Ireland from the stark truth of the drama but that well-meaning cover-up had left the problem hanging unresolved for a century. Hopefully, it has turned what was a family catastrophe into a positive epiphany. I found that the writing of this tragedy a form of catharsis, a healing act in order to redeem a family disaster.

I wondered what would have happened if James Mongan had remained in America, and his son Reg had later married there, I might have been born an American myself. Possible destinies had been radically altered on that fateful October morning in 1903. Michael and his sisters had been just a few of the 2 million Irish people who had emigrated to America between 1850 and 1950. Perhaps they can now rest peacefully in the knowledge that 44 million Americans claim Hibernian roots in the damp misty isle on Europe's Atlantic coast.

I think that it has all been worthwhile, following Michael's stations of the cross and I hope I have brought some peace to his tormented soul, after a hundred years of silence.

I held a personal wake for Michael at exactly 10 a.m. Irish time (4 a.m American east coast time) on 5 October 2003, to commemorate the 100th anniversary of his passing. As a low tin whistle wove a haunting, bittersweet, melancholic Celtic lament, I sensed that his soul was now at peace. The young boy inside me felt sad, yet happy that the truth had been revealed. Now he could let go of the past and move on.

Appendix 1: Written in the stars? Probing deeper into Michael's personality

In a last attempt to gain a deeper understanding of Michael's motivation for his final act, I looked to other ways to comprehend his deeper character and personality. As no images of him seem to have survived, any judgement of his personality based on his physical appearance remains out of reach. Was he narrow-faced like his brother James or broad-faced like his sister Mary Anne? However he did leave behind some fragmentary lines of his fluid handwriting and his signature. I decided to find out what graphology might reveal about him. As I also had his birth date and location I thought by drawing up his astrological portrait it might give a clearer insight into his deeper underlying personality.

Graphology is the analysis of a person's character based on their handwriting. Widely used in business, education and councelling services throughout Europe and America, it can reveal an individual's goals and aspirations, thinking styles, fears and defences, sociability and integrity. I consulted Ms Patricia Field, MA, Assoc IPD, Dip IGA, a UK-based professional graphologist and member of the International Graphology Association, (www.analyse-handwriting.co.uk) who explained that writing is the result of impulses originating in the brain, and is an expression of, and a response to, different outside influences on personality. It can reveal how the inner personality deals with reality, how individuals organise themselves and interact with others.

Normally an in-depth analysis requires a page of handwriting to carry out a full study. However, in Michael's case, only his signature and a fragmentary handwriting example in his medical records 'God save the Commonwealth of Massachusetts' survives in his medical records as a test of his writing ability.

Working within the limitations of the samples available, Ms Field compiled a report on Michael's writing. I have summarised the salient points of the findings:

> His signature indicates that practical needs and material rewards were his 'drivers'. [He had] a need to belong and ties to the past. The wide spacing indicates the writer's need for acceptance, communications, interpersonal and interactive. Clear, legible writing indicates clarity of purpose. [The] letters 'M', 'N', and 'H' show a sharp thinker. In general [his writing] illustrates an extroverted nature, at ease in making contact with others. The slant of the writing is an indication of the emotional responsivness and involvement… how quickly these emotions surface. Characteristics associated with Michael's

writing are restlessness, impulsiveness and strongly spirited, perhaps influences by his likes and dislikes. These people tend to be spontaneous, adaptable and demonstrative, eager and enthusiastic, they respond to people and events. [The] pressure [of the writing] reflects emotional intensity. It seems fairly heavy which can indicate a forceful, dynamic and productive person with good amounts of endurance and determination. Heavy writers have long memories, they can remember emotional pain with the initial intensity for many years after the event. The signature above the line shows optimism, probably connected with the document it appeared on [Michael's citizenship papers].

The writing is dominated by its lower zone. In Freudian terms, this is the area of the 'id' and is essentially concerned with the material, physical and sexual side of life, the raison d'être.

Ms Field explained the significance of Michael's signature;

[The signature] … is merely a trademark and is the face chosen to wear for the world. Its position, style, size, etc., all indicate the needs of one's ego, a public representation. It's about public persona [although] he may have been an underground renegade.

The capital 'M' is believed by some graphologists to have its own importance and is to do with self-image, the association being with early attempts woven into 'mummy, 'me', and 'my' and the shaping of our attitude towards ourselves and others. Though many aspects of our writing may change, surprisingly few capital letter 'M's do!

Ms Field's further detailed analysis of individual areas of Michael's signature suggested other traits;

Personal pride bordering on vanity, self-conciousness, may dislike supervision, influenced by public opinion, likes acknowledgment, controlled anxiety, tries to keep his feelings under control. Close-minded, maybe unwilling to consider other people's views. May be opinionated, protects 'self' from thoughts that cause discomfort, mental images (are) separate from material/practical ideas, jealousy, fear of rivalry or rejection, fear of being supplanted, or by having affection of others removed. Need for security. Plain spoken. Could blurt things out, reticence, is self protective, avoids drawing attention to self. True ideas, feelings, may not always be known.

Ms Field also interpreted other traits which suggested that 'instinctual energies are dominant, materialistic, security paramount. Looking for material gain sometime in the future, restlessness. Discriminating selection of friends, may have been willing to mix socially but would have had a few close and trusted friends. Drawn to people with common interest. Reveals determination, productivity orientated, materialistically inclined values, driver towards success'.

Wherefore, your petitioner prays, that he may be admitted to become a citizen of the said United States of America, according to the forms of the statutes in such case made and provided.

Michael J. Mongan

1893. Sworn to by said Petitioner before the Court.

Attest:

Michael J. Mongan's signature from his citizenship papers in 1893 and his writing ability test from his Worcester State Hospital medical records in 1902.

Ms Field interpreted other characteristics as 'not facing facts realistically, may find hard to see or accept advice, could be manipulative. Someone who can be led, not driven, (a) sense of purpose, maybe headstrong, hard to manage, unreasonable, distruptive. Could be overwhelming in his beliefs. Self-directed [an] ability to take charge, important for leadership. [He had a] definite idea of what he wanted to achieve. If he believes in something, it would have been whole-heartedly.'[1]

From this partial analysis I sensed that Michael, like us all, had made mistakes, had his positive points along with his flaws and failings, yet as an adventurous spirit, had made the transatlantic leap to face the challenges and uncertainties of the New World. Had the streetcar accident with the blow to Michael's forehead triggered his downfall? Had that blow to the forehead, where the personality is 'housed' in the brain's frontal lobes, affected his behaviour? Had his sometimes erratic mood swings been caused by pressure on the brain? Ms Field underlined that at the time mental instability was not fully understood or appreciated and individuals whose troubles may have had a physical cause, i.e., accident, brain tumour, were treated no different from the genuine insane.

Although inconclusive, it does add some revealing insights. Michael comes across a a forceful, dynamic individual who possibly tried to keep his feelings under control because of some anxiety. Has he been affected by an unahppy childhood? Was he overtly jealous of his wife Maria? Had he been headstrong and difficult to manage, and become unreasonable and disruptive? (Anti-social behaviour in 1900s Boston was considered madness at the time.) My general feeling was that these interpretation were uncannily close to my own impressions of Michael's personality I had taken from the verbatim interviews in his medical records and were now confirmed by the findings of the graphology analysis.

Although it has its critics, detractors and sceptics, I then turned to astrology in the hope of finding further clues. I thought that by combining the two disicplines some common themes might emerge to further deliniate Michael's personality.

With its roots traced back to Mesopotamia, where the earliest urban civilisation appeared around 4000 BC, I felt it might add to my knowledge of Michael's character. It hasd been used for millenia as a way for mankind to understand human destinies in nour universe. It is believed that individuals are not only influenced by hereditary factors and their environment but also by the state of the solar system at the moment of their birth. By interpreting the role of the planets and creating a synthesis, astrology can draw up a comprehensive evaluation of a person's character and his potential based on his natal horoscope. Astrology also considers itself to be the elder sister of psychology, as both disciplines explore the human psyche.

A former Freud disciple, Swiss psychologists Carl Gustav Jung, was interested in alchemy and astrology in his later career. In his *Analytical Psychology,* he had insights into the parallels between holistic astrology and psychology which allows them to blend easily, while Freud believed that a child was born as a 'clean slate', with the character beginning to form from birth, Jung, on the contrary, stated in his work *Psychological Types:* 'The individual disposition is already a factor in childhood, and not acquired in the course of life. Today astrology is based on that principle, and the horoscope is considered as "a map of the psyche".'

Michael J. Mongan was born on Monday, 24 August 1863, in Mullingar, County Westmeath, Ireland. As his exact time of birth is not known [an arbitrary time of 12.00 noon was chosen] a 'flat' astrological birth chart was drawn up on 15 November, 2000 by Robert Currey of the House of Astrology in Dublin,[2] (www.astro.com) based solely on the available data. No information on Michael's identity was provided other then his name, date and place of birth. This astrology portrait could not be definite about Michael's rising sign (or ascendant) nor could it give a totally valid reading about the areas connected with the Moon, the fastest moving celestial body from our viewpoint on planet Earth. Otherwise, the remaining planets were located in their correct signs and their inter-relationships could provide interesting and accurate insights. Although other astrologers generally will go along with an interpretation, it should be noted that every astrologer has an original point of view and an an individual way of conveying it. [This chart was transcribed from the first person to the third person and put in to the past tense in order to facilitate legibility.] Afterwards, I also passed the final horoscope to my consultant graphologist Ms Patricia Field to see what recognisable similarities or parallel insights might be found in the chart [indicated below by her remarks in square brackets]. I have summarised the findings in Michael's chart as follow:

With his Sun sign in Virgo, Michael's dominant character traits were those of a pratical, logical and methological type of person [perfectly suited to his original employment as Chief Freight Clerk at Mullingar Station]. As a Virgo, his work meant a lot to him and if things went wrong he tended to worry and get depressed. Most of the time, he could have been very successful in the material world. If only his love life could have been as simple: he sought a partner who shared and could understand his values and ambitions in the world. With his Moon possibly in Sagittarius, essentially Michael was a rather restless type [Yes] who needed space to move around. He had an active mind, with a dry wit and being quite well informed, had a tendancy to dish out blunt advice or critism sugared with a bit of good humour. Outwardly he strove to earn a reputation for perfection, especially in his work environment. One of his greatest skills was at devising techniques and short-cuts to get the job done faster and more efficiently. Inwardly Michael was seen as a cynic who treated life as one joke, who only really let his hair down at home or with intimate company.

A great deal of Michael's identity and sense of self-esteem was derived from maintaining high standards in everything he did, and in improving himself. Whatever he was doing, he put everything into doing it well – working efficently and competently. With the Sun and Moon in harmonoius relationships to each other, Michael was essentially well-adjusted, straightforward and sincere. Being able to take command and respond well to people, he was good at dealing with the public. He was brilliant when offering a service, or working as a personal assistant, agent or broker, a shining example among other workers.

With his Moon possibly in Capricorn, reputation and public image were sensitive issues for him. His whole sense of security was dependent on his career, which was more often then not, in a state of flux. Essentially he fared best in a career where he was needed; dealing with the public [streetcar conductor] and using his gift for sensing their needs and moods. There was a multitude of vocations where he could feel at home, marketing products for women or the home, a caring profession, catering or daily farming. His mother's influence was strong, and may have affected his choice of career. Perhaps his parents were at odds with each other, his mother demanding, his father detached. This pattern may have been repeated in close live-in relationships. He picked up on other people's moods and reactions. Yet he found his own emotional nature muddled. Confusing, though often prophetic, messages came from his subconscious in his dreams. Separating reality from myth or fiction could be quite hard for him so it was not surprising that he worried about his home and his family, even though his fears were usually imaginary. He could also create a special athmosphere within the home. With his masculine/feminine sides so well attuned to each other, he found it easy to alternate between active and passive [No]. His physical reactions and gut feelings enabled him to express himself spontaneously and with confidence [Yes]. An unusual side of Michael's nature was a tendancy to have suddeen and unexpected swings of mood, [Not evident in writing sample?] even becoming hysterical for no apparent reason. It came from a strong need for a thrill, to be un-inhibited and spontaneous like a child. But these needs could not always be immediately satisfied with existing close ties; family or marriage, which left him feeling tense or restless like a cat on a hot tin roof. He was drawn to unusual types, who perhaps share his off-beat sense of humour. With Mercury in Virgo, Michael's mind tended to be analytical [Yes] and observant. Seeking perfection in his speech and thoughts he tended to voice his criticism at sloppy attitudes. At time pedantic or pointing out imprecise use of words and spelling, Michael was competent at classifying information or categorising types, he could have been a collector of stamps, coins, or aware of different species of flora and fauna. In a craft (such as carpentry), his meticulous attention to detail and standards came into operation.

Health was an important concern for Michael. Here his striving for perfection may have resulted in health fads, special diets or fitness regimes. Health matters were often on his mind. On the negative side, this concern in itself could lead to worry, nerves and ill health. He was highly strung with an active central nervous system and found it hard to relax when there was so many little matters left undone. At worse he could bore everyone by making his aches and pains central to his conversation, presenting a kind of 'organ recital'. He might have become involved in other therapies that could have helped him; relaxation through breathing, dialogue, meditation, yoga and other techniques. Generally his health could be fairly good [Strong energy levels] with strong recuperative powers.

Analysing people to know what made them tick, taking apart a clock or motor, was typical of his approach and learning process, Michal thought a problem through by method and classification, rather then by inspired guesses or trial and error. [Yes, joined handwriting is associated with this] By using his high standards of professionalism to tackle a varied and busy schedule, he could be an intelligent and competent worker. Being observant [not evident in sample – 'e' suggests closed-minded] of all that occurred in his working environment, he would be the first to criticise fellow workers who were sloppy or speak up for them if working conditions were unfavourable.

The fact that his mind could be very quick and erratic, enabled him to solve highly complex problems, or look at an ordinary idea or everyday situation from a completely different and original angle. He could use this streak of genius…. for writing. On another level, Michael's mind moved quickly [Yes] sometimes jumping to conclusions or speaking too openly. He found it hard to take 'No' for an answer, and had no time for excuses. Conversations tended to centre around his interests [Yes] as he was better as a talker than as a passive listener, and he tended to take charge of any discussion. Speech and the written word was his primary way of asserting himself. Indeed for him the pen was mightier than the sword! With Venus in Libra, when it came to personal relationships, Michael tended to be rather idealistic, seeking a lover with both mental and physical beauty. Sometimes he would go more for a pretty face then the person inside. Though he disliked rows and would try to keep the peace, one partner dominating a relationship went against his sense of justice. As in romance, he was friendly socially. [Yes] He liked most people who liked him, and with his looks, charm and manners, most people did. He was drawn to beautiful or artistic types… people with whom he would have much in common. Being with someone who was in other people's eyes appealing, made him feel attractive. Consequently, he was attracted to partners who were mature and socially well-established in some way. He valued wisdom, depth and an ethical outlook rather then superficial traits, in his choice of his lovers and friends.

All too often Michael's kind, giving nature [generosity possible] towards those he was attracted to, appeared to other people like an open invitation to take advantage of him… He could waver between the role of saint and victim. Besides the issue of marytrdom, he also had a very refined taste, in his appreciation and composition of music and art.

Mars in Virgo revealed how Michael asserted himself. He tended to be cool [control evident], logical, sometimes cutting and sarcastic. One of the few things that provoked his anger was criticism, even with the best of intentions. Sexually, Michael may have appeared inhibited when he was really being selective in his choice of lover. [Definitely] With the right partner he could become something of an expert in techinique. An aggressive, diligent worker [Yes] Michael loved to improve something and make it more efficent.

Often he blurted out things first [Possibly] that came into his head or made spot decisions but usually his actions turned out to be for the best. His incisive mind could make a good satirist, critic or writer whose narrative was hard to put down. This mental dynamism could also manifest itself in the swift use of hand and mind in rapid co-ordination, like a boxer, croupier, conjuror, percussion player, typist or tennis player. The energy could have given him a nervous tenperament, surfacing in smoking or biting his nails. Eager to penetrate the deepest truths, Michael could pursue social crusades with great dedication. He had a great reserve of energy, the only trouble was, he needed a crisis or danger to harness it.

Jupiter in Virgo suggested that Michael's beliefs were underlined by a sense of fairness and valued quality. Relationsips tended to be a source of wisdom, happiness, as well as much discovery through travel together. By nature gregarious he learned about the world through social interaction. This could have been discoveries through marrying someone from overseas or different from himself, or marrying into money.

With Saturn in Libra, one of Michael's greatest fears was to be considered unjust, rude, or to incur social disapproval. He took his social and partnership obligations seriously. He had a great fear of vunerability of exposing his feelings to the opposite sex. Often he preferred to be distant and aloof. These problems could have been overcome by treating repationships less seriously. He could have worked successfully in the 'beauty business' such as cosmetics, scent or hairdressing. Artistic work was another area where he could have applied his skills. Clearly satisfying his needs was his driving force in his working life even when he lacked nothing. [Yes] Michael felt as if he alternated between emotional security and financial security, which each could be a source of depression. He had a tendancy to worry [?] and got depressed [?] about meaningless problems. Avoiding drugs and too much alcohol [Heavy pressure/thickness of a stroke can be associated with indulging the senses] would have helped to clear up confused fears. A career in art, or in partnership as an agent in that field could have worked.

Uranus in Gemini reveals how Michael (b. 1863) fitted into the wider context of his generation. Generally, he was able and willing to entertain, and even believe many of the enlightened ideas of his age group. The freedom, not only in what he believed in, but also to travel or launch into some exciting new flights of fancy, was something he cherished.

Being prone to nervous tension, he didn't require that much sleep. He was good at juggling with abstract ideas and lateral thinking. Sometimes Michael needed freedom so badly that he was prepared to break away from domestic ties, relationships, his mother, even the task of child rearing or a 'nine to five' existence. [Interesting] It was very easy for him to be cast as 'the black sheep of the family' simply because of his inate need for independence.

Neptune in Aries allows exploration of Michael's compassion, the nature of his deepest spiritual yearings and most elevated ideals. This can only be done by examining the ideals of his generation that were goverened by the passage of Neptune in Aries between 1860 and 1875. Michael and his peers had more then just a fertile imagination; many were able to act out their dreams and become archtypal pioneers. A classic example was the Wright brothers, Wilbur (b. 1867) and Orville (b. 1871) who fearlessly pioneered avation. Mohandas Gandhi (b. 1869) became a master of passive resistance. Missionary Albert Schweitzer (b. 1866) was awarded the Nobel Peace prize. In H.G.Wells (b. 1866) novel *The Wars of the Worlds*, the Martians were defeated by disease, the common cold. Novelists like Kipling, Maughan and Chesterton presented their work through short, punchy, short stories and audacious journalistic pieces.Toulouse-Lautrec (b. 1864) and Mattisse (b. 1869) used stronger images and bolder colours.[Associated with heavy pressure] than their Pisean immpressionist predecessors.'Bolero' by Ravel (b. 1869) summed up the era in musical terms.'

As part of that generation, Michael no doubt had the spirit of a pioneer. By seeing only the good in people or falling in love with an idealised image of a person, rather then the actual person, he set himself up for situations where he was let down and dissillusioned. Falling in love, for him, required a touch of fantasy. It was only by his twenty-ninth year [1898] that he was able to confront his fears and weaknesses.

Being so intuitive, Michael's feelings were easily hurt. Periodically he needed to withdraw into a world of tranquility. The danger came, if this became a substitute for reality, an escape into a fantasy world, or dependence on drink or drugs [again 'muddy writing']. Living near the proverbial slippery slope Michael had to ensure that this escape could take place, through meditation or yoga, in a serene home life, near water of sea.

This reponsiveness to moods and vibrations could have led to uncertainties, worries and problems of relying on those closest to him, especially women. Maybe all this started with his mother whom he felt was not around when he needed her.

Pluto in Taurus shows tha Michael's self concious motivations were part of the Victorian generation where certain principles particularly towards materialism and propriety were upheld at all costs. Powerful tycoons like Henry Ford (b. 1863) and William Randolph Hearst (b. 1863) built up commercial empires. Changing land use and agricultural developments created food surpluses during Michael's prime years. Through materialism was the driving force that enabled the late industrial revolution to flourish, there were many, notably Sigmund Freud (b. 1856), Carl Jung (b. 1857) amd Helen Keller (b. 1880) who went beyond the prevailing superficial understanding of the limitations and working of the mind and the body. In Michael's case, suffice to say that possessions and material values were important to him [Yes] and during his life his attitudes towards them changed in the light of experience. If he had chosen to use it, Michael could exert his authority and power quite constructively [Large initial capitals]. He could get to the root of a problem and had the ability to motivate a team around him especially in an emergency. Sometimes this force could come out in a destructive way, through his temper which could be quite spectacular but usually very effective.

As I perused Michael's handwriting analysis and astrological profile, I was struck by the number of concordant similarities which I found quite uncanny and intriguing. The interpretations certainly gave deeper insights into his character and personality, and how this may have impacted on his destiny in America. He certainly had a sensitive nature, an inate artistic temperament that suggested his fate as an incurable romantic drowning in an ocean of harsh urban–industial reality. I trust his troubled soul can now rest in peace.

Appendix 2: Michael's ancestry.
The O'Mongans of Monganstown

This quest began with a few dilettante searches in the in the National Library in 1973. The few names and dates I found encouraged me to find out more about my ancestors.

Over a number of years, I slowly began to piece together details showing that the entire first millennium of the history of the O Mongans of Monganstown had taken place within a 15-20 kilometre radius of Lough Ennel and Lough Owel in County Westmeath. A contrasting landscape of rolling hills, widespread bogs and tranquil lakes that lay between Kinnegad, Mullingar and the Hill of Uisneach had been my family's ancestral backdrop for many centuries. As a small obscure clan, there was not much recorded evidence of the O Mongans, however, I gleaned glimpses of their existence from scant references in varied sources. A rapid survey of their history showed how closely they were linked to the landscape, and how they had interacted with other tribes, clans and families during that time-span.[1]

One mediaeval manuscript text compiled around AD 1122 mentions, in a graceful, uncial calligraphy the words 'Uí Manchain i Lís na Cluana' ('The O Mongans of the Meadow Homestead'). The manuscript – known as *Betha Colmáin maic Lúacháin* (The Life of St Colmán, son of Lúacháin) – has survived down to the present through a 16th-century copy which is preserved in Rennes Town Library in Brittany. It contains the earliest mention of the O Mongan sept in the Mullingar area.[2] At that time, they were erenaghs (hereditary guardians) of St Colman's Church at Clongawney, 6 kilometres east of Mullingar. I explored the ancient church ruins on the site in the late 1970s, before they were sadly covered over during the building of the Mullingar bypass in the 1980s.[3] Ten kilometres farther east of the church lay the original homeland of the O Mongan sept at Baile Uí Mancháin, now Monganstown townland, just northeast of Kinnegad town on the Westmeath/Meath border.

As I began to seek information on my earliest ancestors, I gradually became involved in researching a book on an ancient Celtic maritime tribe called the Menapii, from whom the O Mongans are descended.[4] It was a search that took me all over Ireland, Scotland and northern France. The Menapii were a Belgic tribe from northern Gaul, who inhabited the dense forests of the Rhine estuary on the North Sea coast before they extended their trading by headland-hopping, up through the Irish Sea. They were unique as they turned out to be the only tribe for whom historical evidence has survived both in Ireland and on the continent. First mentioned by Julius Caesar in his Gallic Wars in ad 574 the Menapii

A page from the manuscript *Betha Colmain mac Luachain*, or 'Life of St Colman' first compiled at Lynn monastery on Lough Ennell, c. 1122 AD, near Mullingar, County Westmeath. The top two lines (underlined) refer to the Ui Manchain i Lis na Cluain, or O Mongan of Monganstown sept, who were the erenaghs, Hereditary Guardians of Clongawney Church, east of Mullingar. (*Courtesy Rennes Municipal Library*)

were singled out by him as the *only* tribe never to surrender to his legions.[5]

From Menapia, the tribe's initial trading enclave founded around Wexford (*c.* 216 BC), the Menapii eventually spread across Ireland, becoming known as the Fir Manach and evolving into historic clans whose descendants are today found worldwide. Names including Mooney, Monaghan, Mannion, Mongan, Mangan, Minogue, Mannix, McMenamin, MacWeeney, McMonagle and MacManninann can all trace back to an original Menapian root. Offshoots of the tribe headed inland, settling along the lakes on the western reaches of the Kingdom of Meath. Here they settled as hunters, fishermen and then graziers.

For centuries, the O Mongan clan were sub-chieftans and tenants-in-chief to their bellicose O'Connor Faly overlords in war and peace. By the 1500s, as kern (clansmen armed with javelins, swords and leather shields) they were resisting encroaching Cambro-Norman Fitzgeralds, D'Arcys, Petits, Tuites and Nugents. Teig Duffe and Gilpatrick Duffe O'Mongan were bodyguards to Cormac Óg Ó Connor Faly of Castlejordan, near Monganstown in 1575.

Their descendant, Brian Mungan, Gent, is mentioned in the aftermath of the

1641 Rising against Cromwell. Religious persecution and the threat of further land confiscations and plantations led to a revolt that brought together the Gaelic chieftains and the Cambro-Norman lords together in their fight against the Parliamentarian forces in Ireland. The Cromwellian land confiscations that followed were to radically change the pattern of land ownership across the island. Cromwell's policy slogan 'To Hell or to Connacht' planned to uproot large proportion of Catholic tenants from the fertile lands in the eastern counties to transport them to the bogs of Connemara by May 1654, though the peasantry were not affected. Others were to be transported as indentured slaves to Barbados as Cromwellian ethnic-cleansing cleared Catholics from their ancestral homelands.

It appears that Brian Mungan's connections to the local landowning Nugent family allowed him and his family to survive those turbulent times.

The 1659 'Census' was compiled in the immediate post-Cromwellian period to ascertain the names of landowners and their holdings. It refers to Brian Mungan, 'Gent, Titulado' who held 8 acres in Ballinalack townland in Leny parish, 15 kilometres north of Mullingar, together with eight other persons, probably his wife, children and household retainers. I suspect that one of Brian's grandsons served with Colonel Christopher Nugent's regiment of Horse in France and, later, as one of the Wild Geese troopers, settled in northwest Spain, to found the Spanish branch of the clan around 1715. By then, the O Mongans had settled on the Nugent estate lands at Walshestown South and became faithful retainers to the Nugent family down to the 1900s.

Monganstown House, a two-storey, three-bay, late Georgian manor, probably dating to the turn of the 19th century, still stands on the ancestral clan homelands of the O Mongans of Monganstown. It was probably built on the site of an earlier smaller thatched dwelling dating from the 17th-century. About 1 kilometre southwest of the house is the site of a ruined rath, or early fortified circular homestead, 40 metres in diameter, sited on a slight slope down to the Kinnegad river. Surveyed in 1981, it faced south with views over gently undulating pasture land. I have often wondered if this was the original O Mongan clan residence in the early mediaeval period.[6]

During my 1973 summer trip to Dublin, I had extraordinary luck in finding that the Mullingar Parish birth, marriage and death registers had entries stretching back in an unbroken line to the 1730s. That in itself was pure serendipity, as much research in Ireland has been frustrated by lack of documentation prior to 1864 when civil registration was introduced.

Then the Mullingar Cathedral birth registers revealed a plethora of Mungans (an 18th-century spelling) linking them with Walshestown South townland. Some forty males bearing the Mungan name were listed as born there between 1750 and 1850. These entries chronicled the gradual drift of family members to Mullingar from the late 18th century. They also showed family names that

The original Monganstown House, dated *c.*1620, was built by Capt. Henry Fitzgerald of Monganstown and Kinnegad Castle, younger brother of Sir Edward of Teocroghan Castle, near Clonard, County Westmeath, descended from the 7th Earl of Kildare. He served with the Archduke in the Low Countries in 1607. He married Bridget D'Arcy of Hyde Park, Rathwire: their Jacobite son Henry (1626-1716) was attainted in 1691. Monganstown House (Baile Ui Manchain) stands on the ancient territory of the O'Mongan clan.

recurred across generations – Patrick, John, James, Joseph, Michael, William, Thomas, Matthew and Denis, along with the less familiar names of Roger, Lewis, Phillip, Hugh, Matthias and Garrett. There were also recurring names among twenty-five female Mungan births – Jane, Judith, Elizabeth, Rose, Catherine, Anne, Elen, Bridget, Mary-Theresa and Mary.

The earliest record I could find was for William Mungan of Walshestown, who was born in 1731 and married a Judy Allen. He had four brothers – Patrick, Joseph, John and Matthew – and three sisters – Jane, Judith and Mary – all of whom were listed as residents of Walshestown South townland. The registers showed that William and Judith had three sons – Michael, Hugh and James – who were later residents 'of Mullingar'.[7]

In 1854, the Valuation Office Books showed a Denis Mangan (another variant spelling) had inherited the 2-acre homestead, still rented from Sir John Nugent of Ballinlough Castle, near Clonmellon. His children, Bridget and John, were the last Mongans to own the ancestral homestead before it passed to John Grimes in 1906. Bridget 'Biddy' Mongan was believed to have lived there as a tenant of John Grimes until the 1920s, and had married a Naughton of nearby Sonna, Slanemore. Among the neighbours were several artisan families: the Allens were chimneysweeps; the Cassidys, farmers; the Ryans, land agents; the Nallys, tailors; while the Mongans were carpenters. In the 1870s, a Thomas Dignam rented a 40-acre farm farther along the road from my family's homestead.

In 1973, I had also visited Mullingar and Walshestown South for the first time, and I drove around the area just to get a sense of the place where the ancestors had lived for so many generations.

Over twenty years later, I returned to Walshestown South and I talked to local residents. Through pure chance I met James Geoghegan, whose Mac Geoghegan clan chieftain ancestors were originally seated at Castletown-geoghegan, near Horseleap. He lived just opposite the site of the former Mongan family cottage site on the Walshestown-Hopestown road. He was able to tell me that the old Mongan homestead had been a typical thatched cottage in the shade of a willow tree on the road that ran along the eastern edge of the former estate. Ironically, he had personally pulled down the old ruins in 1957.

He recalled that his father, Christopher, had talked about Bridget, the last Mongan resident on the homestead, who paid her £2.10 rent to Lady Letitia Nugent. James produced an old Nugent estate map showing the exact locations and holdings of the different tenants on the estate when it was put up for sale in 1900.

Many Mongans had lived and died in this place and were buried at Walshestown cemetery nearby. As I listened to him, I rejoyced in the fact that I had reconnected with the place where the Mongan clan had lived for over two centuries. This was Michael's Irish ancestry.

Appendix 2: Family Trees

The Burns family of Holbrook, MA

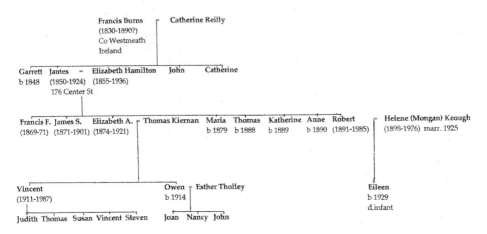

Francis Burns (1830-1890?) = Catherine Reilly
Co Westmeath Ireland

Garrett b 1848 | James (1850-1924) = Elizabeth Hamilton (1855-1936) 176 Center St | John | Catherine

Francis F. (1869-71) | James S. (1871-1901) | Elizabeth A. (1874-1921) = Thomas Kiernan | Maria b 1879 | Thomas b 1888 | Katherine b 1889 | Anne b 1890 | Robert (1891-1985) = Helene (Mongan) Keough (1898-1976) marr. 1925

Vincent (1911-1987) | Owen b 1914 = Esther Tholley | Eileen b 1929 d.infant

Judith Thomas Susan Vincent Steven | Joan Nancy John

The Mongan family of Boston, MA

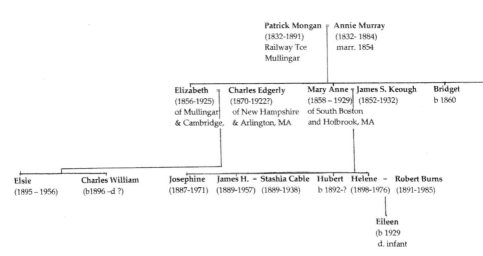

Patrick Mongan (1832-1891) Railway Tce Mullingar = Annie Murray (1832-1884) marr. 1854

Elizabeth (1856-1925) of Mullingar & Cambridge, = Charles Edgerly (1870-1922?) of New Hampshire & Arlington, MA | Mary Anne (1858–1929) of South Boston and Holbrook, MA = James S. Keough (1852-1932) | Bridget b 1860

Elsie (1895–1956) | Charles William (b1896 –d ?) | Josephine (1887-1971) | James H. (1889-1957) = Stashia Cable (1889-1938) | Hubert b 1892-? | Helene (1898-1976) = Robert Burns (1891-1985)

Eileen (b 1929 d. infant

The Hurd family of Cambridge, MA

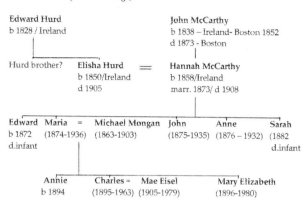

Edward Hurd
b 1828 / Ireland

John McCarthy
b 1838 – Ireland- Boston 1852
d 1873 - Boston

Hurd brother?   Elisha Hurd   ===   Hannah McCarthy
                 b 1850/Ireland   b 1858/Ireland
                 d 1905   marr. 1873/ d 1908

Edward Maria = Michael Mongan John   Anne   Sarah
b 1872 (1874-1936) (1863-1903)   (1875-1935) (1876 – 1932) (1882
d.infant   d.infant

Annie   Charles = Mae Eisel   Mary Elizabeth
b 1894   (1895-1963) (1905-1979)   (1896-1980)

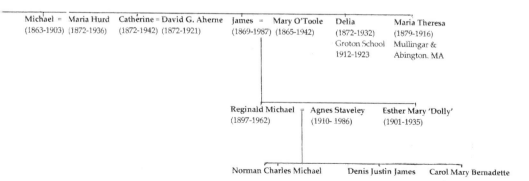

Michael = Maria Hurd   Catherine = David G. Aherne   James = Mary O'Toole   Delia   Maria Theresa
(1863-1903) (1872-1936) (1872-1942) (1872-1921)   (1869-1987) (1865-1942) (1872-1932)   (1879-1916)
                                                                               Groton School Mullingar &
                                                                               1912-1923   Abington. MA

Reginald Michael = Agnes Staveley   Esther Mary 'Dolly'
(1897-1962)   (1910- 1986)   (1901-1935)

Norman Charles Michael   Denis Justin James   Carol Mary Bernadette

The Aherne family of Abington, MA

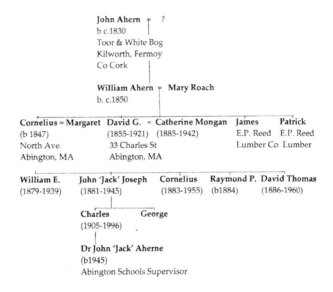

John Ahern ⊤ ?
b c.1830
Toor & White Bog
Kilworth, Fermoy
Co Cork

William Ahern = Mary Roach
b. c.1850

Cornelius = Margaret   David G. = Catherine Mongan   James   Patrick
(b 1847)   (1855-1921) (1885-1942)   E.P. Reed E.P. Reed
North Ave.   33 Charles St   Lumber Co Lumber
Abington, MA   Abington, MA

William E.   John 'Jack' Joseph   Cornelius   Raymond P. David Thomas
(1879-1939)   (1881-1945)   (1883-1955) (b1884)   (1886-1960)

Charles   George
(1905-1996)

Dr John 'Jack' Aherne
(b1945)
Abington Schools Supervisor

Bibliography

Andrews, G.H. and Davies. K.M. *Irish Historic Towns Atlas - Mullingar*, R.I.A., Dublin, 1988

Ashburn, Frank D., *Fifty Years On – Groton School 1884-1934*, Gosden Head, New York, 1934

Ashburn, Frank D., *Peabody of Groton–A Portrait of Endicott Peabody*, Riverside Press, Cambridge, 1967

Barnard, T.C., *Cromwellian Ireland*, Oxford University, 1976

Barthorp, Michael, & Turner, Pierre, *The British Army on Campaign (4) 1882-1902*, Osprey Publishing, 1988

Bastarreche, Fernando Fernandez, *El Ejercito Espanol en el siglo XIX*, Madrid, 1979

Beatty, Jack, *The Rascal King: The Life and Times of James Michael Curley. 1874-1958*, Reading MA. 1992

Bence-Jones, Mark, *Twilight of the Ascendancy*, London, 1987

——*A Guide to Irish Country Houses* London, 1988, revised ed.

Berresford-Ellis, Peter, *The Celtic Empire – The First Millennium of Celtic History, 1000 BC-51 AD*, Constable, London, 1990

——*Erin's Blood Royal – The Gaelic Noble Dynasties of Ireland*, London, 1999

Betjeman, John, *John Betjeman's Collect Poems*, John Murray, London, 1970

Bowers, Fergal, *Suicide in Ireland*, Colour Books Ltd, 1994

Burke's Peerage& Baronetage, 106th edition, Vol II, London, 1999

Burns, Eric, *The Spirit of America: A Social History of Alcohol*, Philadelphia University Press, 2004.

Brady, Rev. J., *Parish of Mullingar* Mullingar,

Byrne, F.J., *Irish Kings and High Kings*. B.T. Batsford, London, 1973

Casey, Christine, and Rowan, Alistair, *North Leinster: the counties of Longford, Louth, Meath and Westmeath*, The Buildings of Ireland series] Penguin Books, 1993

Cogan, Anthony *Diocese of Meath, Vol III,*

Clark, Samuel, and Donnelly, Jr., James S. *Irish Peasants - Violence and Political Unrest, 1780-1914*, Gill & McMillan, 1983

Clarke, Bradley H. and Cummings, O.R. *Tremont Street Subway – A Century of Public Service*, Boston, 1997

Craig, Maurice, *The Architecture of Ireland from the Earliest Times to 1880,* London and Dublin 1982

——*Classic Irish Houses of the Middle Size*, The Architectural Press, London, 1976

Crespo-Pozo, Fray Jose-Santiago, Blasones y Linages de Galicia, *Enciclopedia Gallego II (tomo II)*, Parte Genealogica, Santiago de Compostella, 1965

Curley, James Michael, *I'd Do It Again: A Record of All My Uproarious Years*, Englewood Cliffs, N.J., 1957

Dickson, W.K. *The Jacobite Attempt of 1719* Edinburgh, 1895

Dinneen, Joseph F. *The Purple Shamrock: The Hon. James Michael Curley of Boston*, New York, 1949

Dallek, Robert, *John F. Kennedy. An Unfinished Life*, Penguin Books, 2003

Daly, Leo, (ed.) *Life of Colman of Lynn- Betha Colmain Lainne*, Lilliput Press, 1999

Dauwer, Leo P. *I Remember Southie*, Christopher Publishing House, Boston, 1975

Dease, Edmund F. *A Complete History of the Westmeath Hunt*, Dublin, 1898

De Cadenas y Vicent, D. Vincente, *Repertorio de Blasones de la Communidad Hispanica*, Hidalguia, Madrid, 1966

——*Elenco de Grandeza y Titulos Nobiliarios Espagnoles*, Hidalguia, Madrid, 1975

De Cosson, Maj. E.A. *Fighting the Fuzzy-Wuzzy*, Greenhill Books, London, 1990

Dickenson-Fally, M., *Irish and Scotch-Irish Ancestral Research*, Vol 1,

Diner, Hasia R. *Erin's Daughters in America*, John Hopkin's University Press, 1983

Dooley, Terence, *The Decline of the Big House in Ireland – A Study of Irish Landed Families, 1860-1960,* Wolfhound Press, 2001

Donovan, Charles F., et al. *A History of Boston College,* Chestnut Hill.MA, 1990

Duffy, Richard A. *Arlington,* Arcadia Publishing, 1997

Duffy, Sean (ed.) *Atlas of Irish History,* Gill & McMillan, 2000

Duggan, John P. *A History of the Irish Army,* Gill & McMillan, 1991

Ellis, P.B. *Hell or Connaught- The Cromwellian Colonisation of Ireland, 1652-60,* Hamish Hamilton, 1975

Emden, A.B., *Biographical Register of Oxford University to A.D. 1500,* Oxford, 1958

Estorick, Michael, *Heirs and Graces: The Claim to the Dukedom of Leinster,* London, 1981

Faulkner, H.U., *Politics, Reform and Expansion, 1890-1900,* Harper & Row, New York, 1950

Finegan, John, *The Story of Monto- An Account of Dublin's notorious Red Light District* Mercier Press, Cork, 1978

Fitzgerald, B., *The Geraldines, an experiment in Irish Government,* London, 1956

Fitzsimons, Fiona, The Lordship of O'Connor Faly, 1520-1570, in *Offaly-History and Society,* Kevin Whelan (ed.) Geography Publications, Dublin. 1999

Fortesque, John, *The Royal Army Service Corps-History of Transport and Supply in the British Army,* Cambridge University Press, 1930

Frank, Gerold, *The Boston Strangler,* New American Library, 1966

Godley, Gen. Sir Alex, *Life of an Irish Soldier,* Dublin, 1939

Goodwin, Doris Kearns, *The Fitzgeralds and the Kennedys: An American Saga,* New York, 1987

Garcia Carraffa, J.A., *Enciclopedia Heraldica y Genealogica,* Madrid, 1915

Grenham, John, *Tracing your Irish Ancestors,* Gill & McMillan, 1992

Grob, Gerald N. *The Mad Among Us – A History of the Care of America's Mentally Ill,* Harvard University Press, 1994

——*The State and the Mentally Ill; a history of Worcester State Hospital in Massachusetts, 1830-1920,* Chapel Hill, University of North Carolina Press, 1966

Guinness, Desmond and Ryan, William, *Irish Houses and Castles* London, 1971

Handcock, S.A. (ed.) *Caesar. The Conquest of Gaul,* Penguin Books, Harmondsworth, 1984

Handlin, Oscar, *Boston's Emmigrants, 1780-1880,* Cambridge, MA. 1941

Hayman, Ronald, *A Life of Jung,* New York, 2001

Hitchcock, F.R.M., *The Midland Septs and the Pale,* Dublin, 1908

Horgan, John, *Sean Lemass- The Enigmatic Patriot,* Gill & McMillan, 1999

Howard-Bury, Charles, *Mountains of Heaven: Travels in the Tian Shan Mountains, 1913,* Marian Keaney (ed.) London, 1990

——Lt.Col. C.K. *Mount Everest: the reconnaissance,* London, 1921

Hussey De Burgh, U.H., *The Landowners of Ireland: An Alphabetical List of Owners of Estates of 500 acres or £500 Valuation and Upwards in Ireland* (Dublin, 1878)

Illingworth, R. (ed.) *When the Train Came to Mullingar–150 Years of Mullingar Railway Station, 1848-1998,* Mullingar, 1998

James, Henry, *The Bostonians,* MacMillan & Co, London and New York, 1886

Keaney, Marian, *Westmeath Authors,* Mullingar, 1969

——*Westmeath Local Studies: A Guide to Local Sources,* Mullingar, 1982

Kelly, Susan, *Boston Stranglers: The Wrongful Conviction of Labert DeSalvo and the True Story of Eleven Shocking Murders,* Carol Publishing Group, 1995

Kenny, Kevin, *The American Irish: A History,* Boston, 2000

Killanin, Lord, and Duignan, M.V. *The Shell Guide to Ireland,* Gill & McMillan, 1989

Lehr, Dick, and O'Neill, Gerard, *Black Mass, The true Story of an Unholy Alliance Between the FBI and the Irish Mob,* Perseus, New York, 2000

Lewis, Samuel, *The Topographical Dictionary of Ireland* Vol II, Dublin, 1837

Loftus, Patrick J. Jr., *That Old Gang of Mine: A History of South Boston*, South Boston, 1991

Lord, Robert H., Sexton, John E., and Harrington, Edward, *History of the Archdiocese of Boston*, 3 vols., Boston. MA, 1945

Lyons. J.C. *The Grand Juries of Westmeath, 1727 to 1853,* Lediston, 1878

Mac Curtain, M. *Tudor and Stuart Ireland,* Gill & McMillan, 1972

Masters, John, *Casanova*, Penguin Books, 2001

Matheson, Sir Robert, *Surnames in Ireland,* Genealogical Publishing, Baltimore, 1988

McGrath, F., S.J. *Education in Ancient and Medieval Ireland,* Scellig Press, Tralee, 1979

McKisack, M., The Fourteenth Century, 1307-1399, in *The Oxford History of England* (ed. Sir George Clarke), Oxford, 1959

McLaughlin, M.G., *The Wild Geese, the Irish Brigades in the service of Spain and France*, Osprey Publications, London, 1980

Meagher, Timothy J., *Inventing Irish America: Generation, Class and Ethnic Identity in a New England City, 1880-1920*, Notre Dame University, 2001

——*From Paddy to Studs: Irish-American Communities in the Turn of the Century Era, 1880 – 1920*, Greenwood Press, 1986

Meyer, K. *Betha Colmain maic Luachain (Life of St Colman of Lann)*. R.I.A., Dublin, 1911

Miller, Kirby A. *Emigrants and Exiles – Ireland and the Irish Exodus to North America*, Oxford University Press, 1985

Mongan, Norman, *The Menapia Quest*, The Herodotus Press, Dublin, 1995

Loftus, Patrick J. *That Old Gang of Mine-A History of South Boston*, Boston, 1976

Moody, T.W., and Martin, F.X., (eds.) *The Course of Irish History*, Mercier Press, Cork, 1967

——F.J. Byrne, *A New History of Ireland*, Vol III, Early Modern Ireland, 1534-1691, Oxford, 1976

Morrissey, Joseph P., Goldman, Howard H., Klerman, L.V., *The Enduring Asylum: cycles of institutional reform at Worcester State Hospital*, Grune & Stratton, New York, 1980

Mulligan, Fergus, *Railways in Ireland, 1834-1984*, Dublin, 1985

Nalson, David, *The Victorian Soldier*, Shire Publications Ltd, 2000

Nolan, Janet A. *Ourselves Alone- Women's Emigration from Ireland, 1885-1920*, University Press of Kentucky, 1989

Nolan, Matt, *Mullingar- Just For the Record*, Crigean Press, 1999

Neill, Kenneth, *The Age of Steam and Steel- Ireland, Britain and Europe in the Nineteenth Century*, Gill and McMillan, 1976

Nichols, Kenneth., *Gaelic and Gaelicised Ireland in the Middle Ages*, Gill & McMillan, 1972

Nugent, Sir Hugh, *The Sir*, privately published. Mullingar, 1990

O'Brien, Gearoid, *Belvedere House Gardens & Park-The Official Guide*, Temple Printing, 2000

O'Brien, M.A., *Corpus Genealogiarum Hibernae*, Dublin Institute, Dublin, 1978

O'Connor, Thomas H. *The Boston Irish – A Political History*, Boston, 1995

——*Boston A to Z*, Harvard University Press, Cambridge, MA, 2000

——*South Boston: My Home Town- The History of an Ethnic Neighbourhood*, Northeastern University Press, 1994

O'Farrell, Padraic, *The Book of Mullingar*, Uisneach Press, 1986

O'Hart, John, *Irish Pedigrees*, 2 Vols. Dublin, 1887-88

O Raithbheartaig, T., *Genealogical Tracts* 1, Irish Manuscripts Commission, Dublin, 1932

Orpen, G.H., *Ireland under the Normans*, London, 1939

Pardo, A. Meijide, *La Invasion Inglesa de Galicia en 1719*, Santiago de Compostella, 1970

Pender, Seamus, *A Census of Ireland, 1659*, IMC, Dublin, 1935

Peters, S. Orcutt, *Abington*, Arcadia Publihsing, 2002

Potter, E.B. *The United States and World Sea Power*, Prentice Hall, New York, 1955

Pratt, F. *The Navy-A History*, Doubleday & Doran, New York, 1938

Rhine, J.B., et al., *Extra-Sensory Perception After Sixty Years* Holt, New York, 1940; Humphries, Boston, 1966

——*Parapsychology: Frontier Science of the Mind*, Charles Thomas, Spring-field, Illinois, 1937

Robson, Brian, *Fuzzy-Wuzzy, The Campaigns in Eastern Sudan 1884-85*, Spellmount Ltd, 1993

Ruvigny, Marquis de, *The Titled Nobility of Europe*, London, 1914

Ryan, Dennis P. *A Journey through Boston Irish History*, Acadia Publishing, 1999

——*Beyond the Ballot Box*, Rutherford, N.J., 1983

Sammarco, A. Mitchell, *Cambridge*, Arcadia Publishing, 1999

——*South Boston*, Arcadia Publishing , 1996

——*South Boston* (Vol II) Arcadia Publishing, 2000

Shannon, William V. *The American Irish*, New York, 1966

Share, Bernard, *The Emergency–Neutral Ireland, 1939-45,* Gill & McMillan, 1978

Sharkey, Olive, 'Belvedere House, gem of the Irish Midlands' in *The GPA Irish Arts Review Yearsbook, 1989-90*, pp 248- 253

Shehan, J., *Westmeath: as others saw it*, Moate, 1982

Sheehy, M., *When the Normans Came to Ireland*, Mercier Press, 1975

Shepherd, W. Ernest, *The Midland Great Western Railway of Ireland*, Midland Publishing Ltd, 1994

Smyth, Alfred. P, *Celtic Leinster*, Irish Academic Press, 1982

Smyth, W.J., Society and settlement in the seventeenth century Ireland: the evidence of the' 1659 Census' in *The Common Ground*, Studies in honour of Prof. Hughes, William J. Smyth and Kevin Whelan, (eds.) Cork University Press, 1982

Spellissy, Sean, *Suicide- The Irish Experience*, On Stream Publications, 1996

Sullivan, D. B. and Tighe, J.P. *Weymouth*, Arcadia, 2001

Sutton, John, (ed.) *Wait for the Waggon – The Story of the Royal Corps of Transport and its Predecessors, 1794-1993,* Pen&Sword Books, 1998

Sweetman, Jack, *The Landing at Vera Cruz: 1914*, Naval Institute Press, 1968

Tatlow, Joseph, *Fifty Years of Railway Life*, London, 1920

Tierney, Phillip, *Mullingar in Old Picture Postcards*, European Library, Zaltbommel, Nederlands, 1995

Trustees of Groton School, Groton School, 1884-1985, Groton, MA. 1986

Warner, Sam Bass, *Streetcar Suburbs* New York, 1974

Wallace, Martin, *A Short History of Ireland*, Appletree Press, Belfast, 1986

Wallace, Peter, *Multyfarnham Parish History*, Mullingar, 1987

Walsh, Micheline K., 'Destruction by Peace' *Hugh O Neill after Kinsale*, Cumann Seanchais Ard Macha, Monaghan, 1986

Walsh, Rev. Paul, *The Placenames of Westmeath*, Dublin Institute of Advanced Studies, Dublin, 1957

——*Ancient Westmeath*, Dublin, 1913

——*Some Placenames in Ancient Westmeath*, 1946

White, D.G., *The Tudor Plantations in Ireland before 1571*, Unpublished Ph.D thesis, T.C.D., 2 vols (1968)

Wilkinson-Latham, Robert, Roffe, Michael *The Sudan Campaigns, 1881-1898*, Osprey Publishing Ltd, 1976

Wood, Tim, *The Victorians*, Ladybird Books, 1999

Woodham-Smith, Cecil, *The Great Hunger: Ireland, 1848-1849*, New York, 1962

Woods, J, *Annals of Westmeath, ancient and modern*, Dublin, 1907

Newspapers consulted

Cambridge Chronicle
Boston Globe
Boston American Herald
Galway Advertiser
Irish Times
Quincy Patriot Ledger
Westmeath Examiner

Websites consulted

www.opacity.us
www.kirkbridebuildings.com/buildings/worcester
www.connection.ebscohost.com/
wswww.associatedcontent.com/fighting_for_preservation_worcester.html
www.preservationnation.org/.../demolition-at-worcester.html
www.WorcesterMass.com
www.abandonedasylum.com/photos. html/
http://www.geocities.com/Athens/2008/pcards.htm
www.massnurses.org/files/News/.../032703worcester.petition.pdf
www.flickr.com/photos/2220677@No7/3395882135/
www.yelp.com/biz/worcester-state-hospital-worcester
www.telegraph.com/article/20080416/NEWS02
www.worcestermag.com/archives/2007/01-04.../cover.html
www.surrealnewjersey.com/worcester_clocktowr.htm
www.navsource.org/archives/01/19.htm
www.greatwhitefleet.info

Notes

Introduction

1 Unmarried, Agnes had been the first woman appointed as keeper to the Fogg Art Museum at the Harvard University Art Museum. As an internationally recognised as an expert in 18-19th century Old Master drawings, especially French artists like Ingres, David and Corot, she pioneered women's breakthrough into senior curatorial positions. Revered as an outstanding teacher, she died in 1996 and her legacy is now remembered by the Agnes Mongan Center for the Study of Prints, Drawings and Photographs established in her memory in 1994.

Notes on Chapter 3

Belvedere House. Upstairs, Downstairs

1 Richard Castle (1690-1751), the celebrated 18th-century architect, has been credited with designing the house on its majestic settings overlooking the lake. Born in Kassel, in Hesse, Germany, he was brought to Ireland from London in 1728 by Sir Gustavus Hume to design Castle Hume in County Fermanagh. O'Brien, G., *Belvedere House Gardens & Park, The Official Guide*, Athlone, 2000, p 4.

2 O' Brien, G., *ibid*, p 18

3 Lord Belvedere also ended up at loggerheads with another brother George who had commissioned Richard Castle to design a mansion for him nearby. As the house was considerably larger than Belvedere, Robert was consumed by jealousy and rage. In 1760, he commissioned an elaborate sham Gothic ruin to be built, reminiscent of a large medieval priory. Known as the Jealous Wall, it completely blocked the view of Rochfort House (now Tudenham House) from the Belvedere estate. The Jealous Wall fulfilled its purpose perfectly, becoming one of the most celebrated and spectacular follies in Ireland. Now restored, it stands today as a grim witness of the venomous hate and malice that Lord Belvedere visited on his hapless brother.

4 Reginald Mongan Archives, Dublin. John Duignam, as Coachman, resided with his family in a stone cottage located half way up the entrance avenue to Belvedere House. (The abandoned ruinous building still exists on site) He was replaced after his death c1892-94 by English-born William Yeoman, (1861-1944) of Wanstrow, near Salisbury, Somerset, and his wife Alice Emma (née Boyns). He had been previously employed by Charles Brinsley Marlay at his London home. William Yeoman's sons Richard (b 1894) and Robert (b 1896) were both born at Belvedere. My thanks to Robert Yeoman, Toronto, Canada, and Desmond Yeoman, Mullingar, for providing this information.

5 Keaney, M., The Exquisite Life of Charles Brinsley Marlay in *Offaly Heritage*, Tullamore, Vol 2, 2004, pp 137-48. See also Constable, W.G., *Catalogue of Pictures in the Marlay Bequest*, Fitzwilliam Museum, Cambridge Museum, 1927. The author wishes to thank Marian Keaney for kindly drawing author's attention to this material.

6 *idem*, Reginald Mongan Archives

7 Dooley, T., *The Decline of the Big House in Ireland – A Study of Irish Landed Families, 1860-1960*, Wolfhound Press, Dublin, 2001, p 152

8 Dooley, T., *ibid*, p 157

9 Dooley, T., *ibid*, pp 157-8

10 Dooley, T., *ibid*, p 160

11 Hussey De Burgh, U.H., *The Landowners of Ireland*, Dublin, 1878, p 307

12 *ibid*, Belvedere House Silver Inventory, Marian Keaney Private Collection, Mullingar

13 Howard-Bury, C., *Mountains of Heaven* –

Travels in the Tian Shan Mountains, 1913, (Keaney, M., ed.) Hodder & Stoughton, London, 1990. See also Howard-Bury, C., & Mallory, G.L., *Everest reconnaissance. The First Expedition of 1921.* (Keaney, M.ed.) Hodder & Stoughton, London, 1991

14 Betjeman, J., *Collected Poems*, Enlarged edition, John Murray, London, 1970

15 Editorial Dick Hogan, An Upstairs-Downstairs story from Belvedere, in *Topic* newspaper, Mullingar, May 24, 2001, p 7

16 Author interview with Ms Mary O'Donoghue, Mullingar, April, 2001. Ms O'Donoghue (neé Molloy) recalled that 40 Mount St, built circa 1850, had originally been the home of Mr McNaboe, a vetinary surgeon. The Valuation Office Cancelled Books indicate that Mary Duignam Jr had purchased the property in 1905 from a James Allen, who had been leasing the property from Lord Greville. In 1906 Mary Duignam was a lessor to Christopher Gogarty, and in 1910 to Mary Gaynor, with whom she appears to have shared the property for the next forty years. Mary Duignam Jr retired from Belvedere around 1938, when she began taking in boarders at 40 Mount St. Mary Gaynor died in 1949, when Mary Duignam Jr became the resident-owner until her death in 1956, aged 80. She had apparently mortgaged the property to a local solicitor in return for a regular income in her final years. No family relatives were mentioned were mentioned in any legal documents. The house was sold to James Molloy in 1958 and inherited by Ms O'Donoghue in 1964. Former Westmeath County Librarian Marian Keaney was a boarder at 40 Mount St in her early years in Mullingar. My thanks to Mary O'Donoghue for providing this important information, and for the erection of a memorial stone over Mary Duignam Jr's grave at Meedin cemetery, Tyrrellspass.

Notes on Chapter 4
Patrick Mongan. Mullingar railway pioneer

1 Sheperd, W. E., *The Midland Great Western Railway of Ireland – An Illustrated History*,

Midland Publishing, Leicester, 1994, p 15

2 O'Farrell, P., *The Book of Mullingar*, Mullingar, 1987, p 53

3 Shepherd, W.E., *ibid*, p 109

4 O Conlain, *ibid*, p 3

5 O Conlain, M., Mullingar News A Century Ago, and Mullingar Cabins A Century Ago, in *Westmeath Examiner*. March 23, 1957

6 Morrison, R., *When The Train Came To Mullingar*, ibid, Introduction, v

7 O Conlain, M., Mullingar As A Railway Centre, in *When The Train Came To Mullingar – 150 Years Of The Mullingar Railway Station, 1857-1998*, Mullingar, 1998, p 38

8 Shepherd, W.E., *ibid*, p 110

9 However, employment with the MGWR was not without its risks. In 1869, Mullingar Station was the scene of a brutal murder. On Wednesday, 3 March, the recently appointed stationmaster, Thomas Anketell, was shot as he entered his house near the engine shed at the station and died three days later. Held in such high regard, the directors attended his funeral and offered a £200 reward for information about his murder. They also persuaded the shareholders to grant £700 to his widow. The reward remained unclaimed and the two men suspected of the crime were eventually released for lack of evidence. Anketell had been murdered allegedly as the result of the dismissal of a long-serving railway policeman named Moran for 'irregular habits and addicted to tippling.' Ribbonmen were believed to have carried out the killing in reprisal for the dismissal. Moran, a Catholic, had blamed Anketell for his dismissal, and had referred to him as an Orangeman. Following his dismissal towns people had organised a subscription for him, encouraged by Catholic priest Rev Michael Gogarty, who believed he had been harshly treated, and the dismissal was due to his religion. Sectarian tensions simmered throughout the whole affair.

10 Mullingar Parish Birth Registers, Cathedral House, Mullingar. Transcipts held at Westmeath County Library, Mullingar.

11 O Conlain, M., *Mullingar As A Railway Centre, ibid*, p 38
12 Shepherd, W.E., *Murder At Mullingar, ibid*, p 21

Notes on Chapter 5
Michael. Taking the Queen's shilling

1 He was the son of Rosa, daughter of the last head of the Nugent family, George, eighth Earl of Westmeath, who resided at Clonlyn Castle, in Delvin.
2 Andrews, G.H., and Davies, *Irish Historic Town Atlas–Mullingar*, R.I.A., Dublin, 1988.
3 Nolan, M., *Just For The Record – A Window On The Millenium*, Crigean Press, Mullingar, 1999, 'A Millenium History'
4 Worcester State Hospital, Medical Records File No 22242: Michael J. Mongan. Interview with doctors, July 1, 1902. p 3. He mentions his teacher in Ireland as Mr 'Kartin' [possibly a mis-spelling by doctors for 'Curtin' ?].
5 Shepherd, W.E., *The Midland Great Western Railway of Ireland–An Illustrated History*, Midland Publishing Ltd, Leicester, 1994, p 29
6 *Westmeath Examiner*, September, 6, 1884, Newspaper Collection on Microfilm, National Library of Ireland, Dublin.
7 Daly, L., *James Joyce and the Mullingar Connection*, Dolmen Press, Dublin, 1957
8 *Westmeath Examiner*, September, 6, 1884
9 Public Records Office, Kew, Richmond, Short Service Record No 5831, Michael Mongan, PRO Ref No: WO 97/3485
10 In 1807, the War Department had pur-chased the site for a barracks, and the 78th Highlanders were the first regiment to occupy the it in 1819. From then on, it was the base for many different regiments over the years. It could even boast of hav-ing the world's 'longest lease', when, in 1868, Colonel Fulke Southwell Greville Nugent, of the Westmeath Militia, leased a right of way to the Secretary of State for War – for a peppercorn. The lease was for an astounding 10 million years.
11 Nolan, M., *Just For The Record, A Millenium History*
12 'D', for 'deserter', was branded on a sol-dier's chest and 'BC', for 'bad character', was branded 2 inches below and 1 inch in rear of the left nipple.
13 Public Record Office, Kew, Richmond, PRO Ref No: WO 97/3485
14 Robson, B., *Fuzzy Wuzzy – The Campaigns in the Eastern Sudan, 1884-85*, Spellmount, Tunbridge Wells, 1993, p 2, pp 16-27
15 Public Record Office, *ibid*, PRO Ref No: WO 97/3485
16 Public Record Office, *ibid*, PRO Ref No: WO 16/2557
17 Public Record Office, *ibid*, PRO Ref No: WO 16/2566, p 27
18 Joslin, E.C., et al, *British Battles & Medals*, London, 1995, p 161
19 Public Records Office, *ibid*, PRO Ref No: WO 16/2566
20 Public Records Office, *ibid*, PRO Ref No: WO 16/2591
21 Public Records Office, *ibid*, PRO Ref No: WO 16/2579
22 Public Records Office, *ibid*, PRO Ref No: WO 16/2573
23 Public Records Office, *ibid*, PRO Ref No: WO 16/2577
24 History of the 12th Company, C&T Corps, *ibid*, p 4
25 Finegan, J., *The Story Of Monto – An Account Of Dublin's Notorious Red Light District*, Mercier Press, Cork, 1978, pp 6-9
26 Public Records Office, *ibid*, PRO Ref No: WO 97/3485
27 Public Records Office, *ibid*, PRO Ref No: WO 97/3485
28 Public Records Office, *ibid*, PRO Ref No: WO 97/3485
29 Robert O'Hara, London, Letter to author, October, 1999, (Public Records Officer advisor Malcolm Mercer estimated that it would have cost Lance-Corporal Michael J. Mongan about £25 to buy his way out of the Army in 1888.)

Notes on Chapter 6
'Southie'. Michael's home away from home

1 List of Passengers, Cunard steamship SS *Cephalonia*, Capt Henry Walker manifest, Boston, Feb 4, 1888, Michael J. Mongan

(mispelt 'Morgan'). Passenger No 50. No 2 compartment, National Archives & Records Administration, North Eastern section, Waltham, MA,

2 Cunard Line website, Cunard Heritage,- The Fleet: SS *Cephalonia*, 1882-1904 www.cunardline. com

3 Ryan, D. P., *A Journey Through Boston Irish History, Images of America*, Arcadia Publishing, Charleston, SC, 1999, p 13

4 David Ahearn, employed Reed's lumber-yard, *Abington Resident Directory*, 1889, p 85

5 Worcester State Hospital, Medical Records File No: 22713, Michael J. Mongan, Interview with doctors, May 13, 1903, p 3. Worcester State Hospital, Medical Records File No: 20965, Michael J. Mongan, Interview with doctors, May 18, 1900, p 1

6 Naturalisation Papers, US Circuit Court, Boston MA, Michael J. Mongan, Feb 3, 1893, Record Group No 21, National Archives & Records Administration, North Eastern section, Waltham, MA

7 Naturalisation Papers, US Circuit Court, Boston, *ibid*,

8 Naturalisation Papers, US Circuit Court, Boston, *ibid*

9 O'Connor, T. H., *The Boston Irish – A Political History*, Back Bay Books, Boston, 1995, p141

10 O' Connor, T. H., *The Boston Irish, ibid*, pp 141-48

11 Thomas H.O'Connor, Boston College, Boston MA, Interview with author, Oct, 2002

12 O'Connor, T.H., *The Boston Irish – A Political History*, Boston, 1995, p 128,

13 O'Connor, T.H., *ibid*, p 132

14 O'Connor, T.H., *ibid*, p 133

15 O'Connor, T.H., *ibid*, p 161

16 Clarke, B.H., and Cummings, O.R., Tremont Street Subway – A Century of Public Service, *Bulletin No 22, Boston Street Railway Association*, Inc, Boston, MA, 1997, p 5. My thanks to Charles Bahne, Vice – President, Boston Street Railway Association, Inc. for guiding me to this valuable source.

17 Clarke, B.H., and Cummings, O.R., *Tremont Street Subway*, p 7

18 Clarke, B.H., and Cummings, O.R., *Tremont Street Subway* p 8

19 Clarke, B.H., and Cummings, O.R., *Tremont Street Subway* p 9

20 Clarke, B,H., and Cummings, O.R., *Tremont Street Subway* p 35

21 O'Connor, T.H., *South Boston, My Home Town – The History Of An Ethnic Neighbourhood*, Quinlan Press, Boston, 1988, reprinted by Northeastern University Press, Boston, 1994, pp 16-17

22 Loftus, P.J., *That Old Gang Of Mine – A History Of South Boston*, Boston, 1991, pp 214- 17

23 Loftus, P.J., *That Old Gang Of Mine*, p 214

24 Loftus, P.J., *That Old Gang Of Mine*, pp 21-22

25 Loftus, P.J., *That Old Gang Of Mine*, p 32

26 Sammarco, A.M., *South Boston, Images of America*, Arcadia Publishing, Dover, NH, 1996, p 32

27 Sammarco, A.M., *South Boston, Vol II, Images of America*, Arcadia Publishing, Dover, NH, 2000, p 100

28 O'Connor, T.H., *South Boston, My Home Town*, p 108

29 O'Connor, T.H., *South Boston, My Home Town*, p 125

30 Cambridge Street Directories, 1898-1904, Cambridge Public Library, Cambridge, MA.

31 Michael J. Mongan & Maria E. Hurd, Marriage Cerificate, Vol. 434, p 98, No 41, Massachusetts State Archives, Boston, MA. See biography of Rev Dr George W. Bicknell, (1837-1916) in *The Universalist Leader, Vol. XIX*, No 25, June 17, 1916. The Universalist denomination in the United States originated with John Murray, a convert to Universalism as taught by James Relly in England. Murray arrived in New Jersey in 1770 and preached in New York and throughout New England. He later settled in Gloucester, Massachusetts, where, in 1779, he became pastor of the First Universalist Church in the country. Murray's Universalism was of the Calvinist type.

The movement spread – in 1790 a convention in Philadelphia decided upon a congregational polity and drew up a profession of faith, now merged with the Unitarian Church since 1961

32 Edward Hines, Boston, Letter to author, Nov 16, 1981

33 Edward Hines, Boston, Letter to author, Nov 3, 1985

34 Annie E. Mongan, born March 21, 1894, 112 Second St, South Boston, MA, Birth Index Book, Vol. 441, p 27

35 Sammarco, A.M., *South Boston, Vol II*, p 118

36 See www. Financialhistory. org website: Niedringhaus, L.I., The Panic Of 1893, in *The Depression of 1893* Whitten, D.O. (ed.) Auburn University, 1998, pp 1-5

37 Annie E. Mongan, died July 29, 1894, Malden MA, Death Index Book, Vol. 446, p 135

38 O'Connor, T.H., *South Boston, My Home Town*, p 117

39 Fouhey, David, *Poems*, (Courtesy John M. & Barbara Tivnan, Woodbridge, VA.). David S. Fouhey was born in Carrigtohill, Co Cork in 1848, son of Jeremiah and Bridget Buckley. Educated in local national schools, he emigrated to America in 1868 and settled in Salem, Mass, where he married Margaret Collins in 1868. They went on to have twelve children together. Fouhey worked as a tanner until 1886 and then as a labourer until 1908. He was appointed caretaker of reservoir and roads, a position he held until 1926.

40 Edward Hines, Letter to author, Nov 3, 1985

41 Gate of Heaven Church, 609 East Fourth St, South Boston, MA, Baptism Registers, 1887-1894, Catholic Archdiocese of Boston Archives, Brighton, MA. My sincere thanks to Mss Mary Lou Dennehy and Mary Lowe, who extracted this baptismal information.

42 Sammarco, A.M., *South Boston*, pp 99-108

43 Worcester State Hospital, Medical Records File No: 20965, Michael J. Mongan, Interview with doctors, May 18, 1900

44 Boston Street Directories, 1894 -1898, Microtexts Department, Boston Public Library, Boston, MA

45 City of Cambridge, Massachusetts website, www.ci.Cambridge.ma.us, 'A Brief History Of Cambridge', p 2

46 The Hurd family (also spelt Heard) were of Cromwellian stock in Ireland, where they settled in the 1650s. Humphrey Hurd became Mayor of Galway, and later became a substantial landowner near Kilkenny city. See Barnard, T.C., *Cromwellian Ireland*, Oxford University Press, 1976.

47 Cambridge Street Directories, 1898 - 1918, Cambridge Public Library, Cambridge, MA

48 Cambridge Historical Commission, Cambridge, MA, *Cambridge Architectural Inventory Report*, - 32 Bay St/ 86 Kinnaird St, August, 1965

49 Valuation Cancelled Books, 1864-1900, Longford town, Valuation Office, Dublin (*This source follows the changes in ownership of any property from 1864 to the present*).

Notes on Chapter 7
Michael's sisters. Exodus to America

1 Diner, H.R. *Erin's Daughters in America – Irish Immigrant Women in the Nineteenth Century*, The John Hopkins University Press, Baltimore and London, 1983, p 8

2 Diner, *ibid*, p 38

3 Diner, *ibid*, p 40

4 Diner, *ibid*, p 81

5 Diner, *ibid*, p 84

6 Diner, *ibid*, p 90

7 Diner, *ibid*, p 91

8 Diner, *ibid*, p 91

9 Diner, *ibid*, p 93

10 Diner, *ibid*, p 93

11 Diner, *ibid*, p 95

12 Marriage Register, Cambridge MA, Vol 13, Folio No 175, No 417, Charles A. Edgerly and Elizabeth (Lizzie) E. Mongan, (spelt Morgan) Cathedral of the Holy Cross, 1400 Washington St Boston, MA, July 19, 1894. The Archidiocese of Boston Archdiocesan Archives, Brighton, MA. The handwritten original marriage register entry had the Latin phrase ' super imped disp. cult.obb.' meaning that a dispensation had been given for a marriage that arises from the

union of a baptised person and a non-baptised person. My thanks to Phyllis Danehy for extracting this information. Many congregational churches trace their descent from the early 16th century congregational church, arising from the non-conformist movement in England during the Puritan Reformation. In America, the Congregationalists include the pilgrims of Plymouth and the Puritans of the Massachusetts Bay colony, organised in Union by the Cambridge platform in 1684. In New England, they later became linked with the Prespyterian Church.

13 Meagher, T.J., *Inventing Irish America: Generation, Class and Ethnic Identity In A New England City, 1880 – 1928*, University of Notre Dame. Notre Dame, 2001 p 333

14 Ryan, D.P., *A Journey Through Boston Irish History, Images of America*, Arcadia Publishing, Charleston, SC, 1999, p 78

15 Arlington Town Directories, 1894 - 1897, Robbins Library, Arlington, MA

16 Denis Ahern, Interview with author, Oct. 2002

17 Duffy, R.A., Arlington, *Images of America*, Arcadia Publishing, Dover, NH, 1997, p 69

18 Duffy, R.A., Arlington, *ibid*, p 32

19 Duffy, R.A., Arlington, *ibid*, p 93

20 Duffy, R.A., Arlington, *ibid*, p 69

21 Duffy, R.A., Arlington, *ibid*, p 101

22 Births Register, 1895, Vol. 449, p 70, No 151, Arlington Town Hall, Arlington, MA

23 Births Register, 1897, Vol. 467, p 315, No 231. Mary Gallant Reference Dept, Medford Public Library, Medford, MA

24 Plymouth County 300th Anniversay Commorative Guide, Plymouth, 1990, Shoemaking, p 66

25 Marriage Register, David Ahearne and Catherine (Kate) Mongan (spelt Mongan), St Bridgit's Church, Abington MA, January 7, 1886, Abington Town Hall archives, Abington MA. My thanks to Abington Town Clerk Patricia McKenna for providing this information.

26 Peters, S.Orcutt., *Abington, Images Of America*, Arcadia Publishing, Charleston, SC, p 15, p 55

27 Abington Resident Directory, 1889, p 85, My thanks to Pamela Whiting, Dyer Memorial Library, Abington, MA, for kindly providing this information.

28 Peters, S.Orcutt., Abington, *ibid*, pp 47 - 51

29 Peters, S.Orcutt., Abington, *ibid*, p 40

30 US Census, 1900, Delia Mongan, domestic maid with William H. Partridge, 23 Pembroke St, Newton, MA, National Archives & Records Administration, Waltham, MA

31 Ashburn, F.D., *A Portrait of Peabody of Groton*, Riverside Press, Inc., 1967, p 77

32 Ashburn, F.D., *Fifty Years On – Groton School, 1884-1934*, At the Sign of the Gosden Head, New York, 1934, p 69

33 Ashburn, F.D., *Fifty Years On, ibid*, p 70

34 Ashburn, F.D., *Fifty Years On, ibid*, p 42-43

35 Brown, D.V.D., (ed.) Groton School, 1884-1985, The Trustees of Groton School, Groton, MA, 1986, p 10

36 Douglas Van Dyck Brown, Letter to author, Aug 11, 1998. The author wishes to express his gratitude to Groton archivist Douglas Brown, who kindly provided essential information on Delia Mongan's years at Groton School.

37 Death Index Books, Vital Records Office, Boston MA, Delia Mongan, 275 Clarendon St, Boston, died May 4, 1932 at Mass General Hospital, Boston.

38 Death Index Books, Abington Town Hall records, Vol. 1, p 18, Maria Teresa Josephine Mongan (spelt Mongon), died February 25, 1916, at 33 Charles St, Abington, MA

39 List of Names in the Town Of Rockland Of Persons Assessed A Poll Tax in 1937, Rockland, MA, p 58

40 Death Index Books, Abington Town Hall records, Rockland, Vol. 74, p 482, Catherine Ahearn, died July 20, 1942, Lonergan Rest Home, 56 W. Water Street, Abington, MA

Notes on Chapter 8
Michael. A first descent into Hell

1 Death Registers, Vol. 13, line 221, Cambridge City Clerk's Office, Cambridge, MA

2 Edward Hines, Boston, MA, Letter to author, May 5, 1983
3 Edward Hines, Boston, MA, Letter to author, Oct 5, 1985
4 Edward Hines, Boston, MA, Letter to author, Nov 3, 1985
5 Edward Hines, Boston, MA, Letter to author, Aug 3, 1984
6 Edward Hines, Boston, MA, Letter to author, May 7, 1983
7 Baptism Register, St Mel's Cathedral, Longford, Parish of Templemichael and Ballymacormack, Michael Reginald Mongan, born 29 April, 1897, baptised May 2, 1897, Rev F. Duffy, Godparents: William Byrne and Elizabeth Shanley
8 Edward A. Riquier, Worcester, MA, Letter to author, Dec 5, 1984
9 Carole A.. Persia, Worcester, MA, Letter to author, Nov 2, 1998
10 Mary Alice Herman, Medical Records Dept, Worcester State Hospital, Worcester, MA, Letter to author, July 29, 1999
11 Worcester City website, www.ci.worcester.ma.us History, p 1. A major fire at Worcester State Hospital in June 23, 1991 destroyed large parts of the original Kirkbride complex, leaving only the right wing and the administration building. The burnt out shells of other areas were later bulldozed. There is now an ongoing campaign to preserve the surviving old building as a memorial to all those unfortunate enough to have been inmates and died there. Although due to safety concerns entry is to the building is forbidden, some brave individuals have been able to enter and photograph poignant night-time images of the interiors. The nearby Worcester State Hospital cemetery contains some 1600 inmate graves. Several website now carry photos of the interior, notably www.opacity.us/site56. htm.
12 Grob, G. N., *The Mad Among Us – A History of the Care Of America's Mentally Ill,* Harvard University Press, Cambridge, MA, 1994, p 44
13 Grob, G.N., *The State And The Mentally Ill – A History Of Worcester State Hospital,*

1830-1920, Chapel Hill, University of North Carolina Press, 1966, p 235
14 Grob, G.N., *ibid,* p 236
15 Grob, G.N., *ibid,* p 62
16 Morrissey, J.P., and Goldman. H.H., et al, *The Enduring Asylum – Cycles of Institutional Reform at Worcester State Hospital,* Grune & Stratton, New York, 1980, p 62
17 Grob, G.N., *The State And The Mentally Ill, ibid,* p 248
18 Grob, G.N., *ibid,* p 248-49
19 Grob, G.N., *ibid,* p 249
20 Grob, G.N., *ibid,* p 265
21 Grob, G.N., *ibid,* pp 266-67
22 Grob, G.N., *ibid,* pp 267-68
23 Morrissey, J. P., and Goldman, H.H., *The Enduring Asylum, ibid,* p 65
26 Grob, G.N., *The State And The Mentally Ill, ibid,* p 280
27 Grob, G.N., *ibid,* p 281
28 Grob, G.N., *ibid,* p 288
29 Grob, G.N., *ibid,* p 289
30 Grob, G.N., *ibid,* p 289
31 Grob, G.N., *ibid,* p 295
32 Worcester State Hospital Archives, Medical Records File No 20965, Michael J. Mongan, Interview with doctors, May 18, 1900. Michael was actually born in 1863 but we don't know if he gave the date wrongly or if the stenographer noted the date incorrectly. Grob, G.N., *ibid,* p 295
33 Charles Bahne, Vice President, Boston Street Railway Association, Inc. Cambridge, MA, Letter to author, Aug 29, 2000. He wrote 'A check of corporate annual report for Boston's transit companies – the West End Street Railway prior to 1897, and the Boston Elevated after that date, reveals no references to any strikes in the late 1890s. Quite frankly, we are puzzled by you granduncle's references to such a strike. We have no idea what he is referring to....One possibility is that there was a minor 'wildcat' strike, perhaps involving just one carbarn and only lasting a day or two. Another is that a strike was threatened but never actually occurred.' The 1900 US census, taken on 4 June, listed Michael as an inmate of Worcester Insane

Hospital. The census, under letter M, also listed the names of many other Irish-born inmates; Meaney, Mulvaney, McGrath, MacDermott, McKenna, McNamara, McManus, O'Donnell, O'Leary, etc,.

34   Grob, G.N., *The Mad Among Us*, ibid, p 80

Notes on Chapter 9
1900s Boston. Yankee versus Irish

1   Census of Ireland, 1901, Longford Town, James Mongan, 11 Ward's Terrace, Longford, House Carpenter

2   Worcester State Hospital, Medical File No 21479, Michael J. Mongan, Statement of wife Maria Mongan, Interview with doctors, April 12, 1901

3   Grob, G.H., *The Mad Among Us, ibid,* p 171

4   Grob, G.H., *ibid*, pp 83-4

5   Worcester State Hospital, Medical Records File No 21 479, Michael J. Mongan, Physician's Certificate, April 2, 1901, p 3

6   Worcester State Hospital, Medical Records File, No 21 479, Michael J. Mongan, Assessment by doctors, April 2, 1901, p 3

7   Worcester State Hospital, Medical Records File, No 21 479, Michael J. Mongan, Interview with doctors, April 2, 1901, pp 3-4

8   Worcester State Hospital, Medical Records File, No 21 479, Michael J, Mongan, Interview with doctors, April 2, 1901, p 4

9   Worcester State Hospital, Medical Records File, No 21 479, Michael J. Mongan, Doctors Assessment, April 2, 1901, p 4

10   Worcester State Hospital, Medical Records File, No 21 472, Michael J. Mongan, Interview with doctors, April 2, 1901, p 4

11   Worcester State Hospital, Medical Records File, No 21 472, Michael J.Mongan, Interview with doctors, April 2, 1901, p 5

12   Worcester State Hospital, Medical Records File, No 21 472, Michael J. Mongan, Interview with doctors, April 5, 1901, p 5

13   Worcester State Hospital, Medical Records File, No 21 472, Michael J.Mongan, Interview with doctors, May 20, 1901, p 5-6

14   Worcester State Hospital, Medical Records File, No 21 472, Michael J. Mongan, Doctors Report, May 26, 1901.p 6 [Erysipelas, or St Anthony's Fire, was an acute streptococcal infection accompanied by a diffused inflammation of the skin. Staring from a single point, it spreads over a wider area of the facial dermis layer, and regarded as contagious and occurred epidemically. Skin can begin flaking off infected area.]

15   Worcester State Hospital, Medical Records File, No 21 472, Michael J. Mongan, Doctors Report, June 10, 1901, p 6

16   Worcester State Hospital, Medical Records File, No 21 472, Michael J. Mongan, Doctors Report, June 11, 1901, p 6

17   Worcester State Hospital, Medical Records File, No 21 472, Michael j. Mongan, Doctors Report, June 12, 1901, p 6

18   Worcester State Hospital, Medical Records File, No 21 472, Michael J. Mongan, Interview with doctors, July 5, 1901, p 7

19   Worcester State Hospital, Medical Records File, No 21 472, Michael J. Mongan, Interview with doctors, August 9, 1901. p 7

20   Worcester State Hospital, Medical Records File, No 21 472, Michael J. Mongan, Interview with doctors, September 18, 1901, p 7

21   Worcester State Hospital, Medical Records File, No 21 472, Michael J. Mongan, Doctors Report, October 11, 1901, p 8

22   Worcester State Hospital, Medical Records File, No 21 472, Michael J. Mongan, Doctors Report, November 8, 1901, p 8

Notes on Chapter 10
Michael. 'Living with the Loonies'

1   Johns, A.S., *The Man Who Shot McKinley*, A.S. Barnes & Co, London, 1970, p 23

2   O'Connor, T.H., *The Boston Irish – A Political History*, Back Way Books, Boston, 1995, p 161

3   Worcester State Hospital, Medical Records File, No 22 242, Michael J.Mongan. Statement by wife Maria, July 9, 1902, p 1

4   Worcester State Hospital, Medical Records File, No 22 242, Michael J. Mongan. Statement by wife Maria, July 9, 1902, p1. The 1901 Boston Street Directory lists a Samuel Whitehead, a shipwright, and his electrician son, living at 856 East Broadway in South Boston, who rented rooms to guests.

5   Worcester State Hospital, Medical Records

File, No 22 242, Michael J. Mongan.
Doctors Report, July 1, 1902, p 1
6 Worcester State Hospital, Medical Records
File, No 22 242, Michael J. Mongan.
Physicians' Certificate, July 1, 1902, p 2
7 Worcester State Hospital, Medical Records
File, No 22 242, Michael J. Mongan.
Doctors Report, July 1, 1901, p 2
8 Worcester State Hospital, Medical Records
File, No 22 242, Michael J. Mongan
Interview with doctors. July 1, 1902, p 2
9 Worcester State Hospital, Medical Records
File, No 22 242, Michael J. Mongan.
Doctors Report, July 2, 1902, pp 2-3
10 Worcester State Hospital, Medical Records
File, No 22 242, Michael J.Mongan.
Interview with doctors, July 2, 1902, p 3
11 Worcester State Hospital, Medical Records
File, No 22 242, Michael J.Mongan.
Interview with doctors, July 2, 1902, p 5
12 Worcester State Hospital, Medical Records
File, No 22 242, Michael J.Mongan.
Doctors Report, July 3, 1902, p 6
13 Worcester State Hospital, Medical Records
File, No 22 242, Michael J.Mongan.
Interview with doctors, July 4, 1902, p 7
14 Worcester State Hospital, Medical Records
File, No 22 242, Michael J.Mongan.
Interview with doctors, July 7, 1902, p 7
15 Worcester State Hospital, Medical Records
File, No 22 242, Michael J.Mongan.
Interview with doctors, July 14, 1902, p 7
16 Worcester State Hospital, Medical Records
File, No 22 242, Michael J.Mongan.
Interview with doctors, November 21,
1902, P 8

Notes to Chapter 11
Michael. Slipping back into Hell
1 O'Connor, T.H., *The Boston Irish – A Political History*, Boston, 1995, p 161
2 Worcester State Hospital, Medical Records File, No 22 713, Michael J. Mongan. Physicians' Certificate, April 30, 1903, p 1
3 Worcester State Hospital, Medical Records File, No 22 713, Michael J. Mongan. Interview with doctors, April 30, 1903, p 1
4 Worcester State Hospital, Medical Records File, No 22 713, Michael J. Mongan.

Interview with doctors, May 1, 1903 p 2
5 Worcester State Hospital, Medical Records File, No 22 713, Michael J. Mongan. Doctors' Report, May 13, 1903, p 3
6 Worcester State Hospital, Medical Records File, No 22 713, Michael J. Mongan. Interview with doctors, May 13, 1903, p 3
7 Worcester State Hospital, Medical Records File, No 22 713, Michael J. Mongan. Interview with doctors,May 13, 1903, pp 3-4
8 Worcester State Hospital, Medical Records File, No 22 713, Michael J. Mongan. Interview with doctors, July 22, 1903, pp 5-6 Taka-Diastase, made from Aspergillus Oryzae powder, is a pure amylase enzyme preparation for digesting starch. A mixture of enzymes made from malt, it converts at least fifty times its weight of potato starch into sugars in 30 minutes. Taka-Diastase digestive enzyme pills were produced by the major US pharmaceutical firm Parke Davis & Co in the 1890s. The name is made up of two parts: 'taka' meaning 'superior' or 'best' in Greek, and 'diastase' which is identified as an enzyme by the '-ase' ending.
9 Worcester State Hospital, Medical Records File, No 22 713, Michael J. Mongan. Doctors Report, October 5, 1903, p 6 Ironically, American interest in psychotherapy received a major boost in August, 1909 when Sigmund Freud, Carl Jung and Sandor Ferenczi, visited Worcester Insane Hospital on the occasion of Clark University's twentieth anniversary. At Clark, Freud and Jung delivered a series of lectures on psychoanalysis to a distinguished audience of leading American psychologists, educators and behavioural scientists. As Freud's first official recognition by an academic institution, and his only personal appearance at an American university, his visit led to his theories becoming more widely accepted in the United States. Jung gave three lectures, one on the word-association test, a second on recurring family complexes, and the third on psychic conflicts in children. In a ceremony held before three hundred dis-

tinguished guests, Freud and Jung were awarded doctorates; Freud in psychology, Jung in education and social hygiene. However, they had come six years too late to alter the sad destiny of an Irish emigrant named Michael J. Mongan.

Notes on Chapter 12
Life after Death. Grieving a Suicide

1   State Medical Examiner's Records, Michael J. Mongan, No 132, Letter M. Massachusetts State Archives, Boston, MA

2   Obituary, Michael J. Mongan, *Boston Globe*, Boston, MA, October 7, 1903.

3   Cambridgeport - In And About Central Square, in *Cambridge Chronicle*, Cambridge, MA, October 17, 1903

4   Another commentator, Hasia Diner, remarked on the large numbers of Irish immigrants who made their home in a 19th-century American institution – the insane asylum. She argued that figures on 19th-century admission figures to mental hospitals had to be read with a degree of scepticism: 'Americans typically defined individuals with radically different values and behaviour patterns as deviants who ought to be isolated from the rest of society. Irish men and women seemed particularly inappropriate by the standards of Yankee Protestants.'

5   Joseph P. Morrissey, Letter to author, April 30, 2001

6   Joseph P. Morrissey, *ibid* Emile Durkheim, the noted French sociologist, writing in 1897 in *Suicide – A Study in Sociology*, believed that vulnerability to suicide in society depended on the strength of bonds between the individuals; the weaker the bonds the greater the risk. He pointed to the increase in suicide in industrialised area such as inner cities where cohesion of society was at its weakest. He felt that a person who commits suicide may not necessarily be mentally ill, although at least temporarily deeply disturbed. In most countries men commit suicide more often than women; in America, the ratio was 3:1.10 A recent report on prison deaths found that seventeen of the twenty-three

suicides examined over a sixteen-year period were as the result of hanging from cell windows bars. Durkheim coined the term 'anomie' to explain the disintegration (or transformation) of a society. The loss of meaningful work identity and its relationships, led to the proliferation of self-destructive tendencies, such as alcoholism, depression or suicide.

7   Dr Morrissey later communicated the response by this psychiatrist friend at Worcester University of Massachusetts Medical Center who replied to Dr Morrissey's question on the use of the term 'constitutional inferiority' in Worcester at the turn of the 20th century and whether or not it was a euphemism for 'poor Irish' as viewed by the Yankee medical officers. 'The terminology was incredibly loose. Most historians don't even discuss the subject in this time period: Grob, Stone, Shorter. The likelihood that the diagnoses were valid or reliable is close to zero. Probably, the only way to understand the term would be to look at a few hundred cases of the era and examine who did and did not get such a label.'

8   Sammarco, A.M., South Boston, Vol II, Images of America, Arcadia Publishing, Charleston, SC, 2000, see cover photo

Notes on Chapter 13
Transatlantic Cousins. Charlie and Reg

1   Baptism Register, Charles Joseph Mongan, Gate of Heaven Church, 609 East Fourth St, South Boston, MA, baptism May 12, 1895, witness Annie E. Hurd, Archdiocese of Boston archives, Brighton, MA.

2   Military Records file, Charles Joseph Mongan, Military Service No 143 4049, Statement of Service, Navy Reference Branch, National Personnel Records Center, (Military Personnel Records), St Louis, MS

3   Sweetman, J., The Landing At Veracruz, 1914, *ibid*, p 42

4   Office of the Chief of Naval Operations, Naval History Division, *The Dictionary Of American Naval Fighting Ships, Vol IV*, Washington, 1969, pp 147-8. My sincere

thanks to Michael J. Crawford, Head, Early History Branch, Department of the Navy, Washington, D.C. for guidng me to this important source.

5 By 1912 American investment exceeded one billion dollars. Standard Oil, United States Steel, Anaconda Corporation, Mexican Petroleum, along with Hearst and Guggenheim interests, accounted for the most extensive holdings. American firms ended up owning 75 percent of all the mines, and 50 percent of the all oil fields in Mexico.

6 Sweetman, J., The Landing At Veracruz, 1914, *ibid*, p 137

7 Sweetman, J., The Landing At Veracruz, 1914, *ibid*, p 149

8 Charles J. Mongan, Veteran's File No: 301/272 – XC# 01-009-137/00, *ibid*

9 Charles J. Mongan, Veterans File No: 301/272 – XC# 01-009-137/100. *ibid*

10 Marriage Certificate, Charles J. Mongan and Mae Elizabeth Eisel, St Paul's Church, 34 Holyoke St, Mount Auburn, Cambridge, MA, June 1, 1925, See also Cambridge Chronicle, Marriages, June 14, 1925, 'Charles Joseph Mongan, 112 Kinnaird Street, and Mae Elizabeth Eisel (mispelt Cecil), 1525 Kenset St, Baltimore, MD. on June 14th at St Paul's Church by the Rev. William W. Gunn'.

11 *Census of Ireland*, 1901, James Mongan, House Carpenter, 11 Ward's Terrace, Longford town, Longford Urban No 1 DED, Longford Parish Ref 54/14/2

12 Birth Register, St Mel's Cathedral, Longford, Parish of Templemichael and Ballymacormack, Esther Mary Mongan, born April 7, 1901, sponsors John Murray and Elexia Heany

13 Permanent Way Staff Ledger, MGWR Archives, Irish Railway Record Society, Iarnrod Eireann, Hueston Station, Dublin

14 St Michael's National School, Longford, Attendance Records, November, 1904 – July, 1906, Longford Roots, Longford Museum and Heritage Center, Church St, Longford. My thanks to Mr Jude Flynn for extracting this information from the archives.

15 Census of Ireland, 1911, James Mongan, 11 Ward's Terrace, Longford town, Longford Urban No 1 DED, Longford Parish Ref: 54/14/2

16 Civil Service File, Reginald Michael Mongan, Employment Application Form, January 7, 1923, Department of Industry and Commerce archives, Dublin

17 Permanent Way Staff Ledger, MGWR Archives, Irish Railway Record Society, Iarnrod Eireann, Hueston Station, Dublin

18 Wallace, M., A *Short History of Ireland*, Appletree Press, Belfast, 1986, pp 69-70

19 Permanent Way Staff Ledger, MGWR Archives, Irish Railway Record Society, *ibid*

20 See Costello, P., *James Joyce – The Years of Growth, 1882 – 1915*, Kyle Cathie Ltd, 1992, p 279 p 290 Writer James Joyce, and his son Giorgio, had stayed with his father John, and his sisters, when they lived at 44 Fontenoy St from August to December 1909.

21 Permanent Way Staff Ledger, MGWR Archives, Irish Railway Record Society, *ibid*

22 Permanent Way Staff Ledger, MGWR Archives, Irish Railway Record Society, *ibid*

23 Officers' History Sheet, supplementary, Reginald M. Mongan, Irish Free State Army records, Military Archives, Cathal Brugha Barracks, Dublin

24 Wallace, M., *A Short History of Ireland*, ibid, pp 73-73

25 Officers' History Sheet, Reginald M. Mongan, Irish Free State Army records, *ibid*

26 'By our special commissioner', The Salvage Corps, in *An t-Oglac*, May 5, 1923, pp 3-6

27 Reginald Mongan Archives, Dublin, A wood framed hand-drawn address in ink & coloured crayon, 12x14" (30x36cm) signed by E.J. Campbell, C.Q.M.S. and J. Fox, Private, presented on November 28, 1923

28 Reginald M. Mongan, Clerical Officers' Examination, Exam No 545, SDR/1843, Military Archives, Cathal Brugha Barracks, Dublin

29 Marriage Register, Reginald M. Mongan,

and Mary Taggart, Church of the English
Martyrs, Whitington, Manchester, August
17, 1927, witnesses Leonard and Maria
Hulme.
30 Charles J. Mongan, Veterans File No
301/272–XC# 01–009–137100, Death
Certificate
31 Dallek, R., John F. Kennedy, *ibid*, pp 130-31
32 Marguerite Lechiaro, Watertown MA,
Letter to author, October 1997
33 Marguerite Lechiaro, Interview with
author, Charles Hotel, Cambridge, MA,
October 2002
34 Susan Ciccone, Reference Librarian,
Cambridge Public Library, Letter to
author, October 30, 2000. Susan Ciccone
kindly provided information on Charles J.
Mongan's salary scale over his career; in
1945 he earned $2054 per annum and by
1963 earned $4844 yearly.
35 Charles J. Mongan, Veterans File No
301/272–XC# 01–009–137100,
36 Edward Hines, Boston, MA, Letter to
author, October 7, 1981
37 Death Index Book, Earl Eisel, Certificate
No 004071, Massachusetts Vital Records,
Boston, MA, (Edward Hines, Letter to
author, October 17, 1981)
38 Permanent Way Staff Ledger, MGWR
Archives, Irish Railway Record Society, *ibid*

Notes on Chapter 14
Mary's story. A spiritual journey
1 Baptism Register, Mary Elizabeth
Mongan, Gate of Heaven Chucrh, 609
East Fourth St, South Boston, MA, May
29, 1896, sponsors John McCarthy,
Gertrude Daly, Archdiocese of Boston
archives, Brighton, MA
2 *Cambridge City Directories, 1898–1903*,
Cambridge City Hall, Cambridge, MA
3 Burial Records, Hurd Family graves, Holy
Cross Cemetery, Malden, MA, Edward
Hines, Letter to author, February 24, 1983.
4 *Cambridge City Directories, 1910–1937*,
Cambridge City Hall, Cambridge, MA,
Edward Hines, Letter to author,
November 11, 1982
5 Rao, K.R., (ed.) *Introduction to J.B. Rhine:*

On the Frontiers of Science, Duke University,
Durham, NC, 19XX
6 Hayman, R., *A Life Of Jung*, W.W. Norton
& Co, New York, 2001, p 50
7 Hayman, R., *A Life Of Jung*, *ibid*, p 389
8 Hayman, R., *A Life Of Jung*, *ibid*, p 415
9 Hayman, R., *A Life Of Jung*, *ibid*, p 416
10 Mary Elizabeth Mongan, 675 Boylston St,
Letter to Dr J.B. Rhine, Duke University,
November 18, 1957. My sincere gratitude
to Mary Mongan's attorney and executor,
J. Edward Foster, Tremont St, Boston, MA,
(Letter to author, December 17, 1980) for
providing the author with these documents
now held in his archives.
11 Dr Louisa E. Rhine, Duke University,
Letter to Mary Mongan, December 9, 1957
12 Mary Mongan, Letter to Ms Louisa E.
Rhine, Duke University, January 8, 1958
13 Ms Louisa E. Rhine, Duke University,
Letter to Mary Mongan, Boston, MA,
January 23, 1958
14 Bardsley, M. and Bell, R.S., *The Boston
Strangler*, Crime Library, www.crimeli-
brary.com, See also Frank, G. *The Boston
Strangler*, New American Library, 1966;
Kelly, S,. *The Boston Stranglers: The Public
Conviction of Albert DeSalvo and the True Story
of Eleven Shocking Murders*, Kensington
Publishing Group, 1995; Rae, G.W.,
Confessions of the Boston Strangler,
Pyramid Books, New York, 1967
15 Ms Prescilla Hughes, Methuen, MA,
Letter to 'Good Morning' Editor, *Boston
Herald American*, August 10, 1981
16 Mr Joseph Viglione, Boston, Letter to
author, October, 1981,
17 Ms Arlene G. Fitzpatrick, Medford. MA,
Letter to author, August 7, 1981
18 Ms Ann Feragamo, Letter to author, 17
December 1980.
19 Edward J. Foster, Boston, MA, Letter to
author, December 17, 1981
20 Ryan, D. P., *A Journey Through Boston Irish
History, Images of America*, Arcadia
Publishing, Charleston SC, 1999, p 35
21 Ms Eileen L. Higgins, Quincy, MA. Letter
to author, August 11, 1981.

Notes on Chapter 15
Helene and Bob. A South Shore romance

1   Baptism Registers, Gate of Heaven Church, 609 East Fourth St, South Boston, MA, Archdiocese of Boston, Brighton, MA

2   Death Certificate, James J. Keough, Hyde Park, Boston, MA, August 27, 1932, Register No 7261

3   Cote, W.C., The First Settlers of Holbrook, Mass., unpublished manuscript, Holbrook Public Library, Holbrook, MA. 1964, p 1. My thanks to Wesley Cote and his wife for his kind guidance and hospitality during my research trip to his home town.

4   Cote, W.C., The First Settlers of Holbrook, Mass., *ibid* p 2

5   Cote, W.C., The First Settlers of Holbrook, Mass, *ibid* p 3

6   Cote, W.C. The First Settlers of Holbrook, Mass., *ibid*, p 5

7   Cote, W.C., The First Settlers of Hollbrook, Mass., *ibid*, p 8

8   Holbrook Inventory, 176, Center St, Holbrook, MA, Holbrook, Form No 3, Kathleen Kelly Broomer, Historical Commission Report, 176 Center St, Holbrook, MA. See also Cote. W.E., *Colonial and Revolutionary War Soldiers of Holbrook, MA*, Holbrook, MA, and Dedham Land Court records, Dedham, MA, Book 386, p 135, and Book 85, p 151. My thanks to Ruth A. Hathavy, Reference Librarian, Holbrook Public Library, Holbrook, MA, for providing this material.

9   Mike Burns, Weymouth, MA, Letter to author, August 1, 2002

10 Fourteenth Census of the United States, 1920, Holbrook, MA,

11 Marriage Certificate, Robert Hamilton Burns and Mary Helene Keough, January 17, 1925, Rev John F. Dunn, witnesses James Graham and Florence Osborn.

12 Polk's *Weymouth Directory, Vol 1*, 1926-27, p 165, 'Keough Jas J. (Mary M) h20 Oakdale Ave, South Weymouth, MA; Keough, Josephine F. saleslady, resident, 20 Oakdale Ave, South Weymouth, MA.' My thanks to Ms Elizabeth Murphy, Tufts Library, Wey-mouth, MA, for providing this document, and to Phillip Smith, President of Weymouth Historical Society, and his colleague Debbie Sergent Sullivan for their generous assistance during my research in Weymouth.

13 Death Certificate, Holbrook Town Hall, archives, Holbrook, MA, Mary Eileen Burns, March 25, 1929

14 Death Certificate, Holbrook Town Hall archives, Holbrook, MA, Mary Keough, 62 Pleasant St, Holbrook, MA, July 13, 1924, Informant Thomas Burns.

15 Death Certificate, Boston, MA, James J. Keough, 940 Hyde Park Ave, Boston, MA, August 27, 1932, Informant Ms R.Burns

16 Mary MacAvoy, Norwood, MA, Letter to author, February, 2001

17 Mary MacAvoy, Norwood, MA, Interview with author, April, 2001

18 Mary MacAvoy, Norwood, MA, ibid

19 Bob Burns, (Mary Elen McLaughlin) Holbrook, MA, Letter to author, October 10, 1982

20 Bob Burns Interview, with Janet Colozone and Anna Kapmann, recorded in August, 1977, 176 Center St, Holbrook, MA. Transcription by the author.

21 Wager, R., *Golden Wheels*, Western Reserve Historical Society, Cleveland, 1975, pp 25-38

22 Massachusetts National Guard, Military Museum and Archives, Worcester, MA, James H. Keough File, 25 Center St, Holbrook, MA, Private, enlisted Rockland, MA, March 28, 1918, Army Serial No 1,686,608, 151st Depot Brigade, May 1, 1918, 58th Massachusetts Infantry Regiment, overseas from May 10, 1918 – June 30, 1918. Honorable discharge July 2, 1919 at Camp Devens, MA. My thanks to Dana Essigmann, Archivist, Massachusetts National Guard Military Museum and Archives, Worcester, MA, for providing this document.

23 See 'American Memory' *The Stars and Stripes, 1918-1919*, website, (http://memory. locgov/ ammem/sgphtml/sachtml/aef.html), The American Expeditionary Force, p 1,

24 See Weaver, J.C. The American Expeditionary Force, World War 1, website,

(htt[://www.ls.net/~newriver/ww1/ 1-5 div.htm) Fourth Division (Regular Army), p 4, based on Beamish, R..J., and March. F.A., *America's Part in the World War,* 1919,

25 See 'American Memory', *The Stars and Stripes,* 1918-1919, The American Expeditionary Force, pp 1-2

26 See 'American Memory' *The Stars and Stripes,* 1918-1919, The American Expeditionary Force, p 2, See also Weaver, J.C., The American Expeditionary Force, World War 1, Fourth Division, (Regular Army) p 4

27 US Department of Veterans Affairs, Boston, MA, James H. Keough, File No: 301/272 – C# 20 445 460/00, Army Serial No: 1686608, Veterans Affairs Correspondence,

28 Department of Veterans Affairs, Boston, MA, James H. Keough, File No: 301/272 –C# 20 445 460/60, Change of Address Notice, June 5, 1938

29 See Hermalyn, G., and Ultan, L., One Hundred Years of the Bronx, Bronx Historical Society website, (www.bronxhistoricalsociety.org)

30 *Southbridge Evening News,* Southridge, Worcester, MA, Monday, February 14, 1938, Jacob Edwards Library, Southbridge, MA. My thanks to Ms Margaret Morrissey, Librarian, Jacob Edwards Library for kindly providing this material.

31 *Southbridge Evening News,* Southridge, Worcester, MA, Tuesday, February 15, 1938, Jacob Edwards Library, Southridge, MA, See also *New York Times,* New York, NY, obituary, Stashia Mae Keough, Wednesday, February 16, 1938

32 Death Certificate, Town Clerk's Office archives, Southridge, MA, Stashia Mae Keough, February 15, 1938

33 Department of Veterans Affairs, Boston, MA, James H. Keough, File No: 301/272 – C# 20 445 460/000, Ms Claude Curtis letter, February 21, 1938

34 Department of Veterans Affairs, Boston, MA, James H. Keough, File No: 301/272 – C# 20 445 460/000, James H. Keough, letter, may 6, 1938

35 See Spring Valley, NY, website, (www.villagespringvalley.com), History of the Spring Valley,

36 Department of Veterans Affairs, Boston, MA, James H. Keough, *ibid,* Letter from Ms Helene Burns, May 23, 1957

Notes on Chapter 16
Helene Burns. A West Side story

1 Department of Veterans Affairs, Boston, MA, James H. Keough, File No: 301/272 – C# 20 445 460/000, Named relatives, Helene Burns and Josephine Keough, 315 W 74th St, New York, 23, N.Y.

2 The name United Nations had been first coined by US President Franklin D. Roosevelt in 1942 at the height of WWII, when representatives of 26 nations had pledged their Governments' support to continue fighting together against the Axis Powers. After the war in 1945, representatives of 50 countries met in San Francisco at the United Nations Conference to draw up a UN Charter. The Charter was formally signed on June 26, 1945 by the representatives of the 50 nations. The United Nations officially came into existence on October, 24, 1945, when the Charter had been ratified by China, France, the Soviet Union, the United Kingdom, the United States and by a majority of other signatories.
Norman Burns, Braintree, MA, Interview with author, October, 2000. My thanks to Norman Burns for providing this information.

3 See Waxman, S., *The History Of The Upper West Side,* p 1, (www.ny.com website) and Salwen, P, Upper West Side Story, Abbeville Press, New York, N.Y. 1988

4 Waxman, S. *The History of the Upper West Side, ibid,* p 2

5 Ruskin-Sewall, Y., *High On Rebellion: Inside The Underground at Max's Kansas City,* Thunder's Mouth Press, New York, 1988. See also (www.max'skansascity.com) website

6 Rick McGaughey, Holbrook, MA, Interview with author, October 2000.

7 Dr Owen Kiernan, Cape Cod, MA,

Interview with author, 2001
8 Vincent Kiernan, East Falmouth, MA, Interview with author, January, 2005.

Notes on Chapter 17
Family reconnections. A happy ending
1 Death Certificate, Abington Town Hall archives, Abington, MA, David G. Ahearn, 33 Charles St, Abington, MA, December 18, 1921
2 Death Certificate, Boston, MA, Delia Mongan, 275 Clarendon St, Boston, MA, May 4, 1932
3 Kevin Donovan, Abington, MA, Letter to author, March, 2002. My sincere thanks to Kevin Donovan, Abington selectman, for his generous assistance in pinpointing the Aherne family in the area.
4 Dr Owen Kiernan, Cape Cod, MA, Interview with author, October, 2001

Notes on Chapter 18
Michael. A last goodbye to Worcester
1 Denis Ahern, Acton, MA, Ahern Family website, (www.ahern@world.std.com)

Notes on Chapter 19
Reflections. On finding the needle in the haystack
1 Death Certificate, Boston, MA, Death Index Book, Vol. 2, p 97, Elizabeth (Mongan) Edgerly, died, July 30, 1925
2 Fourteenth Census of the United States, 1920, Boston, MA, Vol. 107, Sheet 21, John and Grace Edgerly, 40 Lawrence St, (Roxbury), Boston, MA. My thanks to researcher Margaret Jenkins for locating this information.
3 Death Certificate, Boston, MA, Death Index Book, Vol 28, p 90, Elsie E Edgerly, 22 Kempton St, Roxbury, Boston, MA, died November 24, 1956
4 Fourteenth Census of the United States, 1920, Holyoke, MA, Bridget Monaghan, age 50,
5 President John Fitzgerald Kennedy, Remarks on Eyre Square' speech, Galway, July, 1963, *Galway Advertiser*, July 9, 196

Notes on Chapter 20
Written in the stars? Probing deeper into Michael's personality
1 Graphology consultation, Ms Patricia Field, MA, August 2002.
2 Astrological Portrait, Michael J. Mongan, by Robert Currey, House of Astrology, Dublin, Noember 15, 2000

Notes on Appendix 1 - *Michael's ancestry. The O Mongans of Monganstown*
1 Andrews, G.H., and Davies, K.M., *Irish Historic Town Atlas – Mullingar*, R.I.A., Dublin, 1988, pp 1-7
2 Meyer, K., *Betha Colmáin maic Lúacháin* (Life of St Colman of Lynn) R.I.A., Dublin, 1911, folio 76 a 1, p 8
3 Andrews, G.H., and Davies, K.M., *Irish Historic Town Atlas – Mullingar*, R.I.A., Dublin, 1988, pp 1-7
    The Uí Manchain (Mongan/Mangan) were mentioned on several occasions in the early Leinster genealogies where they were given descent from Daire Bairrche, second son of Cathair Mor, legendary ancestor-deity of all the leading Leinster clans. In turn they were given direct descent from Monach, an early King of Leinster, whose descendants became known as the Uí Monaig, Uí Manach, Uí Manchain and Uí Manachain. Cathair Mor's eldest son, Rus Failige, was the ancestor of the Ui Failige tribe, whose leading O'Connor Faly sept, reigned as Kings of Offaly until they lost their territories during the English Plantation of the area in the 1550s.
4 Mongan. N., *The Menapia Quest*, The Herodotus Press, Dublin, 1995
5 Handcock, S.A., (ed.) *Caesar, The Gallic Wars*, Penguin Books, Harmondsworth, 1984
6 Ordnance Survey Map, OS Sheet 27, Office of Public Works, Dublin
7 Mullingar Parish Birth, Marriage and Death registers, Cathedral House, Mullingar. Transcripts held at Westmeath County Library, Mullingar.

Index

9157542R0

Made in the USA
Charleston, SC
16 August 2011